Ideology and Curriculum

Ideology and Curriculum
Third Edition

Michael W. Apple

ROUTLEDGEFALMER

NEW YORK AND LONDON

Published in 2004 by
RoutledgeFalmer
29 West 35th Street
New York, New York 10001
www.routledge-ny.com

Published in Great Britain by
RoutledgeFalmer
11 New Fetter Lane
London EC4P 4EE
www.routledge.co.uk

RoutledgeFalmer is an imprint of the Taylor & Francis Group.
Printed in the United States of America on acid-free paper.

10 9 8 7 6 5 4 3

Library of Congress Cataloging-in-Publication Data

Apple, Michael W.

Ideology and curriculum / By Michael W. Apple.-- 3rd ed.

p. cm.

Includes bibliographical references and index.

ISBN 0-415-94911-4 (Hardcover : alk. paper) -- ISBN 0-415-94912-2 (Paperback : alk. paper) 1. Educational sociology--United States. 2. Education and state--United States. 3. Education--Social aspects--United States. 4. Curriculum evaluation--United States. I. Title.

LC191.4.A66 2004

306.47--dc22

2003027158

Contents

Preface to the 25th Anniversary Third Edition

Placing *Ideology and Curriculum* in Context

Any analysis of the ways in which unequal power is reproduced and contested in society must deal with education. Educational institutions provide one of the major mechanisms through which power is maintained and challenged. These institutions and the manner in which they are organized and controlled are integrally related to the ways in which specific people get access to economic and cultural resources and power. Yet, because education is usually part of the public sphere and is regulated by the state, it is also a site of conflict, since in many nations there are serious questions about whether the state is organized in ways that benefit the majority of its citizens. Certainly the current and seemingly unremitting attacks by conservative forces on anything that is "public" in this society document how politicized this has become.

There are other, equally important issues that can be raised, of course. Education is also a site of conflict about the kind of knowledge that is and should be taught, about whose knowledge is "official" and about who has the right to decide both what is to be taught and how teaching and learning are to be evaluated. Thus, as I argue throughout this volume, a truly critical study of education needs to deal with more than the technical issues of how we teach efficiently and effectively—too often the dominant or only questions educators ask. It must think critically about education's relationship to economic, political, and cultural power.

For more than three decades I have sought to uncover the complicated connections among knowledge, teaching, and power in education. I have argued that there is a very real set of relationships among those who have economic, political, and cultural power in society on the one hand and the ways in which education is thought about, organized, and evaluated on the other. As I mentioned in the Preface to the previous edition, *Ideology and Curriculum* is the first volume of a long series of books that I have written about these issues. It is the first volume of what some have called the two "Apple trilogies," although the second trilogy has now been extended to a fourth book. As the first, it is largely concerned with the dynamics of ideological domination. Later books devote more attention to the realities of struggles against dominance and to the ways in which new articulations of power are now operating.[1] It is very interesting, and certainly gratifying, to me that *Ideology and Curriculum* has been selected as one of the most important books in the history of Western education. I believe that this is due to the long history of groups that have struggled for a more socially critical and democratic education in so many nations. That is, the book itself responds to the desires of millions of people in a considerable number of nations who believe that they have been denied the basic human right of a truly free and democratic process of schooling. In many ways these people are the real authors.

But the book also responds to the beliefs among many scholars in education that new and more socially critical perspectives are necessary to give the field of educational research more vitality. It is important to remember that what actually *counts* as educational research is a construction. Academic boundaries are themselves culturally produced and are often the results of complex "policing" actions on the part of those who have the power to enforce them. This "policing" action involves the power to declare what is or is not the subject of "legitimate" inquiry or what is or is not a "legitimate" approach to understanding it. Yet, as I say in the Preface to the second edition of *Ideology and Curriculum* and as the French sociologist Pierre Bourdieu reminds us, it is the ability to "trespass" that may lead to major gains in our understanding.[2]

The continued development of a field—especially one as diverse as education—is often dependent on epistemological and conceptual "breaks" in which previous traditions are disrupted, displaced, and regrouped under new problematics. It is these breaks that tend to transform the questions to be asked and the manner in which they are answered. The "break" that *Ideology and Curriculum* provided centered around the development and use of a set of critical theoretical tools and cultural and political analyses that enabled us to understand the real functioning of curriculum, teaching, and evaluation much more honestly than before. These tools were based on two major concepts— ideology and hegemony—that had not had a long history of use in Western educational scholarship.

As I noted, over the course of writing the many books that followed the one you are about to read, I have refined both these concepts and their use. However, the concepts still have provided essential building blocks for critical analyses of the politics of "legitimate" and "illegitimate" knowledge. Of course it needs to be said that my arguments here are based on an understanding of a particular sets of countries. Thus, they cannot be automatically transferred to countries with different histories, although it has become clear over the years that the arguments provided in this book have resonated with the experiences of many dissidents and critical educators in a considerable number of nations. They too continue to be my teachers and I publicly thank them.

Although *Ideology and Curriculum* does not incorporate the story-telling style that characterizes parts of many of the books that came after it, rereading it reminded me of my own biography as both a teacher and political/educational activist. As someone who has taught or worked in inner-city and rural schools, it brought back the realities that helped shape me, many of which confront educators, students, parents, and activists in these communities every day. These memories were both compelling and sometimes painful. I began my teaching career in the schools of a decaying urban neighborhood in the largely poor and working-class city in which I grew up. These were the same schools I had attended. It's an odd experience to reread one's own book and relive the experiences I had as both a student and a teacher there.

In *Educating the "Right" Way*,[3] I tell the story of one of these experiences, a story about one of my students, a sensitive but at times troubled boy named Joseph. I want to retell it here since it speaks to many of the reasons that *Ideology and Curriculum* took the form it did and why it stresses differential power and the role that education plays in legitimating it. Here is the story.

Joseph sobbed at my desk. He was a tough kid, a hard case, someone who often made life difficult for his teachers. He was all of nine years old and here he was sobbing, holding on to me in public. He had been in my fourth grade class all year, a classroom situated in a decaying building in an east coast city that was among the most impoverished in the nation. There were times when I wondered, seriously, whether I would make it through that year. There were many Josephs in that classroom and I was constantly drained by the demands, the bureaucratic rules, the daily lessons that bounced off of the kids' armor. Yet somehow it was satisfying, compelling, and important, even though the prescribed curriculum and the textbooks that were meant to teach it were often beside the point. They were boring to the kids and boring to me.

I should have realized the first day what it would be like when I opened that city's "Getting Started" suggested lessons for the first few days and it began with the suggestion that "as a new teacher" I should circle the students' desks and have them introduce each other and tell something about themselves. It's not that I was against this activity; it's just that I didn't have enough unbroken desks (or even chairs) for all of the students. A number of the kids had nowhere to sit. This was my first lesson—but certainly not my last—in understanding that the curriculum and those who planned it lived in an unreal world, a world *fundamentally* disconnected from my life with those children in that inner-city classroom.

But here's Joseph. He's still crying. I've worked extremely hard with him all year long. We've eaten lunch together; we've read stories; we've gotten to know each other. There are times when he drives me to despair and other times when I find him to be among the most sensitive children in my class. I just can't give up on this kid. He's just received his report card and it says that he is to repeat fourth grade. The school system has a policy that states that failure in any two subjects (including the behavior side of the report card) requires that the student be left back. Joseph was failing gym and arithmetic. Even though he had shown improvement, he had trouble keeping awake during arithmetic, had done poorly on the mandatory citywide tests, and hated gym. One of his parents worked a late shift and Joseph would often stay up, hoping to spend some time with her. And the things that students were asked to do in gym were, to him, "lame."

The thing is, he had made real progress during the year. But I was instructed to keep him back. I knew that things would be worse next year. There would still not be enough desks. The poverty in that community would still be horrible; and health care and sufficient funding for job training and other services would be diminished. I knew that the jobs that were available in this former mill town paid deplorable wages, and that even with both of his parents working for pay, Joseph's family income was simply insufficient. I also knew that, given all that I already had to do each day in that classroom and each night at home in preparation for the next day, it would be nearly impossible for me to work any harder than I had already done with Joseph. And there were another five children in that class whom I was supposed to leave back.

So Joseph sobbed. Both he and I understood what this meant. There would be no additional help for me—or for children such as Joseph—next year. The promises would remain simply rhetorical. Words would be thrown at the problems. Teachers and parents and children would be blamed. But the school system would look like it believed in and enforced higher standards. The structuring of economic and political power in that community and that state would again go on as "business as usual."

The next year Joseph basically stopped trying. The last time I heard anything about him, he was in prison.

The personal account I have related here speaks to what has changed and what has stayed the same in the years since the first and second editions of this book. The account might be called a history of the present, a present so well illuminated in recent books such as Pauline Lipman's *High Stakes Education* and Linda McNeil's *The Contradictions of School Reform.*[4] An unyielding demand—perhaps best represented in George W. Bush's policies found in *No Child Left Behind*—for testing, reductive models of accountability, standardization, and strict control over pedagogy and curricula is now the order of the day in schools throughout the country. In urban schools in particular, these policies have been seen as not one alternative, but as the *only* option. In many ways, reforms of this type serve as a "political spectacle" rather than as a serious and well thought out set of policy initiatives that deal honestly with the depth of the problems now being faced in schools throughout the nation.[5] In fact, we are now increasingly aware of a number of the negative and even truly damaging effects of such policies.[6] Joseph's story is now being retold in the lives of thousands of children caught in underfunded schools. The global restructuring of markets, of paid and unpaid labor, of housing and health care, of communities large and small and so much more—all of this is having differential effects in terms of race and class and gender. And all of this has had profound effects on the financing and governance of schools, on what is to count as "official knowledge" and "good" teaching, and ultimately on the many Josephs who walk through the halls of the schools of our cities and towns.

Neo-liberalism and neo-conservatism are in the driver's seat right now and this is not only happening in education. In his history of the dismantling of the crucial social and economic programs that enabled many of our fellow citizens to have a chance at a better life, Michael Katz argues that current economic and social policies have "stratified Americans into first- and second-class citizens and have undermined the effective practice of democracy."[7]

We cannot understand what has happened unless we connect this to trans-formations in urban political economies (although similar destructive tenden-cies are having powerful effects in rural and many suburban areas as well). The social and labor structures of large cities have, in essence, split into "two vastly unequal but intimately linked economies." These economies are intimately linked because jobs that are less well paid, nonunionized, often part-time, and with few benefits are required to make urban life attractive to the affluent. This is due not only to an increasingly globalized corporate sector that pits the workers of one nation against another and demands ever lower taxes no mat-ter what the social costs to local communities, although such things are indeed crucial parts of any serious explanation. It is also due to the needs of affluent urban workers "who have created lifestyles that depend on a large pool of low wage workers." In Katz's words again, the result is a new "servant class." "Like corporations, affluent urbanites have outsourced their domestic tasks for much the same reasons of economy and flexibility and with much the same re-sults"—poverty wages and an often heartbreaking exposure to the risks associ-ated with no health care, no insurance, no unions, no childcare, and no social benefits.[8]

Yet, class relations do not totally cover the reasons for this situation. The political economy of race enters in absolutely crucial ways. As Charles Mills re-minds us, underpinning so much of the social structure of American life is an unacknowledged *racial contract*.[9] Current neo-liberal and neo-conservative policies in almost every sphere of society—marketization, national curricula and national testing are representatives of these policies in education—have differential and racializing effects. While they are often couched in the lan-guage of "helping the poor," increasing accountability, giving "choice," and so on, the racial structuring of their outcomes is painful to behold in terms of re-spectful jobs (or lack of them), in health care, in education, and in so much more. For reasons of economy, health, education, nutrition, and so on, for black children, Latino/a youth, and so many more, the American city is often a truly dangerous place not only for their present but their future as well.[10] Yet we then ask the school to compensate for all of this.

My points here are ratified in Lipman's *High Stakes Education*, which pro-vides a detailed examination of the effects of the dismantling and reconstruc-tion of urban political economies and social networks on schools in our cities and towns, especially on schools that serve poor children of color. A better un-derstanding of some of the less talked about and hidden effects of widely emu-lated school reforms, one that goes beyond the hype of "TINA" ("there is no alternative" to these tough policies), is absolutely essential for educators throughout the nation and the industrialized world. Lipman and others such as Linda McNeil have shown what actually happens to teachers and children when policies involving strict accountability, massive amounts of testing, and similar things get instituted. The results are striking and should raise serious questions in the minds of all of those who believe that in these sets of policies we have found *the* answers to the problems that beset our schools. The results may certainly not be a more socially critical and democratic education that is connected to principles of thick democracy and social justice. Rather, such policies may re-create conditions that mirror many of those criticized in this book.

We tend to forget that "revolutions may go backwards." And what we are witnessing in education and in many other economic, political, and cultural institutions is exactly this—a politics that wants to radically shift our society so that it mirrors a supposed Eden that once existed. Well that "Eden" was the time of what some wise political commentators called "Satanic mills" and of a politics of cultural control that marginalized the lives, dreams, and experiences of identifiable people. This is a dangerous time and we need to face these dangers directly, if we are not to reproduce the histories, ideological tendencies, and conditions I trace out in this book.

The return to shallow understandings of science, the search for technical solutions based on this (mis)understanding of science, a new managerialism that relies on the massiveness of the resurgent regime of "measuring anything that moves in classrooms," the reduction of education to workplace skills and the culture of the powerful—these are things that are not fictions. We are facing them every day, sponsored by a government that seems intent on giving everything that ordinary people have struggled for over to the most powerful—and often simply rapacious—segments of this society. This must be stopped and education has a role to play in stopping it.

"Really" Beyond Ideological Reproduction

The arguments I made above lead to a crucial question. Is it possible to do something that is different, that interrupts neo-liberal and neo-conservative policies and ideologies, that has a very different politics of legitimate knowledge, and is one that is based on a very real commitment to creating schools that are closely connected to a larger project of social transformation? I think so.

The first and second editions of *Ideology and Curriculum* end with a section titled "Beyond Ideological Reproduction" that speaks to this in general terms, but over the years we have learned more about how such a counter-hegemonic politics can and does go on inside and outside of education. Let me give an example, one taken from Brazil, a nation where I have worked with progressive and socially critical educators for decades. My intense working with and learning from Brazilian activists and educators began in the mid-1980s, right after the military government that was supported by the United States was ultimately removed. It continued with my extensive interactions with Paulo Freire, and has become even more extensive with my efforts to assist and learn from the Workers Party in their attempts to build an education worthy of its name in Brazil.

One of the claims of these rightist forces is that schools are out of touch with parents and communities. While these criticisms are not totally wrong, we need to find ways of connecting our educational efforts to local communities, especially to those members of these communities with less power, which are more truly democratic than the ideas of "thin" democracy envisioned by neo-liberals. If we do not do this, neo-liberal definitions of democracy—ones that I discuss in much greater detail in the last chapter of this new edition and ones based on possessive individualism where citizenship is reduced to simply consumption practices—will prevail. While we need to be very honest about the fact that the current transformations in education, the current attacks on teachers' autonomy, working conditions, and wages, and the current ideological changes in the larger society may make it even harder for us to maintain and expand a truly democratic vision of education, this does *not* make it impossible.

What is happening in Porto Alegre, Brazil provides a powerful example of what is possible if we organize around a coherent set of democratic policies. After many years of electoral losses, the Workers Party has won consecutive elections in Porto Alegre and for a number of years had electoral control of the state of Rio Grande do Sol. One of the reasons it won was that it put forward a very different vision and set of policies for a more substantive set of democratic institutions. More democratic and participatory schooling was a central part of their proposals, as was an immediate and substantial increase in teachers salaries, because they knew that teachers would not support proposals that simply caused them to work even harder for salaries that were declining each year.[11]

The policies being put in place by the Workers Party, such as *participatory budgeting* and the Citizen School, are helping to build support for more progressive and democratic policies there in the face of the growing power of neo-liberal movements at a national level. The Workers Party has been able to increase its majority even among people who had previously voted in favor of parties with much more conservative educational and social programs *because* it has been committed to enabling even the poorest of its citizens to participate in deliberations over the policies themselves and over where and how money should be spent. By paying attention to more substantive forms of collective participation and, just as importantly, by devoting resources to encourage such participation, Porto Alegre has demonstrated that it is possible to have a "thicker" democracy, even in times of both economic crisis and ideological attacks from neo-liberal parties and from the conservative press. Programs such as the Citizen School and the sharing of real power with those who live in favelas (shantytowns), as well as with the working and middle classes, professionals, and others—and with teachers—provide ample evidence that thick democracy offers realistic alternatives to the eviscerated version of thin democracy found under neo-liberalism.

In many ways the policies and practices now being built there extend, in powerful and systemic ways, a number of similar reforms that are being built in other countries. Yet just as important is the pedagogic function of these programs in Porto Alegre. They develop the collective capacities among people to enable them to continue to engage in the democratic administration and control of their lives. This is time-consuming, but time spent in such things now has proven to pay off dramatically later on.[12]

The policies of the Popular Administration in Porto Alegre are explicitly designed to radically change both the municipal schools and the relationships among communities, the state, and education. This set of policies and the accompanying processes of implementation are constitutive parts of a clear and explicit project aimed at constructing not only a better school for the excluded—and for the teachers who work so hard in them—but also a larger project of radical democracy. While the reforms being built in Porto Alegre are still in process, what is being built there may be crucial not "only" for Brazil, but for all of us in so many nations who are struggling in classrooms and schools to create an education that serves *all* of our children and communities. Once again, Joseph is in the forefront of my consciousness as I write these words.

We don't have to look only to Porto Alegre for possibilities, however. In the United States there are outstanding examples of what can be done to counter rightist tendencies and to build an education that responds to the best, not the worst in us. Popular journals such as *Rethinking Schools* document what can be and is being done in real schools and real communities. The widely read book that James Beane and I published, *Democratic Schools*, contains honest and detailed examples of how critical educators, community members, and others—working together—have built counter-hegemonic possibilities that have stood the test of time.[13] But let us be honest; the fact that such possibilities exist, that education can go beyond the reproduction of dominance in important ways, is exactly that—a range of possibilities. If we do not continue to build on them, those in dominance will once again be able reproduce the conditions of their own power.

This is why in this new Preface I have tried to be honest about the complex forces that are having an impact on schools. Sticking our heads in the sand like ostriches will not make these forces go away. Neo-liberal and neo-conservative movements are—aggressively—altering our jobs and our schools. Their effects are increasingly dangerous. Yet as the example of Porto Alegre, the schools described in *Democratic Schools*, and the efforts of *Rethinking Schools* show, this is not only a time for pessimism. The possibility of constructing and defending much more critically democratic schools does exist. Teachers, unions, communities, students, and social activists have joined together to build such schools all over the world. Let us hope that the same is true for other parts of world, including the United States where I live, as well.

Understanding the Present and Future

For historical reasons and for reasons I discuss in the Preface to the second edition, which is included here, the basic text of the original edition of *Ideology and Curriculum* remains unchanged. Yet this new edition contains some important additional material as well. I have included two new chapters. The first, "Pedagogy, Patriotism, and Democracy: Ideology and Education after September 11," connects the conflicts and tensions over education after the horrible events of September 11 to the dangers I discuss in the book. This chapter is rather personal because I believe that the questions of ideological conflict and struggles over power that this book deals with, though at times written in abstract ways here, are not abstract at all. The chapter speaks both to my own experiences during and after the tragedy, and to the hidden effects that the rightist resurgence that accompanied it have had on both the ideological struggles over and the governance of schooling even at a local level. As I shall show, race needs to play a crucial role in understanding the real effects of 9/11 on real schools.

The second additional chapter is an interview with me done with Michael F. Shaughnessy, Kathy Peca, and Janna Siegel for an international journal. The interviewers ask me to reflect on a number of crucial tendencies and relations of differential power that are currently moving education in particular, largely rightist, directions—what I have called "conservative modernization."

I have included this interview for a number of reasons. First, it has a pedagogic intent. Interviews force authors to be clear because speaking is not like writing. It's harder to hide behind the language of the academy when one is face to face with people who really want to know how and why you are critically interrogating an unequal reality. Because the interviewers ask me to lay out my arguments about some of the most significant ideological and material transformations now affecting educational policy and practice, to basically describe things I've written about extensively in later books such as *Cultural Politics and Education, Official Knowledge,* and especially *Educating the "Right" Way* and *The State and the Politics of Knowledge,* the interview can serve as a good brief introduction to these analyses.

There's a second reason for including it, and this has to do with the positive responses I received to an interview that was included as an appendix to *Official Knowledge.* Many readers thought that it was very useful because it helped to clarify a number of the points I was talking about, and because its more approachable style enabled them to better sense the author behind the words. No book is ever disembodied. Real people with backgrounds, lives, intuitions, arguments, worries, and perhaps not a few flaws, write books. And it's not a bad idea for readers to see this.

As in previous books, I want to include a way of contacting me so that I can learn from your thoughts, questions, agreements, and disagreements with this book. (Here's my email address: apple@education.wisc.edu) Like many others I am sure, one of the ways I personally learn is through discussions and debate with people who care just as deeply as I do about the lives and futures of students and their educators, as we all try our best to create educative experiences that make a real difference in schools and the larger society. *Ideology and Curriculum* may be a book that I first completed 25 years ago, but it is still very much a part of me. No book (and no author) is ever complete, and I welcome your comments.

Michael W. Apple
John Bascom Professor of
Curriculum and Instruction
and Educational Policy Studies
University of Wisconsin, Madison
August 2003

Acknowledgments to the Third Edition

This new edition of *Ideology and Curriculum* comes at a time when the book is being celebrated as a "classic" in the literature in education. While the text has been associated largely with me, it is important to state that Barry Franklin and Nancy King played a significant role in making this book a lasting contribution.

Over the years since the first edition appeared, a considerable number of people in many nations have been my teachers about how one should critically analyze the limits and possibilities of education in societies like our own. I've acknowledged them in other books and thus shall not do so here. However, in doing this particular edition, there are friends and colleagues who do need to be singled out. Rima Apple, James Beane, Diana Hess, Bob Lingard, Steven Selden, Amy Stuart Wells, and Kenneth Zeichner all made very useful suggestions on specific parts of the new material included in this edition. As usual, the members of the Friday Seminar at the University of Wisconsin deserve thanks for their perceptive criticisms and support.

Let me also do something unusual here as well. An author knows that she or he has made an impact when one's opponents have to respond. For this very reason, I paradoxically would like acknowledge the conservative writers at the Fordham Foundation and in the pages of *The Wall Street Journal* for their rather vitriolic comments on my arguments in some of the new material included here. Oddly, that they responded in this way gives me hope for the future.

Finally, special praise needs to be given to Catherine Bernard, my editor at Routledge. In an era when everyone's work has become intensified, including the labor of being an editor at a major press, Catherine's advice and efforts were exceptional.

This edition is dedicated to Alexander Seth Apple and Alyssa Lee Cotton. I hope that the schooling they experience and the society in which they live will enable them to become the kinds of persons who cherish equality.

Preface to the Second Edition

Spencer was not wrong when he reminded educators that one of the most fundamental questions we should ask about the schooling process is "What knowledge is of most worth?" This is a deceptively simple question, however, since the conflicts over what should be taught are sharp and deep. It is not "only" an educational issue, but one that is inherently ideological and political. Whether we recognize it or not, curriculum and more general educational issues have always been caught up in the history of class, race, gender, and religious conflicts in the United States and elsewhere.

Because of this, a better way of phrasing the question, a way that highlights the profoundly political nature of educational debate, is "Whose knowledge is of most worth?" That this is not simply an academic question is made strikingly clear by the fact that right-wing attacks on the schools, calls for censorship, and controversies over the values that are being taught and not being taught have made the curriculum into what can best be described as a political football. When one adds to this the immense pressure on the educational system in so many countries to make the goals of business and industry into the primary if not the only goals of schooling, then the issue takes on even greater salience.

Educators have witnessed a massive attempt—one that has been more than a little successful—at exporting the crisis in the economy and in authority relations *from* the practices and policies of dominant groups *onto* the schools. If teachers and curricula were more tightly controlled, more closely linked to the needs of business and industry, more technically oriented, with more stress on traditional values and workplace norms and dispositions, then the problems of achievement, of unemployment, of international economic competitiveness, of the disintegration of the inner city, and so on would largely disappear, or so goes the accepted litany.[1] I predicted a rapid increase in these conservative tendencies when I first wrote *Ideology and Curriculum*. And while any author is pleased to see that her or his predictions were accurate, it is not with any real sense of joy that I note these events, for the conservative restoration that lies behind them is having tragic effects on many people not only in the United States but in other nations as well.

One thing these alterations and tendencies do help make very clear, however, is the fact that discussions about what does, can, and should go on in classrooms are not the logical equivalent of conversations about the weather. They are fundamentally about the hopes, dreams, fears, and realities—the very lives—of millions of children, parents, and teachers. If this isn't worth our best efforts—intellectual and practical—then nothing is.

As a political activist, as a former elementary and secondary school teacher, and as a past president of a teachers union, for me these efforts came increasingly to focus on the political nature of curriculum and teaching and of education in general. *Ideology and Curriculum* represented one of the first major syntheses of these political issues. It seemed to me when I was originally writing it, and I am even more convinced now, that until we take seriously the extent to which education is caught up in the real world of shifting and unequal power relations, we will be living in a world divorced from reality. The theories, policies, and practices involved in education are *not* technical. They are inherently ethical and political, and they ultimately involve—once this is recognized—intensely personal choices about what Marcus Raskin calls "the common good."[2]

To be concerned with issues of power—in my case with how class, race, and gender inequalities work through schools in the control of teachers and students and in the content and organization of the curriculum—is to stand on the shoulders of the many women and men who helped form those of us who work for a more democratized society. Even though I believed that it was essential that we politicize these issues much further than had been done in the past, the questions I asked in this volume have their roots in a long tradition—in Dewey's and Counts's attempts to define a democratic education, in past moments of democratic curriculum reform, and in efforts to teach "the knowledge of all of us" rather than only elite knowledge in schools,[3] in Huebner's eloquent insistence that we cannot purge the personal, ethical, and political from the discourse of curriculum, in Greene's compelling arguments for the "existential situatedness" of ourselves as educators. We must choose and we must act. There really is no other choice.[4]

Of course, we never act in a vacuum. The very realization that education is deeply implicated in the politics of culture makes this clear. After all, the decision to define some groups' knowledge as worthwhile to pass on to future generations while other groups' culture and history hardly see the light of day says something extremely important about who has power in society. Think of social studies texts that continue to speak of "the Dark Ages" rather than the historically more accurate and much less racist phrase "the Age of African and Asian Ascendency" or books that treat Rosa Parks as merely an African American who was simply too tired to go to the back of the bus, rather than discussing her training in organized civil disobedience at the Highlander Folk School. The realization that teaching, especially at the elementary school level, has in large part been defined as women's paid work (with nearly 90 percent of elementary school teachers and over 65 percent of teachers overall being women) documents the connections between teaching and the history of gender politics as well.[5] Thus, whether we like it or not, differential power intrudes into the heart of curriculum and teaching.

By asking us to see education relationally, to recognize its intimate connections to the inequalities in the larger society, I am self-consciously aligning myself with a program aimed at what I earlier called "the common good." This program of criticism and renewal asserts the principle that "no inhuman act should be used as a short cut to a better day," and, especially, that at each step of the way any social program "will be judged against the likelihood that it will result in linking equity, sharing, personal dignity, security, freedom, and caring."[6] This means that those pursuing such a program "must . . . assure themselves that the course they follow, inquire into, [and] analyze . . . will dignify human life, recognize the playful and creative aspects of people," and see others not as objects but as "co-responsible" subjects involved in the process of democratically deliberating over and building the ends and means of all their institutions.[7]

As some of you may know, *Ideology and Curriculum* is the initial volume of a trilogy. It was followed by *Education and Power*[8] and *Teachers and Texts*,[9] as well as by a number of edited volumes that extended its original problematic and explored even more deeply the questions it raised, the actual content, organization, and control of curriculum and teaching, and student and teacher responses to these issues.[10] As the first volume, however, *Ideology and Curriculum* established the problematic. It set the path for all that came after it.

In writing *Ideology and Curriculum* I sought to do a number of things. First, I wanted educators, particularly those specifically interested in what happens inside classrooms, to critically examine the assumptions they had about what education does. These assumptions concern some very deep seated, but often unconscious, presuppositions about science, the nature of men and women, and the ethics and politics of our day-to-day curricular and pedagogic theories and practices. I strongly believed then and still do today that the major way to accomplish this critical examination is to place our institutions of formal education back into the larger and unequal society of which they are a part.

Second, I wanted to bring a particular conceptual, empirical, and political approach to bear on this task. This approach had to illuminate how education was linked in important ways to the reproduction of existing social relations. Yet at the same time, it had to avoid some of the mistakes of previous investigations of schooling in our kind of economy. It had to be critical and still resist the tendency to deal *only* with economic controls and "determinations." It had to speak directly to cultural and ideological dynamics that were not totally reducible to economic relations, even though they were clearly influenced by them.

Finally, I felt it was necessary to get inside the school and rigorously scrutinize the actual curriculum—both overt and hidden—that dominated the classroom and then compare it to the commonsense assumptions educators had. My aim was to synthesize and reconstruct, and then go beyond, previous investigations of the social role of our widely accepted educational theories and practices. My arguments drew on aspects of "critical theory" and on some exceptionally insightful critical cultural and sociological work done in Europe to complement work already done by myself and others in the United States.

Behind all of these issues lay a particular set of questions. What is the relationship between culture and economy? How does ideology function? It is not enough to answer these questions in the abstract, however. As people concerned with education, we need to answer them in relation to one major institution, the school. Thus, we must rigorously scrutinize the form and content of the curriculum, the social relations within the classroom, and the ways we currently conceptualize these things, as cultural expressions of particular groups in particular institutions at particular times.

At the same time, and this is important for my arguments in *Ideology and Curriculum,* it is important to realize that while our educational institutions do function to distribute ideological values and knowledge, this is not all they do. As a system of institutions, they also ultimately help produce the type of knowledge (as a kind of commodity) that is needed to maintain the dominant economic, political, and cultural arrangements that now exist. I call this "technical knowledge" here. It is the tension between distribution and production that partly accounts for some of the ways schools act to legitimate the existing distribution of economic and cultural power.

My treatment of these issues is only in its initial form in this book and is expanded considerably in *Education and Power* and *Teachers and Texts.* But I hope it is clear enough for the reader to begin to see that what schools do ideologically, culturally, and economically is very complicated and cannot be fully understood by the application of any simple formula. There *are* very strong connections between the formal and informal knowledge within the school and the larger society with all its inequalities But since the pressures and demands of dominant groups are highly mediated by the internal histories of educational institutions and by the needs and ideologies of the people who actually work in them, the aims and results will often be contradictory as well. Whatever the aims and results, however, there are real people being helped and harmed inside these buildings. Wishful thinking and not confronting what may be some of the more powerful effects of the educational system will not make this fact go away.

In the years since *Ideology and Curriculum* first appeared, I have been more than pleased with its reception. The fact that it has been translated into many languages, that it is seen as a path-breaking book, and is widely read speaks eloquently I think to the honesty and openmindedness with which many educators, social scientists, policymakers, cultural and political activists, and others approach their tasks. Just as importantly, it also documents the constant struggle by these same people to question their present conditions so that they may act in more responsible ways. Not to engage in such continual questioning is to abrogate one's responsibility to the current and future lives of the thousands of students who spend so many years in schools. Self-reflection and social reflection are joined here.

The perspectives embodied in the book you are about to read are most concerned with the forces of ideological reproduction. What is dealt with in less detail is a set of concerns involving what has been called contradictory tendencies, resistances, and conflicts over these ideological forces. That is, cultural and economic reproduction is not all that is happening in our educational institutions. Even though *Ideology and Curriculum* focuses largely on one moment of a larger historical progression—that of the politics of domination—I cannot see how we can begin to understand "how relations of domination, whether material or symbolic, could possibly operate without implying, activating resistance."[11] There are often people who, either singly or in organized groups, are now acting in ways that may provide significant bases for "counter-hegemonic" work as well. This should give us some reason for optimism, an optimism (without illusions) that is expressed and developed in my later books. The recognition of such "counter-hegemonic" work, however, means that analyzing the manner in which powerful conservative interests operate is even more important so that we can better understand both the conditions under which education operates and the possibilities for altering these conditions.

One other point needs to be made in this preface. Not only is the focus in this volume more strongly on forms of reproduction in education, it tends to stress class relations as well. Class dynamics are of immense significance and cannot be ignored. However, I have become more and more convinced that *gender* relations—and those involving *race*, which in the United States and in so many other countries are critically important—are of equal significance in understanding what the social effects of education are and how and why curriculum and teaching are organized and controlled. These arguments, as well, are elaborated at greater length elsewhere.[12] It is sufficient, I think, to note here only how the problematic first established in *Ideology and Curriculum* has been markedly expanded to include the ways the contradictory dynamics of gender, race, and class operate in all their complexity in our institutions and how they may be leading in progressive, not only retrogressive, directions.

Parts of the argument made here rest on a critique of liberalism as the framework for social policy and educational theory and practice. While these criticisms of liberalism are essentially correct, liberalism itself is under concerted attack from the right, from the coalition of neo-conservatives, "economic modernizers," and new right groups who have sought to build a new consensus around their own principles. Following a strategy best called "authoritarian populism," this coalition has combined a "free market ethic" with a populist politics. The results have been a partial dismantling of social demo-cratic policies that largely benefited working people, people of color, and women (these groups are obviously not mutually exclusive), the building of a closer relationship between government and the capitalist economy, a radical decline in the institutions and power of political democracy, and attempts to curtail liberties that had been gained in the past. And all this has been very cleverly connected to the needs, fears, and hopes of many groups of people who feel threatened during a time of perceived crisis in the economy, in au-thority relations, in the family, and elsewhere.[13]

These attacks, and the ease with which certain gains were lost, have led to a partial rapprochement with social democratic "liberal" positions. While liberal policies often acted to cover up the depth of our problems in education, the economy, and elsewhere, these policies did often include some real gains. Be-cause of this, our approach to liberalism has to be more subtle. Our task is to de-fend the partial gains and rights won under the social democratic banner, and to expand and go beyond them to a more fully democratized economy, polity, and culture.[14] Thus, while I still agree with my analysis of the ultimate weaknesses of liberal positions in this book, the context has changed. In a context where even liberal policies and rights are threatened, we need to focus our attention more on the threats coming from the authoritarian populism of the right.

Let me discuss this just a bit more. The resurgence of conservative positions is an attempt to regain hegemonic power that was threatened by women, peo-ple of color, and others. One need only read the pronouncements of William Bennett, the former Secretary of Education of the United States—with its em-phasis on a common culture based on "our" western heritage and on a roman-ticized past in which all students sat still and internalized "our" values—to understand how powerful is the current urge to regain a lost consensus over what counts as legitimate knowledge.[15] The questions surrounding what counts as legitimate knowledge and an analysis of the attempt to create a false cultural and political consensus lie at the very heart of this book. This makes many of its arguments about ideology perhaps even more important today than when they were first written.

The current call to "return" to a "common culture" in which all students are given the values of a specific group—usually the dominant group—does not to my mind concern a common culture at all. Such an approach hardly scratches the surface of the political issues involved. A common culture can never be the general extension to everyone of what a minority mean and be-lieve. Rather, and crucially, it requires not the stipulation of lists and concepts that make us all "culturally literate," *but the creation of the conditions necessary for all people to participate in the creation and recreation of meanings and values.* It requires a democratic process in which all people—not simply those who are the intellectual guardians of the "western tradition"—can be involved in the deliberations over what is important. It should go without saying that this necessitates the removal of the very real material obstacles—unequal power, wealth, time for reflection—that stand in the way of such participation.[16] As Williams put it:

> The idea of a common culture is in no sense the idea of a simply consenting, and certainly not of a merely conforming, society. [It involves] a common determination of meanings by all the people, acting sometimes as individuals, sometimes as groups, in a process which has no particular end, and which can never be supposed at any time to have finally realized itself, to have become complete. In this common process, the only absolute will be the keeping of the channels and institutions of communication clear so that all may contribute, and be helped to contribute.[17]

In speaking of a common culture, then, we should not be talking of something uniform, something all of us conform to. Instead, what we should be asking is "precisely, for that free, contributive and common *process* of participation in the creation of meaning and values."[18] It is the blockage of that process in our formal institutions of education, and its very real negative effects, that I wished to deal with in *Ideology and Curriculum*.

Our current language speaks to how this process is being redefined. Instead of people who participate in the struggle to build and rebuild our educational, political, and economic relations, we are defined as consumers. This is truly an extraordinary concept, for it sees people by and large as either stomachs or furnaces.[19] We use and use up. We don't create. Someone else does that. This is disturbing enough in general, but in education it is truly disabling. Leave it to the guardians of tradition, the efficiency and accountability experts, the holders of "real knowledge." As I demonstrated in this book, we leave it to these people at great risk, especially at great risk to those students who are already economically and culturally disenfranchised by our dominant institutions.

Part of the reason I took, and still take, these issues of cultural politics and empowerment to be of such importance is autobiographical. I came of age in a poor family (but *only* in the economic sense of that word), in a very poor neighborhood in a dying industrial city in the Northeast—Paterson, New Jersey. The all too real struggles and insecurities of working-class life, its forms of solidarity and its politics and culture in the face of this, all formed me in significant ways. I have too many memories of the ways this rich culture was degraded in the media, in educational institutions, and elsewhere. I am all too aware of how whatever I have made of myself is rooted in the feelings, sensibilities, and richly contextualized meanings of the women and men of that neighborhood to feel comfortable with an economic system in which profit counts more than people's lives and an educational system that—despite the immensely hard and all too little respected labors of the people who work in it—still alienates millions of children for whom schooling could mean so much.

I cannot accept a society in which more than one out of every five children is born in poverty, a condition that is worsening every day. Nor can I accept as legitimate a definition of education in which our task is to prepare students to function easily in the "business" of that society. A nation is not a firm.[20] A school is not part of that firm, efficiently churning out the "human capital" required to run it. We do damage to our very sense of the common good to even think of the human drama of education in these terms. It is demeaning to teachers and creates a schooling process that remains unconnected to the lives of so many children.

These are, of course, complicated issues and, because of this, parts of *Ideology and Curriculum* are densely argued and I have sometimes made use of unfamiliar concepts. I end a more recent book of mine—*Teachers and Texts*—by calling for greater attention to the politics of writing, to writing in a way that makes one's arguments more accessible to the reader. In another way, however, it is important to realize that reality is very complicated, as are the relations of dominance and subordination that organize it. Sometimes understanding these relations requires that we develop a new language that may seem uncomfortable when first tried out. Learning how to use this set of concepts to look anew at our daily lives will take hard work, but it may in fact be necessary if we are to make headway in recognizing (rather than our all too usual misrecognizing) the contradictory ways education functions in our society.

Ideology and Curriculum was the result of nearly a decade long struggle to understand the politics of educational reality, and it shows the marks of that struggle in its concepts, language, and analysis. Yet so much of it still seems accurate and so many of the questions and issues it examines remain critical in a period of conservative restoration[21]—of what Aronowitz and Giroux call "an age of broken dreams"[22]—that I think on balance it was written as it had to be.

In *Ideology and Curriculum,* I sought to integrate into educational discourse a set of concepts and concerns that I believe continue to be essential to our deliberations about what and whose knowledge is of most worth. Much of my life as an activist, researcher, and teacher has been spent trying to bridge the artificial boundaries between, say, politics and education, between curriculum and teaching on the one hand and questions of cultural, political, and economic power on the other. These boundaries, as Pierre Bourdieu would say, are "pure products of academic reproduction."[23] The foundation of such boundaries is shaky on conceptual grounds and is immensely disabling if we are to deal with the political realities of schooling in an honest fashion. Hence, part of my method here is "trespassing," using tools built in critical theory, the sociology of knowledge, philosophy, and so on, and applying them to our commonsense thoughts and actions as educators. Again, following Bourdieu, "trespassing . . . is a prerequisite for . . . advance."[24]

This advance requires that the system of meanings and values that this society has generated—one increasingly dominated by an "ethic" of privatization, unconnected individualism, greed, and profit—has to be challenged in a variety of ways. Among the most important is by sustained and detailed intellectual and educational work.[25] This work will not be easily done; after all, so much of the cultural apparatus of this society is organized so that we don't get a clear picture of what lies beneath the surface. Ten second "news bites" and "sound bites" can't convey this. In the face of this, it is even more important that we do the work of cultural excavation, of uncovering the positive and negative moments of power, and restoring to our collective memories what differential cultural power has meant to a society in crisis.

There are, of course, some risks in doing this. Criticism makes people uncomfortable, and often criticism needs to be aimed at oneself as well. Also, saying things that challenge commonly accepted policies and practices can adversely affect one's career, and this has predictably occurred a number of times recently to critical educators at universities and elsewhere.

That taking such arguments seriously is itself a political act was documented very clearly to me by the firing of a teacher who wrote a review of *Ideology and Curriculum* in a journal for teachers in a country in Asia that has a history of repressive regimes. It was again made clear when I was placed under a form of house arrest and prevented from speaking to certain people in the same country. Ideas are weapons (if you will forgive the militaristic and somewhat masculinist turn of phrase); and spreading them in authoritarian contexts is a subversive, sometimes dangerous, and yet utterly essential act.

Yet could we, as educators, do less? Our task is to teach and to learn; to take our inquiries as seriously as the subject deserves; to take criticism of what we say respectfully and openly; to hunger for it so that we too can be called upon to challenge and reformulate our own commonsense as we ask others—like you the reader—to challenge your own. The journey we are embarking on—what Raymond Williams so correctly called the long revolution[26]—requires such challenge and reformulation. It is a journey of hope, but one that is grounded in an unromantic appraisal of what confronts us as educators for whom democracy is not a slogan to be called upon when the "real business" of our society is over, but a constitutive principle that must be integrated into all of our daily lives. *Ideology and Curriculum*—with its limitations and silences acknowledged—is part of my journey on that path to cultural democracy. If it assists you as well, what else could any author wish for?

Michael W. Apple
The University of Wisconsin, Madison

Acknowledgments to the Second Edition

With any volume, but with this one in particular, a number of people have contributed both argument and affirmation. Not all of them will agree with everything written here, but all of them share one characteristic. They have each taught me something that has contributed—sometimes in small but often in large ways—to this book. Among those individuals are Ann Becker, Basil Bernstein, Roger Dale, John Eggleston, Walter Feinberg, Michael Flude, Barry Franklin, Maxine Greene, Dwayne Huebner, Carl Kaestle, Daniel Kallos, Nancy King, Herbert Kliebard, Alan Lockwood, James Macdonald, Steve Mann, Vandra Masemann, Fred Newmann, Michael Olneck, Daniel Pekarsky, Francis Schrag, Steven Selden, Jonas Soltis, Robert Tabachnick, Gary Wehlage, Philip Wexler, Geoff Whitty and Michael F. D. Young. I also owe a good deal to David Godwin of Routledge & Kegan Paul. Bonnie Garski and Barbara Seffrood as always proved their excellence, friendship, and humanity in typing the manuscript, offering suggestions, and being patient with my rethinking.

A word must also be said about the individuals in the ongoing seminar on "Ideology and School Knowledge" at the University of Wisconsin. Much of what has been written here has been influenced by them. They are more than students, but now friends and participants in a collective search for a more thorough and critical appraisal of what schools do.

It is usual in acknowledgments to say a few words about the dedication of one's wife and children. Yet I am afraid that words may not be enough to convey the debt I owe to my wife Rima, whose support, criticism, and continued tutelage in both the history of women and the history of science, have been so very important in my own growth. Her support, and those members of my family whose origins and political struggles against oppression have led to the search for my own political roots on the American left, have made this book a reality.

Finally, I want to dedicate this book to my sons, Peter and Paul. May both they and we be strong enough to enable them to stand on our political shoulders.

Earlier versions of a number of these chapters have appeared elsewhere: Chapter 2 in *Comparative Education Review*, XXII (October 1978), Chapter 3 in *Curriculum Inquiry*, VI (no. 4, 1977), Chapter 4 in *Community Participation in Education*, Carl Grant (ed.) (Boston: Allyn & Bacon, 1979), Chapter 5 in *Interchange*, II (no. 4, 1971), Chapter 6 in *The Journal of Educational Research*, LXVI (September 1972), and Chapter 7 in *Schools in Search of Meaning*, James

B. Macdonald and Esther Zaret (eds) (Washington: Association for Supervision and Curriculum Development, 1975). My thanks are due to Raymond Williams and *New Left Review* for permission to quote from "Base and Superstructure in Marxist Cultural Theory" (1973).

CHAPTER 1

On Analyzing Hegemony

I

Introduction

A few years ago I was asked to write a personal statement for a volume that was reprinting a number of my papers. In that piece, I tried to document the kinds of political and personal commitments that I felt provided an irreducible minimum set of tenets which guided my work as educator.[1] In summary, I argued strongly that education was not a neutral enterprise, that by the very nature of the institution, the educator was involved, whether he or she was conscious of it or not, in a political act. I maintained that in the last analysis educators could not fully separate their educational activity from the unequally responsive institutional arrangements and the forms of consciousness that dominate advanced industrial economies like our own.

Since writing that statement, the issues have become even more compelling to me. At the same time, I have hopefully made some progress in gaining a greater depth of understanding into this relationship between education and economic structure, into the linkages between knowledge and power. In essence, the problem has become more and more a *structural* issue for me. I have increasingly sought to ground it in a set of critical questions that are generated out of a tradition of neo-Marxist argumentation, a tradition which seems to me to offer the most cogent framework for organizing one's thinking and action about education.

In broad outline, the approach I find most fruitful seeks to "explicate the manifest and latent or coded reflections of modes of material production, ideological values, class relations, and structures of social power—racial and sexual as well as politico-economic—on the state of consciousness of people in a precise historical or socio-economic situation."[2] That's quite a lot for one sentence, I know. But the underlying problematic is rather complicated. It seeks to portray the concrete ways in which prevalent (and I would add, alienating) structural arrangements—the basic ways institutions, people, and modes of production, distribution, and consumption are organized and controlled— dominate cultural life. This includes such day-to-day practices as schools and the teaching and curricula found within them.[3]

I find this of exceptional import when thinking about the relationships between the overt and covert knowledge taught in schools, the principles of selection and organization of that knowledge, and the criteria and modes of evaluation used to "measure success" in teaching. As Bernstein and Young, among others, have provocatively maintained, the structuring of knowledge and symbol in our educational institutions is intimately related to the principles of social and cultural control in a society.[4] This is something on which I shall have more to say in a moment. Let me just state now that one of our basic problems as educators and as political beings, then, is to begin to grapple with ways of understanding how the kinds of cultural resources and symbols schools select and organize are dialectically related to the kinds of normative and conceptual consciousness "required" by a stratified society.

Others, especially Bowles and Gintis,[5] have focused on schools in a way which stresses the economic role of educational institutions. Mobility, selection, the reproduction of the division of labor, and other outcomes, hence, become the prime foci for their analysis. Conscious economic manipulation by those in power is often seen as a determining element. While this is certainly important, to say the least, it gives only one side of the picture. The economistic position provides a less adequate appraisal of the way these outcomes are *created* by the school. It cannot illuminate fully what the mechanisms of domination are and how they work in the day-to-day activity of school life. Furthermore, we must complement an economic analysis with an approach that leans more heavily on a cultural and ideological orientation if we are completely to understand the complex ways social, economic, and political tensions and contradictions are "mediated" in the concrete practices of educators as they go about their business in schools. The focus, then, should also be on the ideological and cultural mediations which exist between the material conditions of an unequal society and the formation of the consciousness of the individuals in that society. Thus, I want here to look at the relationship between economic and cultural domination, at what we take as given, that seems to produce "naturally" some of the outcomes partly described by those who have focused on the political economy of education.

On Analyzing Hegemony

I think we are beginning to see more clearly a number of things that were much more cloudy before. As we learn to understand the way education acts in the economic sector of a society to reproduce important aspects of inequality,[6] so too are we learning to unpack a second major sphere in which schooling operates. For not only is there economic property, there also seems to be symbolic property—cultural capital—which schools preserve and distribute. Thus, we can now begin to get a more thorough understanding of how institutions of cultural preservation and distribution like schools create and recreate forms of consciousness that enable social control to be maintained without the necessity of dominant groups having to resort to overt mechanisms of domination.[7] Increasing our understanding of this recreation is at the heart of this volume.

This is not an easy issue to deal with, of course. What I shall try to do in this introductory chapter is to portray, in rather broad strokes, the kinds of questions embodied in the approach and program of analysis which guides this book. In my discussion, I shall often draw upon the work of the social and cultural critic Raymond Williams. While he is not too well known among educators (and this is a distinct pity) his continuing work on the relationship between the control of the form and content of culture and the growth of the economic institutions and practices which surround us all can serve as a model, both personally and conceptually, for the kind of progressive arguments and commitments this approach entails.

There are three aspects of the program that need to be articulated at the beginning here: (1) the school as an institution, (2) the knowledge forms, and (3) the educator him or herself. Each of these must be *situated* within the larger nexus of relations of which it is a constitutive part. The key word here, obviously, is situated. Like the economic analysts such as Bowles and Gintis, by this I mean that, as far as is possible, we need to place the knowledge that we teach, the social relations that dominate classrooms, the school as a mechanism of cultural and economic preservation and distribution, and finally, ourselves as people who work in these institutions, back into the context in which they all reside. All of these things are subject to an interpretation of their respective places in a complex, stratified, and unequal society. However, we must be careful of misusing this tradition of interpretation. All too often, we forget the subtlety required to begin to unpack these relations. We situate the institution, the curriculum, and ourselves in an overly deterministic way. We say there is a one-to-one correspondence between economics and consciousness, economic base "automatically" determining superstructure. This is too easy to say, unfortunately, and is much too mechanistic.[8] For it forgets that there is, in fact, a dialectical relationship between culture and economics. It also presupposes an idea of conscious manipulation of schooling by a very small number of people with power. While this was and is sometimes the case—something I shall in fact document in Chapter 4's treatment of some of the historical roots of the curriculum field—the problem is much more complex than that. Thus, in order to go further, we must first clarify what is meant by the notion that structural relations "determine" these three aspects of schools. As I shall argue, one of the keys to understanding this is the concept of *hegemony*.

It is important to note that there are two traditions of using concepts such as "determine." On the one hand, the notion of thought and culture being determined by social and economic structure has been used to imply what was mentioned a minute ago, a one-to-one correspondence between social consciousness and, say, mode of production. Our social concepts, here, are totally prefigured or predicated upon a pre-existing set of economic conditions that control cultural activity, including everything in schools. On the other hand, there is a somewhat more flexible position which speaks of determination as a complex nexus of relationships which, in their final moment, are economically rooted, that exert pressures and set limits on cultural practice, including schools.[9] Thus, the cultural sphere is not a "mere reflection" of economic practices. Instead, the influence, the "reflection" or determination, is highly mediated by forms of human action. It is mediated by the specific activities, contradictions, and relationships among real men and women like ourselves—as they go about their day-to-day lives in the institutions which organize these lives. The control of schools, knowledge and everyday life can be, and is, more subtle for it takes in even seemingly inconsequential moments. The control is vested in the constitutive principles, codes, and especially the commonsense consciousness and practices underlying our lives, as well as by overt economic division and manipulation.

Raymond Williams's discussion of hegemony, a concept most fully developed in the work of Antonio Gramsci, provides an excellent summary of these points.[10]

> It is Gramsci's great contribution to have emphasized hegemony, and also to have understood it at a depth which is, I think, rare. For hegemony supposes the existence of something which is truly total, which is not merely secondary or superstructural, like the weak sense of ideology, but which is lived at such a depth, which saturates the society to such an extent, and which, as Gramsci put it, even constitutes the limit of commonsense for most people under its sway, that it corresponds to the reality of social experience very much more clearly than any notions derived from the formula of base and superstructure. For if ideology were merely some abstract imposed notion, if our social and political and cultural ideas and assumptions and habits were merely the result of specific manipulation, of a kind of overt training which might be simply ended or withdrawn, then the society would be very much easier to move and to change than in practice it has been or is. This notion of hegemony as deeply saturating the consciousness of a society seems to be fundamental. . . . [It] emphasizes the facts of domination.

The crucial idea embedded in this passage is how hegemony acts to "saturate" our very consciousness, so that the educational, economic and social world we see and interact with, and the commonsense interpretations we put on it, becomes the world *tout court,* the only world. Hence, hegemony refers not to congeries of meanings that reside at an abstract level somewhere at the "roof of our brain." Rather, it refers to an organized assemblage of meanings and practices, the central, effective and dominant system of meanings, values and actions which are *lived.* It needs to be understood on a different level than "mere opinion" or "manipulation." Williams makes this clear in his arguments concerning the relationship between hegemony and the control of cultural resources. At the same time, he points out how educational institutions may act in this process of saturation. I would like to quote one of his longer passages, one which I think begins to capture the complexity and one which goes be-

yond the idea that consciousness is only a mere reflection of economic structure, wholly determined by one class which consciously imposes it on another.
At the same time the passage catches the crux of how the assemblage of meanings and practices still leads to, and comes from, unequal economic and cultural control.[11]

> [Hegemony] is a whole body of practices and expectations; our assignments of
> energy, our ordinary understanding of man and his world. It is a set of meanings
> and values which as they are experienced as practices appear as reciprocally con-
> firming. It thus constitutes a sense of reality for most people in the society, a
> sense of absolute because experienced [as a] reality beyond which it is very diffi-
> cult for most members of a society to move in most areas of their lives. But this is
> not, except in the operation of a moment of abstract analysis, a static system. On
> the contrary we can only understand an effective and dominant culture if we un-
> derstand the real social process on which it depends: I mean the process of incor-
> poration. The modes of incorporation are of great significance, and incidently in
> our kind of society have considerable economic significance. The educational
> institutions are usually the main agencies of transmission of an effective domi-
> nant culture, and this is now a major economic as well as cultural activity; in-
> deed it is both in the same moment. Moreover, at a philosophical level, at the
> true level of theory and at the level of the history of various practices, there is a
> process which I call the *selective tradition:* that which, within the terms of an ef-
> fective dominant culture, is always passed off as "the tradition," *the* significant
> past. But always the selectivity is the point; the way in which from a whole possi-
> ble area of past and present, certain meanings and practices are chosen for em-
> phasis, certain other meanings and practices are neglected and excluded. Even
> more crucially, some of these meanings are reinterpreted, diluted, or put into
> forms which support or at least do not contradict other elements within the ef-
> fective dominant culture.
>
> The process of education; the processes of a much wider social training
> within institutions like the family; the practical definitions and organization of
> work; the selective tradition at an intellectual and theoretical level: all these
> forces are involved in a continual making and remaking of an effective dominant
> culture, and on them, as experienced, as built into our living, reality depends. If
> what we learn were merely an imposed ideology, or if it were only the isolable
> meanings and practices of the ruling class, or of a section of the ruling class,
> which gets imposed on others, occupying merely the top of our minds, it would
> be—and one would be glad—a very much easier thing to overthrow.

Notice what Williams is saying here about educational institutions. It is
similar to the point I argued earlier about the possible relationship between
the school as an institution and the recreation of inequality. Schools, in the
words of the British sociologists of the curiculum, do not only "process people;" they "process knowledge" as well.[12] They act as agents of cultural and ideological hegemony, in Williams's words, as agents of selective tradition and of
cultural "incorporation." But as institutions they not only are one of the main

agencies of distributing an effective dominant culture; among other institutions, and here some of the economic interpretations seem quite potent, they help create people (with the appropriate meanings and values) who see no other serious possibility to the economic and cultural assemblage now extant. This makes the concepts of ideology, hegemony, and selective tradition critical elements in the political and analytic underpinnings of the analyses found in this volume.

For example, as I argue later, the issues surrounding the knowledge that is actually taught in schools, surrounding what is considered to be socially *legitimate* knowledge, are of no small moment in becoming aware of the school's cultural, economic, and political position. Here, the basic act involves making the curriculum forms found in schools problematic so that their latent ideological content can be uncovered. Questions about the selective tradition such as the following need to be taken quite seriously. Whose knowledge is it? Who selected it? Why is it organized and taught in this way? To this particular group? The mere act of asking these questions is not sufficient, however. One is guided, as well, by attempting to link these investigations to competing conceptions of social and economic power and ideologies. In this way, one can begin to get a more concrete appraisal of the linkages between economic and political power and the knowledge *made available* (and *not* made available) to students.[13]

The movement, say, in social studies toward "process oriented" curriculum is a case in point. We teach social "inquiry" as a set of "skills," as a series of methods that will enable students "to learn how to inquire themselves." While this is certainly better than the more rote models of teaching which prevailed in previous decades, at the same time it can actually depoliticize the study of social life. We ask our students to see knowledge as a social construction, in the more disciplinary programs to see how sociologists, historians, anthropologists and others construct their theories and concepts. Yet, in so doing we do not enable them to inquire as to *why* a particular form of social collectivity exists, *how* it is maintained and *who* benefits from it.

There exists in curriculum development, and in teaching, something of a failure of nerve. We are willing to prepare students to assume "some responsibility for their own learning." Whether these goals are ever actually reached, given what Sarason[14] has called the behavioral regularities of the institution, is interesting here, but not at issue. Just as important is the fact that what one is "critically reflecting" about is often vacuous, ahistorical, one-sided, and ideologically laden. Thus, as I shall demonstrate in Chapter 5, for instance, the constitutive framework of most school curricula centers around consensus. There are few serious attempts at dealing with conflict (class conflict, scientific conflict, or other). Instead, one "inquires" into a consensus ideology that bears little resemblance to the complex nexus and contradictions surrounding the control and organization of social life. Hence, the selective tradition dictates that we do not teach, or will selectively reinterpret (and hence will soon forget), serious labor or woman's history. Yet we do teach elite and military history. Whatever economics is taught is dominated by a perspective that grows out of the National Association of Manufacturers or its equivalent. And honest information about countries that have organized themselves about alternative social principles is hard to find. These are only a few examples of the role of school in creating a sense of false consensus, of course.

Neutrality and Justice

The very fact that we tend to reduce our understanding of the social and economic forces underlying our unequal society to a set of skills, to "how to's," mirrors a much larger issue. Let me precurse some of the arguments that I shall develop in greater detail in Chapters 6, 7, and 8. This reduction of understanding speaks to the technicization of life in advanced industrial economies. In Habermas's terms, purposive-rational, or instrumental, forms of reasoning and action replace symbolic action systems. Political and economic, and even educational, debate among real people in their day-to-day lives is replaced by considerations of efficiency, of technical skills. "Accountability" through behavioral analysis, systems management, and so on become hegemonic and ideological representations. And at the same time considerations of the *justice* of social life are progressively depoliticized and made into supposedly neutral puzzles that can be solved by the accumulation of neutral empirical facts,[15] which when fed back into neutral institutions like schools can be guided by the neutral instrumentation of educators.

The claim to neutrality is important in this representation, not merely in social life in general, but in education in particular. We assume that our activity is neutral, that by not taking a political stance we are being objective. This is significantly falsified, however, in two ways. First, there is an increasing accumulation of evidence that the institution of schooling itself is not a neutral enterprise in terms of its economic outcomes. As I shall note, as Basil Bernstein, Pierre Bourdieu, and others have sought to show, and as the quotes from Williams have pointed to in this introductory chapter, while schools may in fact serve the interests of many individuals, and this should not be denied, at the same time, though, empirically they also seem to act as powerful agents in the economic and cultural reproduction of class relations in a stratified society like our own. This is a rather involved issue, yet as will be discussed in the next section of this chapter and in Chapter 2, the literature on the role schools play in economic and cultural stratification is becoming increasingly impressive.

Let me now note, actually reiterate, the second reason a claim to neutrality carries less weight than it might. The claim ignores the fact that the knowledge that now gets into schools is already a choice from a much larger universe of possible social knowledge and principles. It is a form of cultural capital that comes from somewhere, that often reflects the perspectives and beliefs of powerful segments of our social collectivity. In its very production and dissemination as a public and economic commodity—as books, films, materials, and so forth—it is repeatedly filtered through ideological and economic commitments. Social and economic values, hence, are already embedded in the design of the institutions we work in, in the "formal corpus of school knowledge" we preserve in our curricula, in our modes of teaching, and in our principles, standards, and forms of evaluation. Since these values now work *through* us, often unconsciously, the issue is not how to stand above the choice. Rather, it is in what values I must ultimately choose.

But this brings to the fore another part of the problem as well—those deepseated values that already reside not at the top but at the very "bottom" of our heads that I mentioned before. The very categories we use to approach our responsibility to others, the commonsense or constitutive rules we employ to evaluate the social practices that dominate our society, are often at issue. Among the most critical of these categories are both our vision of "science" and, just as importantly, our commitment to the abstract individual. For it is the case that our sense of community is withered at its roots. We find ways of making the concrete individual into an abstraction and, at the same time, we divorce the individual from larger social movements which might give meaning to "individual" wants, needs, and visions of justice.[16] This is strongly supported by the notion that curriculum research is a "neutral scientific activity" which does not tie us to others in important structural ways.

Our inability to think in other than abstracted individualistic terms is nicely expressed once again by Raymond Williams in his argument that the dominance of the bourgeois individual distorts our understanding of our real social relations with and dependence on others.[17]

> I remember a miner saying to me, of someone we were discussing: "He's the sort of man who gets up in the morning and presses a switch and expects a light to come on." We are all, to some extent, in this position, in that our modes of thinking habitually suppress large areas of our real relationships, including our real dependence on others. We think of my money, my light, in these naive terms, because parts of our very idea of society are withered at root. We can hardly have any conception, in our present system, of the financing of social purposes from the social product, a method which would continually show us, in real terms, what our society is and does. In a society whose products depend almost entirely on intricate and continuous cooperation and social organization, we expect to consume as if we were isolated individuals, making our own way. We are then forced into the stupid comparison of individual consumption and social taxation—one desirable and to be extended, the other regrettably necessary and to be limited. From this kind of thinking, the physical unbalance follows inevitably. Unless we achieve some realistic sense of community, our true standard of living will continue to be distorted . . . Questions not only of balance in the distribution of efforts and resources, but also of the effects of certain kinds of work both

on users and producers, might then be adequately negotiated . . . It is precisely the lack of an adequate sense of society that is crippling us.

Williams's points are many here, yet among them are the following. Our concern for the abstract individual in our social, economic, and educational life is exactly that—it is merely an abstraction. It does not situate the life of the individual (and ourselves as educators), as an economic and social being, back into the unequal structural relations that produced the comfort the individual enjoys. It can act as an ideological presupposition that keeps us from establishing any genuine sense of affiliation with those who produce our comforts, thus making it even more difficult to overcome the atrophication of collective commitment. Thus, the overemphasis on the individual in our educational, emotional, and social lives is ideally suited to both maintain a rather manipulative ethic of consumption and further the withering of political and economic sensitivity. The latent effects of both absolutizing the individual and defining our role as neutral technicians in the service of amelioration, therefore, makes it nearly impossible for educators and others to develop a potent analysis of widespread social and economic injustice. It makes their curricular and teaching practices relatively impotent in exploring the nature of the social order of which they are a part.

An exceptionally important element in this kind of argument is the idea of *relation*. What I am asking for is what might best be called "relational analyses." It involves seeing social activity—with education as a particular form of that activity—as tied to the larger arrangement of institutions which apportion resources so that particular groups and classes have historically been helped while others have been less adequately treated. In essence, social action, cultural and educational events and artifacts (what Bourdieu would call cultural capital) are "defined" not by their obvious qualities that we can immediately see. Instead of this rather positivistic approach, things are given meaning relationally, by their complex ties and connections to how a society is organized and controlled. The relations themselves are the defining characteristics.[18] Thus, to understand, say, the notions of science and the individual, as we employ them in education especially, we need to see them as primarily ideological and economic categories that are essential to both the production of agents to fill existing economic roles and the reproduction of dispositions and meanings in these agents that will "cause" them to accept these alienating roles without too much questioning.[19] They become aspects of hegemony.

In understanding these hegemonic relations we need to remember something which Gramsci maintained—that there are two requirements for ideological hegemony. It is not merely that our economic order "creates" categories and structures of feeling which saturate our everyday lives. Added to this must be a group of "intellectuals" who employ and give legitimacy to the categories, who make the ideological forms seem neutral.[20] Thus, an examination of the very categories and procedures that "intellectuals" like educators employ needs to be one of the prime foci of our investigation.

So far I have looked rather broadly at what I perceive to be much of the reality behind schools as institutions, the knowledge forms we selectively preserve, reinterpret, and distribute, some of the categories we use to think about these things, and the role of the educator as "neutral" participant in the large-scale results of schooling. There are still a few final comments to be said about that last aspect of the program and approach I am setting forth here though—the educator him or herself as political being. This is a very personal question, one that is by far the hardest. I am quite aware of the difficulty, in fact often the torture, that one must face in responding to or even adequately asking the question of "Where do I stand?" This kind of question already presupposes at least a beginning awareness of answers to my other queries about the relationship between cultural capital and economic and social control. It requires an analysis of what social and economic groups and classes seem to be helped by the way the institutions in our society are organized and controlled and which groups are not.[21]

The fact that this question *is* so hard to deal with, the helpless feeling we get when we ask it (what can I as one educator do now?) points to the utter importance of Gramsci's and Williams's arguments about the nature of hegemony. To hold our day-to-day activities as educators up to political and economic scrutiny, to see the school as part of a system of mechanisms for cultural and economic reproduction, is not merely to challenge the prevailing practices of education. If it were "merely" this, then we could perhaps change these practices through teacher training, better curricula, and so on. These practices may need changes, of course, and there is still a place for such ameliorative reforms, some of which I shall propose later in the volume. But the kinds of critical scrutiny I have argued for challenges a whole assemblage of values and actions "outside" of the institution of schooling. And this is exactly the point, for if taken seriously, it must lead to a set of commitments that may be wholly different than those many of us commonsensically accept. It requires the progressive articulation of and commitment to a social order that has at its very foundation not the accumulation of goods, profits, and credentials, but the maximization of economic, social, and educational equality.

All of this centers around a theory of social justice. My own inclination is to argue for something to the left of a Rawlsian stance. For a society to be just it must, as a matter of both principle and action, contribute most to the advantage of the least advantaged.[22] That is, its structural relations must be such as to equalize not merely access to but actual control of cultural, social, and especially economic institutions.[23] Now this would require more than mere tinkering with the social engine, for it implies a restructuring of institutions and a fundamental reshaping of the social contract that has supposedly bound us together. This theory of social justice which lies behind such a program needs to be generated out of more than personal ideology. It has its basis in a number of empirical claims as well. For example, the gap between rich and poor in advanced corporate nations is increasing. The distribution and control of health, nutritional, and educational goods and services is basically unequal in these same industrialized nations.[24] Economic and cultural power is being increasing centralized in massive corporate bodies that are less than responsive to social needs other than profit. After some initial gains, the relative progress of women and many minority groups is either stagnant or slowly atrophying. Because of these and other reasons, I am more and more convinced that these conditions are "naturally" generated out of a particular social order. As I shall document in this volume, our educational dilemmas, the unequal achievement, the unequal returns, the selective tradition and incorporation, are also "naturally" generated out of this social arrangement. It may be the case that these institutions are organized and controlled in such a way as to require rather large-scale changes in their relationships if progress is to be made in eliminating any of these conditions.

I realize that this is rather controversial, to say the least. Nor do I expect that everyone will accept all that I have written here. However, I did not first come to the position that our educational issues are *at root* ethical, economic, and political and then search for documentation of it. Rather, and this is important, I have been convinced by evidence available to all of us if we are willing to search and to question, if we can learn to analyze hegemony. In fact this is part of the program I would like to explicate here. One thing should be clear, this program requires a good deal of plain old hard "intellectual" work, as well. It involves more than a modicum of reading, study, and honest debate in areas many of us have only a limited background in. We are unused to looking at educational activity ethically, politically, and economically, not to say critically, given the very difficult (and time-consuming and emotionally draining) nature of being a decent educator. This task is made even more difficult because of what might be called the politics of knowledge distribution. That is, the kinds of tools and frameworks I have noted here are not readily distributed by the prevailing institutions of cultural preservation and distribution like schools and mass media. These critical traditions are themselves victims of selective tradition. If my arguments here and elsewhere in this volume about the nature of whose knowledge gets into schools are correct, this may be unfortunate but it is to be expected. However, if we do not take it upon ourselves to master these traditions, to relearn them, we ignore the fact that the kinds of institutional and cultural arrangements which control us were built by us. They can be rebuilt as well.

I have argued so far that any serious appraisal of the role of education in a complex society must have as a major part of its program at least three elements. It needs to situate the knowledge, the school, and the educator him or herself within the real social conditions which "determine" these elements. I have also argued that this act of situating needs to be guided by a vision of social and economic justice if it is to be meaningful. Hence, I have also maintained that the position of educator is neutral neither in the forms of cultural capital distributed and employed by schools nor in the economic and cultural outcomes of the schooling enterprise itself. These issues are best analyzed through the concepts of hegemony, ideology, and selective tradition, and can only be fully understood through a relational analysis.

As was mentioned, however, there is an evolving tradition of educational scholarship that wants to take this program of relational analysis seriously. Let us now look at it and what this volume examines in somewhat more detail.

II

Educational Scholarship and the Act of "Situating"

In his preface to the English translation of Karl Mannheim's classic work, *Ideology and Utopia,* Louis Wirth states that "The most important things . . . we can know about a man is what he takes for granted, and the most elemental and important facts about a society are those that are seldom debated and generally regarded as settled."[25] That is, to gain insight, to understand, the activity of men and women of a specific historical period, one must start out by questioning what to them is unquestionable. As Marx would say, one does not accept the illusions of an epoch, the participants' own commonsense appraisals of their intellectual and programmatic activities (though these are important to be sure); rather, the investigator must *situate* these activities in a larger arena of economic, ideological, and social conflict.

As I noted, education as a field of study does not have a strong tradition of such "situating." In fact, if one were to point to one of the most neglected areas of educational scholarship, it would be just this, the critical study of the relationship between ideologies and educational thought and practice, the study of the range of seemingly commonsense assumptions that guide our overly technically minded field. Such critical scholarship would lay bare the political, social, ethical, and economic interests and commitments that are uncritically accepted as "the way life really is" in our day-to-day life as educators.

The study of the interconnections between ideology and curriculum and between ideology and educational argumentation has important implications for the curriculum field and for educational theory and policy in general. For as I shall argue throughout this volume, we need to examine critically not just "how a student acquires more knowledge" (the dominant question in our efficiency minded field), but "why and how particular aspects of the collective culture are presented in school as objective, factual knowledge." How, *concretely,* may official knowledge represent ideological configurations of the dominant interests in a society? How do schools legitimate these limited and partial standards of knowing as unquestioned truths? *These questions must be asked of at least three areas of school life: (1) how the basic day to day regularities of schools contribute to students learning these ideologies; (2) how the specific forms of curricular knowledge both in the past and now reflect these configurations; and (3) how these ideologies are reflected in the fundamental perspectives educators themselves employ to order, guide, and give meaning to their own activity.*

The first of these questions refers to the hidden curriculum in schools—the tacit teaching to students of norms, values, and dispositions that goes on simply by their living in and coping with the institutional expectations and routines of schools day in and day out for a number of years. The second question asks us to make educational knowledge itself problematic, to pay much greater attention to the "stuff" of curriculum, where knowledge comes from, whose knowledge it is, what social groups it supports, and so on. The final query seeks to make educators more aware of the ideological and epistemological commitments they tacitly accept and promote by using certain models and traditions—say, a vulgar positivism, systems management, structural-functionalism, a process of social labeling, or behavior modification—in their own work. Without an understanding of these aspects of school life, one that connects them seriously to the distribution, quality, and control of work, power, ideology, and cultural knowledge outside of our educational institutions, educational theory and policy making may have less of an impact than we might hope.

To be sure, there is a growing number of current examples of this act of situating, of placing educational argumentation and techniques in a larger, more comprehensive context. Certain historians of education such as Katz, Karier, Kaestle, Feinberg, and others have given us pictures of the relationship between, say, bureaucratic, economic, and ideological interests and schooling that are less self-congratulatory than some of our previously accepted notions of our past. Added to this are the current analyses of both the political economy of education and the possibilities of educational reform done by Bowles and Gintis, Carnoy and Levin, and others. Less familiar perhaps, though equally as important, have been the relatively recent sociological investigations of the ties between school knowledge and such interests. All of these studies are guided, either tacitly or quite overtly, by the belief that a more thorough and honest appraisal of educational issues can be gained by placing them within a framework of competing conceptions of justice, of social and economic equality, and of what is and who should have legitimate power.

For example, in a recent critical analysis of the sociology of education, *The Sociology of Education: Beyond Equality*, Philip Wexler calls for a thoroughgoing reorientation of sociological research into schools.[26] Drawing upon some of the current European and American work on the relationship between ideology and curriculum, and between schools and the creation of inequality, he points out that to understand fully how schools function we must study schools as institutions that "process knowledge," as institutions that serve an ideological function. The sociology of education is to become the sociology of

school knowledge, in large part. Curriculum scholarship, sociological understanding, and the study of political and economic ideologies, hence, merge
into a unified perspective that enables us to delve into the place of schools in
the *cultural*, as well as *economic*, reproduction of class relations in advanced
industrial society.

Wexler's perception is quite provocative for a number of reasons. It sees social and educational research as a political act in large measure, something I
will discuss in somewhat greater depth later in this volume. It also asks us to
focus on the knowledge and symbols schools and other cultural institutions
overtly and covertly give legitimacy to. This is not to neglect the fact that
schools, as the old saw goes, do not merely "teach knowledge," but they also
"teach children." Rather, it calls for an understanding of how the kinds of symbols schools organize and select are dialectically related to how particular
types of students are organized and selected, and ultimately stratified economically and socially. And all of this is encompassed by a concern for power. Who
has it? Do certain aspects of schooling—the organization and selection of culture and people (for that is what schools in fact do)—contribute to a more equitable distribution of power and economic resources or do they preserve
existing inequalities? Whatever answer one gives to these questions, to understand how schools do this it is essential that one do two things. First, one must
see how schools operate first hand. The researcher must comprehend how the
day-to-day regularities of "teaching and learning in schools" produce these results. Second, one must have that peculiarly Marxist sensitivity to the present
as history, to see the historical roots and conflicts which caused these institutions to be what they are today. Without this dual understanding, it is that
much more difficult to comprehend completely the economic and cultural
"functions" of our educational institutions.

One way to think about culture in society is to employ a metaphor of distribution. That is, one can think about knowledge as being unevenly distributed
among social and economic classes, occupational groups, different age groups,
and groups of different power. Thus, some groups have access to knowledge
distributed to them and not distributed to others. The obverse of this is also
probably true. The *lack* of certain kinds of knowledge—where your particular
group stands in the complex process of cultural preservation and distribution—is related, no doubt, to the absence in that group of certain kinds of political and economic power in society.

This relationship between cultural distribution and the distribution and
control of economic and political potency—or more clearly, the relationship
between knowledge and power—is admittedly quite difficult to understand.
Yet an understanding of how the control of cultural institutions enhances the
power of particular classes to control others can provide needed insight into
the way the distribution of culture is related to the presence or absence of
power in social groups.

Many, if not most, educators are somewhat unfamiliar with this problem. We have tended to perceive knowledge as a relatively neutral "artifact." We have made of it a psychological "object" or a psychological "process" (which it is in part, of course). In so doing, however, we have nearly totally depoliticized the culture that schools distribute. Yet there is a growing body of curriculum scholars and sociologists of education who are taking much more seriously the questions of "whose culture?," "What social group's knowledge?," and "In whose interest is certain knowledge (facts, skills, and propensities and dispositions) taught in cultural institutions like schools?" As I have noted elsewhere[27] the best examples of this work are found in some recent volumes from England. Among them are Michael F. D. Young, ed., *Knowledge and Control,* Richard Brown, ed., *Knowledge, Education and Cultural Change,* Basil Bernstein, *Class, Codes and Control* Volume 3: *Towards a Theory of Educational Transmissions,* Michael Flude and John Ahier, eds, *Educability, Schools and Ideology* and Rachel Sharp and Anthony Green, *Education and Social Control.*[28]

The research program of these volumes and the perspective I am articulating here has been influenced by Raymond Williams's assertion that education is not a product like bread or cards, but must be seen as a selection and organization from all available social knowledge at a particular time. Since this selection and organization involves conscious and unconscious social and ideological choices, then a primary task of the curriculum scholarship is that of relating these principles of knowledge selection and organization to their institutional and interactional setting in schools, and then to the wider arena of institutional structures that surround classrooms.[29] These points mean a number of things when they are applied to what has increasingly been called the sociology of school knowledge. It means that for methodological reasons one does not take for granted that curricular knowledge is neutral. Instead, one looks for social interests embodied in the knowledge form itself. The points also imply that one must study the curriculum in use within schools. Instead of input-output studies of school achievement, the researcher needs to "live" in classrooms, to see the complex forms of interaction that occur in classrooms. In this way, more accurate pictures can be got of which particular "kinds" of students "get" what particular kinds of knowledge and dispositions. This makes analyses of the labeling process in schools of particular importance, obviously. Furthermore, one can see how knowledge is actually created and used in school settings. Finally, the tacit teaching of a less overt, hidden curriculum can be documented.

All of these data are important to our understanding of the kinds of and ways schools act to distribute both popular and elite culture. Yet, in order to take Williams's argument most seriously a further step must be taken. The researcher must think structurally or relationally. He or she must link this process of cultural distribution back to questions of power and control outside the school. Now this brings political and economic elements into the heart of educational investigation. This is a rather significant break with past moments of social and educational scholarship, most of which (inaccurately) argued that their underlying position was apolitical and bore no relationship to how power and resources were distributed in society. In fact, while I shall explore this in greater detail in Chapter 2, the general position being argued by those people concerned with, say, cultural reproduction and economic reproduction is that research into school knowledge, and more general forms of educational research, is at least tacitly a political act. However, at the same time that they argue *for* political commitment, they want to argue *against* one particular political affiliation that has come to dominate educational policy and curriculum discourse, that of the liberal tradition.

Actually, some of the similarities among those individuals concerned with a more critical appraisal of the school as a reproductive force can be seen in just this, their treatment of liberal educational theory, with its reliance on science, neutrality, and education as a form of social amelioration. As Feinberg notes, for example, one major weakness of liberal theory arises from its inability to see events as signs of serious structural issues. It turns educational concerns into administrative "problems" rather than instances of economic, ethical, and political conflict.[30]

Though there are differences among them, those people who, like myself, have sought to situate school phenomena within their social and economic context seem to agree on one important thing. Most major aspects of a liberal view of both society and education need to be questioned. While this view is certainly neither homogeneous nor unitary, nor is it the only basis upon which educational and curricular policy is generated, liberalism as a form of social amelioration is focused upon because its "assumptions and dimensions have penetrated patterns of educational practice more decisively than any other ideology."[31] Liberal educational policy—with its ethic of individual achievement based supposedly on merit—is seen as a language of justification, as an ideological form, rather than a fully accurate description of how education functions. While it does describe certain aspects of schooling (certain individuals and groups do achieve well in school), it fails to see the connection between, say, the "production" of certain kinds of people and knowledge on the one hand and the reproduction of an unequal society which establishes the roles for which these agents are produced on the other hand.

But what is it exactly that is being questioned?[32]

Perhaps the most single most important plank of the liberal ideology of education is that education creates and sustains social change. This faith rests on a number of critical assumptions . . . The first is that schooling critically affects the level of economic growth and progress through its link with technology. The level of technological growth is taken to determine the level of economic growth and is itself seen to be dependent on the level of schooling. The educational system provides personnel both to push back the frontiers of technical knowledge and to consolidate these advances and bring them into our everyday lives. Through manpower planning, the apparent imperatives of the technical production process exert pressure upon the school system to produce a diversely skilled and qualified work force. The expansion and differentiation of educational institutions is underpinned by a belief in the supportive role education can play in technological growth, and this has led not only to the rapid growth of higher education in the 1960's but also to the continuing stress on technical and business education.

The second assumption involves a view of education as capable of redressing social inequalities, of overcoming—through the equalization of educational opportunity—the unfair distribution of life chances. The education system is seen as providing a ladder and an avenue for social mobility, implementing objective selection procedures for the establishment of a meritocracy, in which the only qualification for personal advancement is "ability." The education system becomes the key mechanism of social selection, to the benefit of both society and the individual.

Finally, education and the culture it both produces and transmits are viewed as independent and autonomous features in our society. Educational policies are directed towards the production of both knowledge and knowledgeable individuals through the sponsoring of academic research and curriculum reform. The idealism within the liberal tradition presents both culture and schooling as politically neutral forces for social change.

In contradistinction to this set of assumptions about education and its relation to a social order, the cultural and educational apparatus are interpreted as elements in a theory of *social control* by those individuals who are concerned with cultural and economic reproduction.[33] Hence, challenges are made to at least three interrelated notions: that the selection processes are neutral; that "ability" (rather than the socialization of students to socially and economically related norms and values) is what schools actually *do* focus on; and whether the schools *are* actually organized to teach technical curricular skills and information to all students so that each person has an equal chance at economic rewards.

Thus, as one instance, as people such as Bowles and Gintis have pointed out and as I shall argue later on, schools may not be geared to select and produce neutrally a "diversely skilled and qualified work force." Rather they seem to be less concerned with the distribution of skills than they are with the distribution of norms and dispositions which are suitable to one's place in a hierarchical society. But we must be quite careful here not to overstate this case in too deterministic a way, for not all of these liberal assumptions are totally incorrect. As I shall show in Chapter 2, for instance, education *is* linked to technical growth, but in a more complex and ultimately less just and equitable way than we might commonsensically think. For this very linkage between technical knowledge and schooling helps *generate*, not reduce, inequality. Taken together, though, these kinds of criticisms that are marshalled against the liberal tradition provide the underlying framework for a more critical analysis of schooling and the conventional "wisdom" that guides it. They all involve the claim that a good deal of curricular and more general educational theory has acted as a set of ideological blinders that prevents a more serious and searching inquiry into both the unequal institutional structures of American society and the relationship between the school and these structures.

Yet how can something that seeks so fervently to help—as liberal educational theory and practice so clearly seek to do—be an ideological form that covers the reality of domination? After all, very few educators set out to do less than provide services for their clientele. Can their motives, their actions, be so ideologically laden? In order to unpack this problem, the very notion of ideology is significant here and requires some further treatment.

On the Nature of Ideology

What ideology means is problematic usually. Most people seem to agree that one can talk about ideology as referring to some sort of "system" of ideas, beliefs, fundamental commitments, or values about social reality, but here the agreement ends.[34] The interpretations differ according to both the *scope* or range of the phenomena which are presumably ideological and the *function*—what ideologies actually do for the people who "have" them. Interpretations of the scope of ideology vary widely. The phenomena under it can be grouped into at least three categories: (1) quite specific rationalizations or justifications of the activities of particular and identifiable occupational groups (e.g., professional ideologies); (2) broader political programs and social movements; and (3) comprehensive world-views, outlooks, or what Berger and Luckmann and others have called symbolic universes.

Functionally, ideology has been evaluated historically as a form of false consciousness which distorts one's picture of social reality and serves the interests of the dominant classes in a society. However, it has also been treated, as Geertz puts it, as "systems of interacting symbols" that provide the primary ways of making "otherwise incomprehensible social situations meaningful,"[35] that is, as inevitable creations that are essential and function as shared conventions of meaning for making a complex social reality understandable.

These distinctions about the function of ideology are, of course, no more than ideal types, poles between which fall most positions on the question of what ideology is and what it does. Both ideal typical positions do grow from traditions, though, and have their modern proponents. The former, what has been called the "interest theory" of ideology, rooted as it is in the Marxist tradition, perceives ideology's primary role as the justification of vested interests of existing or contending political, economic, or other groups. The latter pole, the tradition of "strain theory," with Durkheim and Parsons as its more well-known proponents, most often takes as ideology's most important function its role of providing meaning in problematic situations, as giving a usable "definition of the situation," if you will, in this way making it possible for individuals and groups to act.

Even with these rather divergent orientations, there seems to be some common ground among those concerned with the problem of ideology in that ideology is usually taken to have three distinctive features. It always deals with legitimation, power conflict, and a special style of argument. McClure and Fischer describe each of these characteristics quite clearly.[36]

(1) Legitimation—Sociologists seem to agree that ideology is concerned with legitimation—the justification of group action and its social acceptance. This holds whether writers speak of rationalization of vested interests, attempts to "maintain a particular social role," or justificatory, apologetic . . . activity concerned with the establishment and defense of patterns of belief. In each case, writers treat as a primary issue the legitimation of how an activity is socially organized. . . . When the basic assumptions underlying a social arrangement seem to be seriously challenged, the resulting need for legitimation may well take the form of concern with the sacred . . . "Ideology seeks to sanctify existence by bringing it under the dominion of the ultimately right principles."

(2) Power Conflict—All of the sociological literature links ideology to conflicts between people seeking or holding power. But some writers have in mind power, or politics, in a narrower sense, and others in a wider sense. In the narrower sense, these terms refer to a society's formal distribution of authority and resources which by and large takes place within one realm—the sphere of politics. In a broader sense, power and politics involve any sphere of activity, and all of its aspects that deal with the allocation of rewards . . . Power conflict is always at stake in ideological disputes, whether or not those involved expressly acknowledge that dimension.

(3) Style of Argument—Many writers note that quite a special rhetoric, and a heightened affect, mark the argumentation that takes place in the realm of ideology . . . The rhetoric is seen to be highly explicit and relatively systematic . . . At least two reasons may account for the distinctive rhetoric.

First, the fundamental importance of the assumptions at issue to the very survival of a group creates a strain toward more articulate explication of assumptions which mark the group alone, in order to reinforce solidarity and agreement among its members. Conversely, there would seem to be a tendency to articulate the assumptions which are shared—or which are compatible—with those contained in rival thought systems. In this case, explicitness is a tactic which seeks to persuade, to mobilize support, or to convert outsiders.

Second, any explication of the assumptions and ideas implicit in a mode of organizing activity is likely to disguise the vague quality of these assumptions and ideas when they are used in practice.

These varied characteristics of ideology have important implications for analysis of both liberal theory and of education as a hegemonic form, for we shall have reason to see how the language and world-view of science, efficiency, "helping," and the abstracted individual perform these ideological functions for the curriculum field shortly. One can see from this relatively brief discussion, though, that ideology cannot be treated as a simple phenomenon. Nor can it be employed merely as a bludgeon with which one hits an opponent over the head (Aha, your thought is no more than ideology and can be ignored) without losing something in the process. Rather, any serious treatment of ideology has to contend with both its scope and its function, with its dual role as a set of rules that give meaning and its rhetorical potency in arguments over power and resources.[37]

For example, in later chapters I shall examine the role played by the dominant models of management, evaluation, and research in curriculum. I shall explore how each of them seems to help give meaning to, helps organize, our activity as educators in ways we tend to think are both basically economically and culturally neutral and helpful, how these dominant models and traditions serve rhetorical functions by giving funding agencies and "the public" a vision of our seeming sophistication, and, finally, how these models at the same time disguise the real values, interests, and social functioning which underpin them. Both scope and function will have to be joined here to make headway.

Again, the most helpful way of thinking through the complex characteristics, the scope and varied functions, of ideology is found in the concept of hegemony. The idea that ideological saturation permeates our lived experience enables one to see how people can employ frameworks which both assist them in organizing their world and enable them to believe they are neutral participants in the neutral instrumentation of schooling (as we shall see much of the language employed by educators in fact does), while at the same time, these frameworks serve particular economic and ideological interests which are hidden from them. As Wexler noted, in order to see how this happens we shall have to weave curricular, socio-political, economic, and ethical analyses together in such a way as to show the subtle connections which exist between educational activity and these interests.

In the chapters that follow, I shall begin this task by examining in greater detail the three major areas of inquiry that I argued in the second section of this preliminary chapter were essential to a complete understanding of the relationship between ideology and school experience. These were: (1) the basic regularities of school experience and what covert ideological teaching goes on because of them; (2) what ideological commitments are embedded within the overt curriculum; and (3) the ideological, ethical, and valuative underpinnings of the ways we ordinarily think about, plan, and evaluate these experiences. The chapters will proceed in a somewhat dialectical fashion—when necessary reiterating and making more subtle certain critical arguments, building upon previous ones, and at times offering concrete suggestions for action on the part of educators.

The latter point, the offering of concrete suggestions, illuminates a contradiction in this volume of which I am only too well aware. By the very fact that I write this book as an *educator* speaking to other educators, and no doubt to a group of interested social scientists, policy analysts, and philosophers as well, I am aware of being caught. For while a person engages in serious critical analysis, he or she still may have an ethical obligation to make life more livable, more poetic and meaningful, for the students who live in the institutions I analyze here. Thus, there are ameliorative reforms incorporated throughout this volume. Some of them are concerned with student rights, others concerned with the use of more ethical and politically conscious modes of curriculum research, and still others which suggest more honest forms of curriculum. These are given cautiously, almost reluctantly, though they are also important tactically. For action on them can lead to clarification of the real possibilities of altering aspects of school life and, perhaps most importantly, a need for further, more structurally oriented, collective action. Yet, they are also given in the hope that other educators will travel the path that has taken me, personally, from a concern for ethical and poetic understanding in curriculum to what is hopefully the beginnings of a more mature search for a just social order that will enable such understanding to be a constitutive part of our experience once again.

As the table of contents briefly indicates, the chapters which follow cover the relationship between, on the one hand, ideology, politics, and economics and, on the other hand, both the overt and hidden curriculum, and dominant educational theories. The first major area or issue (how the basic regularities or hidden curriculum of schools represent and teach ideological configurations) is dealt with within Chapters 2, 3, and 5. The second area (the relationship between ideology and overt curricular knowledge itself) is analyzed in Chapters 2, 3, 4, and 5. The final issue (how ideological, political, ethical and economic commitments are reflected in our theories and ameliorative policies and practices) is examined in four chapters, 4, 6, 7, and 8. In this way, the reader is given a fairly thorough opportunity to see how the larger society has a major impact on such things as educational theories, the apparent and not so apparent knowledge that schools teach, and the modes of evaluation and amelioration that schools employ.

We shall first examine the school's role in the creation and recreation of hegemony in students. Once this is clear, then we shall examine how hegemony operates "in the heads" of "intellectuals" like educators. The individual chapters will go about these tasks in the following ways:

Chapter 2, "Ideology and Cultural and Economic Reproduction," provides greater depth in the traditions which now dominate curriculum discourse. It focuses more clearly on the sociology and economics of curriculum by analyzing the role of the curriculum in the interplay between cultural and economic reproduction. The chapter will explore the linkages between access to and the *lack* of distribution of "legitimate" knowledge and the recreation of cultural and economic inequality by examining some of the role of schooling in technical growth.

Chapter 3, "Economics and Control in Everyday School Life" (with Nancy King), looks at the other side of the coin. By focusing on the social relations and informal curricula, as well as the formal curricula of schooling, it illuminates the ideological or hegemonic teaching that goes on simply by students living in schooling for extended periods of time. The chapter has two elements. It provides a brief historical analysis of how certain kinds of school knowledge with an avowed interest in social control became the underlying framework for organizing day-to-day school life. Second, it offers empirical evidence of kindergarten experience to document the role of the school in teaching economic and ideological knowledge and dispositions that have quite conservative outcomes.

Chapter 4, "Curricular History and Social Control" (with Barry Franklin) seeks to take seriously the importance of having a "sensitivity to the present as history" by further investigating the ways in which these conservative traditions, especially a commitment to consensus and like-mindedness, entered the field. This chapter continues and considerably deepens the brief historical examination done in the previous section of the book. It probes into the roots of the concrete social and economic forces and commitments that provided the ideological context for the selection of the principles and practices that still dominate the curriculum field and education in general.

Chapter 5, "The Hidden Curriculum and the Nature of Conflict," will examine the social interests still embodied in the dominant forms of curricular knowledge found in schools today, interests which mirror a number of the ideological presuppositions analyzed in Chapter 4. It analyzes overt knowledge in the widely accepted curriculum proposals and material in science and social studies, paying particular attention again to the ideology of consensus that pervades school knowledge and to the lack of distribution of more politically powerful curricular knowledge. It is a study in how the selective tradition operates to maintain an effective dominant culture.

Chapter 6, "Systems Management and the Ideology of Control," turns our inquiry toward how hegemony operates at the bottom of educators' heads by delving into the role of management ideologies in organizing schools and selecting curricular knowledge. It points out both their essential lack of ethical, social, and economic neutrality and their use as mechanisms of political quiescence, consensus, and social control.

Chapter 7, "Commonsense Categories and the Politics of Labeling," continues the investigation into the ideological saturation of educators' consciousness. It focuses on how the cultural capital of dominant groups results in the employment of categories which "blame the victim," the child, rather than the school or society which generates the material conditions for failure and success. It documents how, through a complex process of social labeling, schools play a fundamental role in distributing different kinds of knowledge and dispositions to different kinds and classes of people. This chapter analyzes the way school labels act and how they are generated out of ideological presuppositions. It presents a neo-Marxist analytic framework for linking together school knowledge, labels, and the institutions that surround the school by showing how deviance, "achievement problems," and so on are "naturally generated" out of the everyday functioning of the institution.

Chapter 8, "Beyond Ideological Reproduction," attempts to clarify the roles—political as well as educational—that might be played if we are to counter some of the cultural and economic forces analyzed in this volume. It points again to the importance of understanding the complex interrelationships that exist between schools and aspects of cultural as well as economic reproduction for adequate action to be taken. The chapter suggests a number of paths for further research into the problem of the sociology and economics of school knowledge. It concludes with a redefinition of the educator, one which is not based on the understandings generated from the role of abstract individual, but one which is rooted instead in the definition of an organic intellectual whose understanding and action are joined by active involvement against hegemony. Let us continue with the quest for just such an adequate understanding now.

CHAPTER 2

Ideology and Cultural and Economic Reproduction

Cultural and Economic Reproduction

Many economists and not a few sociologists and historians of education have a peculiar way of looking at schools. They envision the institution of schooling as something like a black box. One measures input before students enter schools and then measures output along the way or when "adults" enter the labor force. What actually goes on within the black box—what is taught, the concrete experience of children and teachers—is less important in this view than the more global and macro-economic considerations of rate of return on investment, or, more radically, the reproduction of the division of labor. While these are important considerations, perhaps especially that dealing, as I noted in Chapter 1, with the role of the school as a reproductive force in an unequal society, by the very nature of a vision of school as a black box, they cannot demonstrate how these effects are built *within* schools. Therefore, these individuals are less precise than they could be in explaining part of the role of cultural institutions in the reproduction they want to describe. Yet, as I shall argue here, such *cultural* explanations need to be got at; but it requires a different but often complementary orientation than the ones these and other scholars employ.

There is a unique combination of elite and popular culture in schools. As institutions they provide exceptionally interesting, and politically and economically potent, areas for the investigation of mechanisms of cultural distribution in a society. Thinking of schools as mechanisms of cultural distribution is important since, as the Italian Marxist Antonio Gramsci noted, a critical element in enhancing the ideological dominance of certain classes is the control of the knowledge preserving and producing institutions of a particular society.[1] Thus, the "reality" that schools and other cultural institutions select, preserve and distribute may need to be particularized, in Mannheim's[2] words, so that it can be seen as a particular "social construction" which may not serve the interests of every individual and group in society.

Now it has become something of a commonplace in recent sociological and educational literature to speak of reality as a social construction. By this, these scholars, especially those of a phenomenological bent, mean two things. (1) Becoming a person is a social act, a process of initiation in which the neophyte accepts a particular social reality as reality *tout court*, as the way life "really is." (2) On a larger scale, the social meanings which sustain and organize a collectivity are created by the continuing patterns of commonsense interaction of people as they go about their lives.[3] Now this insertion of the social element back into what has increasingly become a psychological problem in Anglo-Western society is certainly an improvement over the view of many educators who hold that the patterns of meanings which people use to organize their lives and attempt to transmit through their cultural institutions are independent of social or ideological influences. The notion that there is a "social construction of reality" is a bit too general, however, and not as helpful as we might think in understanding the relationships that exist between cultural institutions, particularly schools, and the framework and texture of social and economic forms in general. As Whitty succinctly puts it,[4]

> The overemphasis on the notion that reality is socially constructed seems to have led to a neglect of the consideration of how and why reality comes to be constructed in particular ways and how and why particular constructions of reality seem to have the power to resist subversion.

Thus, the general principle of the social construction of reality does not explain why certain social and cultural meanings and not others are distributed through schools; nor does it explain how the control of the knowledge preserving and producing institutions may be linked to the ideological dominance of powerful groups in a social collectivity.

The opposite principle, that knowledge is not related in any significant way to the organization and control of social and economic life, is also problematic, of course, though this may be a surprise to many curriculum theorists. This is best stated by Raymond Williams in his critical analysis of the social distribution of culture.[5]

> The pattern of meanings and values through which people conduct their whole lives can be seen for a time as autonomous, and as evolving within its own terms, but it is quite unreal, ultimately, to separate this pattern from a precise political and economic system, which can extend its influence into the most unexpected regions of feeling and behavior. The common prescription of education, as the key to change, ignores the fact that the form and content of education are affected, and in some cases determined, by the actual systems of [political] decision and [economic] maintenance.

Both Whitty and Williams are raising quite difficult issues about what might be called the relationship between ideology and school knowledge, yet the context is generally British. It should not surprise us that there is a rather extensive history of dealing with issues concerning the connections between culture and control on the Continent and in England. For one thing, they have had a less hidden set of class antagonisms than the USA. That the tradition of ideological analysis is less visible in American educational and cultural scholarship speaks to two other concerns though, the ahistorical nature of most educational activity and the dominance of an ethic of amelioration through technical models in most curriculum discourse.[6] The ahistorical nature of the field of curriculum is rather interesting here. Anyone familiar with the intense argumentation both within and on the fringes of the Progressive Education Association during its history soon realizes that one of the major points of contention among progressive educators was the problem of indoctrination. Should schools, guided by a vision of a more just society, teach a particular set of social meanings to their students? Should they concern themselves only with progressive pedagogical techniques, rather than espouse a particular social and economic cause? Questions of this type "plagued" democratically minded educators in the past and the controversy continues, though in a different vocabulary, to this day.

In fact, as Stanwood Cobb, one of the early organizers of the Progressive Education Association, has stated, many progressive educators throughout the early decades of this century were quite cautious about even raising the question of what actual content should be taught and evaluated in schools. They often preferred to concern themselves primarily with teaching methods, in part because the determination of curriculum was perceived as inherently a political issue which could split the movement.[7] Cobb's estimation of the larger structural causes behind these educators' choice of arenas in which to act may or may not be historically accurate. The fact remains though that, at least phenomenologically, many educators recognized that the culture preserved and distributed by schools as well as other institutions was not necessarily neutral. They perceived their own actions as often stemming from that recognition. Unfortunately, as I noted, these recurring historically significant issues have not informed current curriculum argumentation in the United States as much as they have in, say, England and France. Yet, as we also saw, there is a growing recognition that schools in advanced industrial societies like our own may serve certain social classes rather well and other classes not well at all. Thus, I can think of few areas of investigation more pressing than that which seeks to uncover the linkages between meaning and control in our cultural institutions.

While I cannot present a fully worked out theory of culture and control at this time (though individuals such as Raymond Williams, Pierre Bourdieu, and Basil Bernstein have begun such a task),[8] I would like to do a number of things here. First, I want to provide a deeper discussion of the basic framework of assumptions under which the recent work on the relationship between ideology and school experience operates. This will be compared to the traditions which now predominate in curriculum research today. I will, then, take one aspect of the argument about the linkages between curriculum and ideological and economic structure and will outline some general propositions about it. These propositions should be seen more as hypotheses than as final proof, and will undoubtedly require historical, conceptual, and empirical—to say nothing of comparative—investigations to demonstrate their fruitfulness. These hypotheses will concern the relationship between what curricular knowledge is accorded high status in our society and its economic and cultural effects. I shall argue that it is difficult to think through the past and present problems of the form and content of curriculum without attempting to uncover the complex nexus linking cultural and economic reproduction together. Let us begin by briefly examining the extant traditions—as ideal types—that tend to provide the assumptive background of a good deal of current curriculum work.

The Achievement and Socialization Traditions

A large proportion of educational and curriculum theories and scholarship today derive their programmatic impetus and their logical warrant from the various psychologies of learning now available. While Schwab and others have demonstrated that it is a logical error to attempt to derive a theory of curriculum (or pedagogy) from a theory of learning[9]—something all too many curriculum theorists still do not seem to realize—there is another difficulty that is more germane to my own discussion here. As I shall demonstrate more fully later, the language of learning tends to be apolitical and ahistorical, thus hiding the complex nexus of political and economic power and resources that lies behind a considerable amount of curriculum organization and selection. In brief, it is not an adequate linguistic tool for dealing with what must be a prior set of curriculum questions about some of the possible ideological roots of school knowledge. In their simplest aspects, these questions can be reduced to the following issues: "What *is* actually taught in schools?" "What are the manifest and latent social functions of the knowledge that is taught in schools?" "How do the principles of selection and organization that are used to plan, order, and evaluate that knowledge function in the cultural and economic reproduction of class relations in an advanced industrial society like our own?"[10] These questions are not usually part of the language game of psychology. Let us examine the conceptual framework, the board, on which language games of this type are played just a bit further.

There seem to have been two rather distinct ways educators (and psychologists, sociologists, and economists) have investigated school knowledge. One has centered around the issue of academic achievement. The second has been less concerned with questions of achievement than with the role of schools as socialization mechanisms.[11]

In the academic achievement model, curricular knowledge itself is not made problematic. Rather the knowledge that finds its way into schools is usually accepted as given, as neutral, so that comparisons can be made among social groups, schools, children, etc. Thus, academic performance, differentiation, and stratification based on relatively unexamined presuppositions of what is to be construed as valuable knowledge are the guiding interests behind the research. The focus tends to be on determining the variables that have a major impact on an individual's or group's success or failure in school, such as the "adolescent subculture," the unequal distribution of educational resources, or say, the social background of the students. The social goal is maximizing academic productivity.

Unlike the academic achievement model, the socialization approach does not necessarily leave school knowledge unexamined. In fact, one of its primary interests is in exploring the social norms and values that are taught in school. However, because of this interest, it restricts itself to the study of what might be called "moral knowledge." It establishes as given *the* set of societal values and inquires into how the school as an agent of society socializes students into its "shared" set of normative rules and dispositions. Robert Dreeben's well-known little book, *On What Is Learned in Schools,*[12] can provide an excellent example here.

These approaches are not totally wrong, of course, and have in the past contributed to our understanding of schools as cultural and social mechanisms, though perhaps not always in the way the approaches intended. In fact, one advantage of the extended accounts of, say, socialization by Dreeben and others is that they enhance our ability to illuminate what is taken for granted as common sense, as given, for such an approach to actually be *accepted* as a cogent explanation at all.[13] As such, they point beyond themselves to the nature of meaning and control in schools. What they tacitly accept and, hence, fail to question is important for, on closer inspection, each of these two research traditions is problematic in its own way. The academic achievement model, influenced more and more strongly by managerial concerns of technical control and efficiency, has begun to neglect the actual content of the knowledge itself, thus failing to take seriously the possible connection between economics and the structure of school knowledge other than to argue, say, the importance of the "production" of students with strong disciplinary affiliations if "democracy is to be kept strong," and so on. The socialization tradition, while insightful in its own way, focuses on social consensus and on the parallels that exist between the "given" values of a larger collectivity and educational institutions. It, thus, ignores to a very large extent the political and economic context in which such social values function and by which certain sets of social values become *the* (by whose definition?) dominant values.[14] Furthermore, both almost totally disregard some of the latent functions of the form and content of the school curriculum. And this is exactly what the tradition of what has come to be called the "sociology of school knowledge" wants to inquire into.[15]

The Sociology and Economics of School Knowledge

A fundamental starting point in this third and more critical tradition is that articulated by Young in his argument that there is a "dialectical relationship between access to power and the opportunity to legitimize certain dominant categories, and the processes by which the availability of such categories to some groups enables them to assert power and control over others."[16] Thus, to put it another way, the problematic involves examining how a system of unequal power in society is maintained, and partly recreated, by means of the "transmission" of culture.[17] The school, as a rather significant agent of cultural and economic reproduction (after all, every child goes to it and it has important effects as both a credentialing and socializing institution) becomes an important institution here, obviously.

Like the socialization tradition, the focus of these investigations has been on how a society stabilizes itself. What is the place of schools in maintaining the way economic and educational goods and services are controlled, produced, and distributed? However, these questions are guided by a more critical posture than, say, Dreeben. For much of these individuals' commitment to this particular kind of problem stems from an affiliation with socialist movements. They begin with something similar to the position I took in Chapter 1. This is broadly like a Rawlsian theory of justice: i.e., for a society to be truly just, it must maximize the advantage of the least advantaged.[18] Thus, any society which increases the relative gap between, say, rich and poor in the control of and access to cultural and economic "capital" (as recent economic reports show ours does, for instance) needs to be questioned. How is this inequality made legitimate? Why is it accepted? As Gramsci would put it, how is this hegemony maintained?

For many of these researchers, this seeming social and ideological stability is seen in part "as relying upon the deep and often unconscious internalization by the individual of the principles which govern the existing social order."[19] However, these principles are not perceived as being neutral. They are seen as intimately interconnected with economic and political stratification.

For example, in the American, British, and French analyses currently being done by Bowles and Gintis, Bernstein, Young, and Bourdieu, the individual's underlying perception of the social order of which he or she is a part provides the locus of understanding. Thus, to take one instance, in the words of a British commentator on Bowles and Gintis's interesting but too mechanistic book,[20] "In the work of Bowles and Gintis emphasis is given to the importance of schooling in forming the different personality types which correspond to the requirements of a system of work relations within an economic mode of production."[21] In this way, for Bowles and Gintis, not only does education allocate individuals to a relatively fixed set of positions in society—an allocation of positions determined by economic and political forces—but the process of education itself, the formal and hidden curriculum, socializes people to accept as legitimate the limited roles they ultimately fill in society.[22]

Other similarly oriented scholars take a comparable stance in examining the effect schools may have on the formation of the consciousness of individuals. Thus, for instance, Basil Bernstein has argued that, to a significant extent, "through education the individual's 'mental structures' (i.e., categories of thought, language and behavior) are formed, and that these mental structures derive from the social division of labor." In France, the investigation of the relationship between cultural reproduction and economic reproduction is being carried out in a parallel vein by Bourdieu. He analyzes the cultural rules, what he calls the *habitus,* that link economic and cultural control and distribution together.[23]

Bourdieu focuses on the student's ability to cope with what might be called "middle class culture." He argues that the cultural capital stored in schools acts as an effective filtering device in the reproduction of a hierarchical society. For example, schools partly recreate the social and economic hierarchies of the larger society through what is seemingly a neutral process of selection and instruction. They take the cultural capital, the *habitus,* of the middle class, as natural and employ it as if all children have had equal access to it. However, "by taking all children as equal, while implicitly favoring those who have already acquired the linguistic and social competencies to handle middle-class culture, schools take as natural what is essentially a social gift, i.e. cultural capital."[24] Bourdieu asks us, hence, to think of cultural capital as we would economic capital. Just as our dominant economic institutions are structured so that those who inherit or already have economic capital do better, so too does cultural capital act in the same way. Cultural capital ("good taste," certain kinds of prior knowledge, abilities and language forms) is unequally distributed throughout society and this is dependent in large part on the division of labor and power in that society. "By selecting for such properties, schools serve to reproduce the distribution of power within the society."[25] For Bourdieu, to understand completely what schools do, who succeeds and who fails, one must not see culture as neutral, as necessarily contributing to social progress. Rather, one sees the culture tacitly preserved in and expected by schools as contributing to inequality outside of these institutions.

Behind these points, hence, is an argument that states that we shall have to recognize that, like poverty, poor achievement is *not* an aberration. Both poverty and curricular problems such as low achievement are integral *products* of the organization of economic, cultural, and social life as we know it.[26] I shall have more to say about seeing many curriculum problems, such as achievement, as "naturally produced" by our institutions shortly, when we consider the formal corpus of school knowledge further in the next section of this analysis.

Given arguments of this type, then, what is it that this third tradition is basically saying?[27]

> The assumption underlying most of the "reproduction" theories is that education plays a mediating role between the individual's consciousness and society at large. These theorists maintain that the rules which govern social behavior, attitudes,

morals and beliefs are filtered down from the macro level of economic and political structures to the individual via work experience, educational processes and family socialization. The individual acquires a particular awareness and perception of the society in which he lives. And it is this understanding and attitude towards the social order which [in large part] constitute his consciousness.

Schools, therefore, "process" both knowledge and people. In essence, the formal and informal knowledge is used as a complex filter to process people, often by class; and, at the same time, different dispositions and values are taught to different school populations, again often by class (and sex and race). In effect, for this more critical tradition, schools latently recreate cultural and economic disparities, though this is certainly not what most school people intend at all.

Let me pause here to clarify one thing: this is not to maintain that either culture or consciousness is mechanistically determined (in the strong sense of that term) by economic structure. Rather, it seeks to bring to a level of awareness and make historically and empirically problematic the dialectical relationship between cultural control and distribution and economic and political stratification.[28] Our ordinary perceptions—ones taken from the achievement and socialization models—hence, are bracketed. The "cognitive interest" underlying the research program is to look *relationally*, if you will, to think about school knowledge as being generated out of ideological and economic conflicts "outside" as well as "inside" education. These conflicts and forces set limits on (not mechanistically determine) cultural responses. This requires subtlety, not appraisals which argue for a one-to-one correspondence between institutional life and cultural forms. Neither all curricula nor all culture are "mere products" of simple economic forces.[29]

In fact, I want to note a critical caveat at this point. There is an obvious danger here, one that should not go unrecognized. To make the actual "stuff" of curriculum problematic, to hold what currently counts as legitimate knowledge up to ideological scrutiny, can lead to a rather vulgar brand of relativism. That is, to see overt and hidden curricular knowledge as social and historical products ultimately tends to raise questions about the criteria of validity and truth we employ.[30] The epistemological issues that might be raised here are not uninteresting, to say the least. However, the point behind these investigations is not to totally relativize either our knowledge or our criteria for warranting its truth or falsity (though the Marxist tradition has a long history of just this debate as the controversy between, say, Adorno and Popper documents. We have much to learn from the epistemological and political issues raised by this debate, by the way.)[31] Rather, as I just mentioned, the methodological dictum is to think relationally or structurally. In clearer terms, one should look for the subtle connections between educational phenomena, such as curriculum, and the latent social and economic outcomes of the institution.

These points are obviously similar to those often associated with the critical theorists of the Frankfurt School who have argued that the context in which we perceive social facts, the general way we conceptually organize our world, may hide the fact that these seemingly commonsensical appearances serve particular interests.[32] But these interests cannot merely be assumed; they need to be documented. In order to lay some of the foundation of this documentation, we shall need to turn to some of the hypotheses that I mentioned earlier I would suggest. We shall need to explore how cultural distribution and economic power are intimately intertwined, not just in the teaching of "moral knowledge" as in some of the reproduction theorists, but in the formal corpus of school knowledge itself.

On the Problem of High Status Knowledge

The discussion in the previous sections of this chapter centered on deepening our understanding of the general political, economic, and conceptual arguments that those people interested in the problem of ideology and curriculum have focused upon. It compared this critical tradition to the current achievement and socialization models predominant in the field. I should now like to take one aspect of the relationship between cultural distribution and economic power and explore it further. I want to employ this critical framework to engage in some speculations about how certain knowledge—particularly that knowledge which is considered to be most prestigious in schools—may in fact be linked to economic reproduction. In essence, I want to begin to think through some of the issues associated with the distribution of knowledge and the creation of inequality that people like Bourdieu, Bernstein, Young, and others have sought to raise. At the forefront of our minds, I think, should be Bourdieu's point that I noted in the last section. If you want to understand how cultural and economic-political forms work in tandem, then think of both as aspects of capital.

In order to delve into the connections between these forms, I shall be using the language of cultural "transmissions," in effect treating cultural artifacts and knowledge *as if* they were things. However, the notion of "as if" must be understood as exactly that, as a metaphor for dealing with a much more complex process in which, say, students do not merely take in information, cultural attributes, etc., but rather they also transform (and sometimes reject) these expected dispositions, propensities, skills, and facts into biographically significant meanings.[33] Thus, while the act of treating knowledge as a thing makes for ease of discussion, a methodological simplification if you will, it needs to be understood as just such a simplifying act. (The fact that it is usually considered a thing in our society does of course point to its reification as a commodity in advanced industrial societies.)[34]

Once again, one of Michael F. D. Young's arguments is helpful as a beginning here. He states that "those in positions of power will attempt to define what is taken as knowledge, how accessible to different groups any knowledge is, and what are accepted relationships between different knowledge areas and between those who have access to them and make them available."[35] Though this is undoubtedly more related to how hegemony acts to saturate our consciousness and is *not* always or even necessarily a conscious process of manipulation and control, and hence may be a bit overstated, it does raise the issue of the relative status of knowledge and its accessibility. For within this statement is a proposition that might entail something like the following. The possession of high status knowledge, knowledge that is considered of exceptional import and is connected to the structure of corporate economies, is related to and in fact seems to entail the non-possession by others. In essence, high status knowledge "is by definition scarce, and its scarcity is inextricably linked to its instrumentality."[36]

This is an exceptionally critical point and needs to be gone into a bit further. I have argued that schools do not merely "process" people but that they "process" knowledge as well. They enhance and give legitimacy to particular types of cultural resources which are related to unequal economic forms. In order to understand this, we want to think about the kinds of knowledge that schools take as the most important, that they want to maximize. I shall define this as technical knowledge, not to denigrate it, but to differentiate it from, say, aesthetics, physical grace, and so on. The conception of the maximization of technical knowledge is a useful principle, I think, to begin to unpack some of the linkages between cultural capital and economic capital.[37]

Our kind of economic system is organized in such a way that it can create only a certain amount of jobs and still maintain high profit levels for corporations. In essence, the economic apparatus is at its *most efficient* when there is a (measured) unemployment rate of approximately 4–6 per cent (though we know that this is a notoriously inaccurate measure to which must also be added both the issues of much higher rates for blacks, high levels of underemployment and the unpaid work of many women in the home). To provide useful work for these individuals would require cutting into acceptable rates of return, and would probably require at least the partial reorganization of so called "market mechanisms" which apportion jobs and resources. Because of this it would not be a misplaced metaphor to describe our economic system as *naturally generating* specifiable levels of under and unemployment.[38] We can think of this model as one which is primarily concerned with the maximization of the production of profit and only secondarily concerned with the distribution of resources and employment.

Now a similar model seems to hold true when we think about knowledge in its relationship to such an economy. A corporate economy requires the production of high levels of technical knowledge to keep the economic apparatus running effectively and to become more sophisticated in the maximization of opportunities for economic expansion. Within certain limits, what is actually required is not the widespread distribution of this high status knowledge to the populace in general. What is needed more is to maximize its production. As long as the knowledge form is continually and efficiently produced, the school itself, at least in this major aspect of its function, is efficient. Thus, certain low levels of achievement on the part of "minority" group students, children of the poor and so on, can be tolerated. It is less consequential to the economy than is the generation of the knowledge itself. Once again, production of a particular "commodity" (here high status knowledge) is of more concern than the distribution of that particular commodity. To the extent that it does not interfere with the production of technical knowledge, then concerns about distributing it more equitably can be tolerated as well.

Thus, just as in the "economic market place" where it is more efficient to have a relatively constant level of unemployment, to actually generate it really, so do cultural institutions "naturally" generate levels of poor achievement. The *distribution* or scarcity of certain forms of cultural capital is of less moment in this calculus of values than the maximization of the production of the particular knowledge itself.

This, I think, goes a long way in partially explaining the economic role of the debate on standards and open enrollment at universities. It also clarifies some of the reasons schools and curricula seem to be organized toward university life in terms of the dominance of subject centered curricula and the relative prestige given to differing curricula areas. This relationship between economic structure and high status knowledge might also explain some of the large disparities we see in levels of funding for curricular innovations in technical areas and, say, the arts.

The structure of discipline movement provides an interesting example of a number of these points about power and culture. The discipline centered approach was not a serious challenge to the traditional view of curriculum. Rather it was an argument that a particular commodity—here academic knowledge—by a particular community was not being effectively "marketed" in schools.[39] Even when it was accepted by most school people as the most important curricular knowledge and was given large doses of federal support to assist its adoption in schools, competing power claims were evident about what was to be high status knowledge.

For instance, substantial funding was given to mathematics and science curriculum development while less was given to the arts and humanities. This occurred then and still occurs now for two possible reasons. First is the question of economic utility. The benefits of maximizing the production of scientific and technical knowledge are easily visible and, at least at the time, seemed relatively non-controversial. Second, high-status knowledge appears to be discrete knowledge. It has a (supposedly) identifiable content and (again supposedly) stable structure[40] that are both teachable and, what is critically important, testable. The arts and humanities have obviously been seen to be less amenable to such criteria, supposedly because of the very nature of their subject matter. Thus, one has a twofold, nearly circular proposition working here. High status knowledge is seen as *macro-economically* beneficial in terms of long run benefits to the most powerful classes in society; and the socially accepted definitions of high status knowledge preclude consideration of non-technical knowledge.

It is important to note the stress on macro-economic considerations. Obviously, television repair is a subject which, if learned well, may provide economic benefits to its user. However, the economy itself will not be unduly impaired if this is not accorded prestige status. In fact, if Braverman's analysis is correct—that our economic structure requires the continual division and breaking down of complex skills into less complex and more standardized skills—economic control may be helped by the lack of prestige given to such craftsmanship. The same does not seem to hold true for technical knowledge.[41]

We have two levels working here again. The constitutive or underlying social and economic rules make it essential that subject-centered curricula be taught, that high status be given to technical knowledge. This is in large part due to the selection function of schooling. Though this is more complex than I can go into here, it is easier to stratify individuals according to "academic criteria" when technical knowledge is used. This stratification or grouping is important in large part because not all individuals are seen as having the ability to contribute to the generation of the required knowledge form. Thus, the cultural content (legitimate or high status knowledge) is used as a device or filter for economic stratification,[42] thereby enhancing the continued expansion of technical knowledge in an economy like ours, as well. At the same time, however, one might expect that within this constitutive framework, educators would be relatively free to respond (or not to respond) to more immediate economic pressures such as career education and so forth.

In short, one major reason that subject-centered curricula dominate most schools, that integrated curricula are found in relatively few schools, is at least partly the result of the place of the school in maximizing the production of high status knowledge. This is closely interrelated with the school's role in the selection of agents to fill economic and social positions in a relatively stratified society that the analysts of the political economy of education have sought to portray.

With Young, I have suggested here that some of the relations among who controls rewards and power in a society, the patterns of dominant values, and the organization of cultural capital can best be uncovered by focusing on the stratification of knowledge. It would not be illogical to claim that, based on what I have argued here, generally, any attempt to make substantive alterations in the relationship between high status and low status knowledge, by, say, making different knowledge areas equal, will tend to be resisted. This would also probably mean that attempts to use different criteria to judge the relative value of different curricular areas will be looked at as illegitimate incursions, as threats to that particular "order."[43]

Examples of this are not difficult to find in the area of evaluation. For instance, the usual way one evaluates the success of curricula is by employing a technical procedure, by comparing input with output. Were test scores raised? Did the students master the material? This is, of course, the achievement model I described earlier. When educators or policy analysts want to evaluate in another, less technical way, by looking at the "quality" of that curricular experience or by raising questions about the ethical nature of the relationships involved in the interaction, they can be rather easily dismissed. Scientific and technical talk in advanced industrial societies has more legitimacy (high status) than ethical talk. Ethical talk cannot be easily operationalized within an input-output perspective. And, finally, "scientific" criteria of evaluation give "knowledge," while ethical criteria lead to purely "subjective" considerations. This has important implications for our view of ourselves as neutral and will become of increasing significance when we analyze how "science" functions in education later on.

A current example might be helpful here. After massive reanalysis of studies relating schooling to mobility, Jencks, in *Inequality,* concluded that it was quite difficult to generalize about the roles schools play in increasing one's chances at a better future. Thus, he notes that it might be wiser to focus less on mobility and achievement and more on the quality of a student's actual experience in classrooms, something with strangely (though pleasantly) Deweyan overtones. However, Jencks's argument that we must pay greater attention to the quality of life within our educational institutions had its roots in ethical and political considerations and was dismissed rather readily. His *criteria* for making that statement were perceived as being illegitimate. They had little validity within the particular set of language games of which evaluation partakes, and, hence are accorded little status.[44]

Notice something else about what this insistence on technical criteria does. It makes both the kinds of questions raised, and the answers given to them, the province of experts, those individuals who possess the knowledge already. In this way, the relative status of the knowledge is linked to the kinds of questions deemed acceptable, which in turn seems to be linked to its *non-possession* by other individuals. The *form* of the questions becomes an aspect of cultural reproduction since these questions can only be answered by experts who already have had the technical knowledge distributed to them. The stratification of knowledge in this case again involves the stratification of people, though less on an economic level here.

Hegemony and Reproduction

All of this is quite involved, obviously, and rather difficult to untangle, I know. While our understanding of these knotty relationships is still tentative, it does raise anew one of the questions I referred to before. Given the subtle connections in this process of the generation of cultural as well as economic reproduction, how and why do people accept it? Hence, the question of hegemony, of ideological stability, that is raised by the reproduction theorists emerges once more.[45] For it is here than the research of Bowles and Gintis, Bernstein, Bourdieu and others on the social reproduction of the values, norms, and dispositions transmitted by the cultural apparatus of a society offers part of an explanation. One form of reproduction (through "socialization" and what has been called the hidden curriculum) which we shall examine in the next three chapters, complements another (the formal corpus of school knowledge), each of which seems to have ties to economic inequality. It is in the *interplay* between curricular knowledge—the stuff we teach, the "legitimate culture"— and the social relations of classroom life that the reproduction theorists describe, that we can begin to see some of the real relations schools have to an unequal economic structure.

Again notice what I am saying, for it constitutes part of an argument against the conspiracy theories so popular in some revisionist critiques of schooling. This process of reproduction is not caused (in the strong sense of that concept) by an elite group of managers who sat or now sit around tables plotting ways to "do in" their workers at both the workplace and the school. While as we shall see in Chapter 4, such an account may accurately describe some aspects of why schools do what they do,[46] it is not a sufficient explanation of the nexus of forces that actually seem to exist. I am arguing, instead, that given the extant economic and political forms which now provide the principles upon which so much of our everyday lives are organized, this reproductive process is a "logical necessity" for the continued maintenance of an unequal social order. The economic and cultural unbalance follows "naturally."[47]

This may make it hard for educators such as ourselves to deal with the problem. We may, in fact, have to take seriously the political and economic commitments that guide the reproduction theorists. Serious educational analysis may require a more coherent theory of the social and economic polity of which we are a part. While I have explored cultural mechanisms here, it is just as essential to remember Raymond Williams's point that neither culture, nor education are free-floating. To forget that is to neglect a primary arena for collective actions and commitment.

Some of this economic concern is summarized by Henry Levin. In a review of the effects of large-scale educational interventions by the government to try to reduce economic inequality through reforms in curriculum and teaching, he concludes that:[48]

> Educational policies that are aimed at resolving social dilemmas that arise out of the basic malfunctioning of the economic, social and political institutions of the society are not amenable to solution through educational policy and reform.

The leverage available to the most benevolent educational reformer and policy specialist is limited by the lack of a constituency for change and the overwhelming momentum of the educational process in the direction of social reproduction of the existing polity. And, there is a deleterious result in our efforts if educational attempts to change society tend to direct attention away from the focus of the problem by creating and legitimating the ideology that schools can be used to solve problems which did not originate in the educational sector.

Yet once again, we must be cautious of this kind of approach, for it can lead us back to viewing schools as little black boxes once more. And that is what we rejected at the outset.

Some Concluding Questions

I want to stop here, knowing full well that much more could be and needs to be said about the topics I have raised. For example, in order to go further with the relationship between high status knowledge and an "external" social order, one would have to inquire into the history of the concomitant rise of new classes of social personnel and the growth of new types of "legitimate" knowledge.[49] These issues obviously require much more thought to be given to the conceptual problem of the dialectical relationship between cultural control and social and economic structure. How does each affect the other? What role does an educational system itself play in defining particular forms of knowledge as high status? What role does it play in helping to create a credentialing process based on the possession (and non-possession) of this cultural capital, a credentialing system that provides numbers of agents roughly equivalent to the needs of the division of labor in society? These questions imply something important I think, for this relationship is not a one-way street. Education is both a "cause" and an "effect" here. The school is not a passive mirror, but an *active* force, one that also serves to *give legitimacy* to economic and social forms and ideologies so intimately connected to it.[50] And it is just this action which needs to be unpacked.

Questions of this type are not usually asked in curriculum of course. However, we need to remember that these concerns are not something totally new to the discourse surrounding American education. In fact, we must not see this kind of sociologically and economically inclined curriculum scholarship as being an attempt to carry on any "reconceptualization" of the curriculum field, though that name has been applied to some recent analysts of power and school knowledge.[51] Rather, the questions which guide this work need to be seen as having rather deep roots in the curriculum field, roots we may have unfortunately forgotten given the ahistorical nature of education.

We need only recall what stimulated the early social reconstructionists in education (Counts, Smith-Stanley-Shores, and others) to begin to realize that one of the guiding themes in past curriculum work has been the role schools fulfill in the reproduction of an unequal society. While these individuals may have been much too optimistic in viewing schools as powerful agencies in redressing this imbalance, and while a number of them ultimately backed away from large-scale structural alterations in our polity,[52] the principle of examining the linkages between cultural and economic institutions is a valued part of our past. It is time to make it our present and future, as well.

CHAPTER 3

Economics and Control in Everyday School Life

(with NANCY KING)

As we saw in the last chapter, schools seem to contribute to inequality in that they are tacitly organized to differentially distribute specific kinds of knowledge. This is in large part related both to the role of the school in maximizing the production of technical cultural "commodities" and to the sorting or selecting function of schools in allocating people to the positions "required" by the economic sector of society. As we are beginning to understand more fully, though, schools also play a rather large part in distributing the kinds of normative and dispositional elements required to make this inequality seem natural. They teach a hidden curriculum that seems uniquely suited to maintain the ideological hegemony of the most powerful classes in this society. As the reproduction theorists argued in Chapter 2, ideological and social stability rests in part on the internalization, at the very bottom of our brains, of the principles and commonsense rules which govern the existing social order. This ideological saturation will undoubtedly be more effective if it is done early in one's life. In schools this means the earlier the better, in essence from day one in kindergarten. The principles and rules that are taught *will* give meaning to students' situations (schools are, in fact, organized in such a way as to maintain these definitions) and at the same time will also serve economic interests. Both elements of an effective ideology will be present.

Let us begin to look at this more carefully by first laying to rest some of the arguments made by the more romantic critics of schooling that these ideological configurations are taught in schools because teachers do not care enough. Then we can see what economically rooted norms and dispositions *are* actually taught in institutions of cultural preservation and distribution like schools.

Schooling and Cultural Capital

One of the least attractive arguments in recent years has been that schools are relatively unexciting, boring, or what have you, because of mindlessness.[1] The argument has it that schools covertly teach all those things that humanistic critics of schools so like to write and talk about—behavioral consensus, institutional rather than personal goals and norms, alienation from one's products, etc.—and that they do so because teachers, administrators, and other educators do not really know what they are doing.

However, such a perspective is misleading at best. In the first place, it is thoroughly ahistorical. It ignores the fact that schools were in part designed to teach exactly these things. The hidden curriculum, the tacit teaching of social and economic norms and expectations to students in schools, is not as hidden or "mindless" as many educators believe. Second, it ignores the critical task schools perform as the fundamental set of institutions in advanced industrial societies that certifies adult competence. It pulls schools out of their setting within a larger and much more powerful nexus of economic and political institutions that give schools their meaning. That is, just as in their role in the maximization of the production of technical knowledge, schools seem, by and large, to do what they are supposed to do, at least in terms of roughly providing dispositions and propensities "functional" in later life in a complex and stratified social and economic order.

While there is no doubt that mindlessness does exist other than in Charles Silberman's mind, it is not an adequate descriptive device—any more than venality or indifference—in explaining why schools are so resistant to change or why schools teach what they do.[2] Nor is it an appropriate conceptual tool to ferret out what, precisely, is taught in schools or why some social meanings and not others are used in the organization of school life.

Yet, it is not just school critics who present too simple an analysis of the social and economic meaning of schools. All too often, the social meaning of school experience has been accepted as unproblematic by sociologists of education, or as problems merely of engineering by curriculum specialists and other programmatically inclined educators. The curriculum field, more particularly than other educational areas, has been dominated by a perspective that might best be called "technological," in that the major interest guiding its work has involved finding the one best set of means to reach pre-chosen educational ends.[3] As I pointed out, against this relatively ameliorative and uncritical background, a number of sociologists and curriculum scholars, influenced strongly by the sociology of knowledge in both its Marxist (or neo-Marxist) and phenomenological variants, have begun to raise serious questions about the lack of attention to the relationship between school knowledge and extra-school phenomena. We saw that a fundamental starting point in these investigations has been well articulated by Michael Young when he notes that there is a "dialectical relationship between access to power and the opportunity to legitimize certain dominant categories, and the process by which the availability of such categories to some groups enables them to assert power and control over others."[4] In essence, just as there is a relatively unequal distribution of economic capital in society, so too is there a similar distribution of cultural capital.[5] In advanced industrial societies, schools are particularly important as distributors of this cultural capital, and they play a critical role in giving legitimacy to categories and forms of knowledge. The very fact that certain traditions and normative "content" *are* construed as school knowledge is prima facie evidence of their perceived legitimacy.

I want to argue here that the *problem* of educational knowledge, of what is taught in schools, has to be considered as a form of the larger distribution of goods and services in a society. It is not merely an analytic problem (what shall be construed as knowledge?), nor simply a technical one (how do we organize and store knowledge so that children may have access to it and "master" it?), nor, finally, is it a purely psychological problem (how do we get students to learn x?). Rather, the study of educational knowledge is a study in ideology, the investigation of what is considered *legitimate* knowledge (be it knowledge of the logical type of "that," "how," or "to") by specific social groups and classes, in specific institutions, at specific historical moments. It is, further, a critically oriented form of investigation, in that it chooses to focus on how this knowledge, as distributed in schools, may contribute to a cognitive and dispositional development that strengthens or reinforces existing (and often problematic) institutional arrangements in society. In clearer terms, the overt and covert knowledge found within school settings, and the principles of selection, organization, and evaluation of this knowledge, are value-governed selections from a much larger universe of possible knowledge and selection principles. Hence they must not be accepted as given, but must be made problematic—bracketed, if you will—so that the social and economic ideologies and the institutionally patterned meanings which stand behind them, can be scrutinized. The latent meaning and the configuration that lies behind the commonsense acceptability of a position may be its most important attributes. And these hidden institutional meanings and relations are almost never uncovered if we are guided only by amelioration.[6] As Kallos has noted, any educational system has both manifest and latent "functions." These need to be characterized not only in educational (or learning) terms but, more importantly, in politico-economic terms. In short, discussions about the quality of educational life are relatively meaningless if the "specific functions of the educational system are unrecognized."[7]

If much of the literature on what schools tacitly teach is accurate, then the specific functions may be more economic than intellectual.

In this chapter, I would like to focus on certain aspects of the problem of schooling and social and economic meaning. I shall look at schools as institutions that embody collective traditions and human intentions which, in turn, are the products of identifiable social and economic ideologies. Thus, our starting point might best be phrased as the question, "*Whose* meanings are collected and distributed through the overt and hidden curricula in schools?" That is, as Marx was fond of saying, reality does not stalk around with a label.

The curriculum in schools responds to and represents ideological and cultural resources that come from somewhere. Not all groups' visions are represented and not all groups' meanings are responded to. How, then, do schools act to distribute this cultural capital? Whose reality "stalks" in the corridors and classrooms of American schools?

I shall focus on two areas. First, I shall offer a description (one that will be considerably deepened in Chapter 4) of the historical process through which certain social meanings became particularly *school* meanings and thus have the weight of decades of acceptance behind them. Second, I shall offer empirical evidence, from a study of kindergarten experience, to document the potency and staying power of these particular social meanings. Finally, I shall raise the question of whether piecemeal reforms, to deal with eliminating these ideological meanings, be they oriented humanistically or in other directions, can succeed alone.

The task of dealing with sets of meanings in schools has traditionally fallen upon the curriculum specialist. Historically, however, this concern for meanings in schools by curriculists has been linked to varied notions of social control. This should not surprise us. It should be obvious, though it is usually not so, that questions about meanings in social institutions tend to become questions of control.[8] That is, the forms of knowlege (both overt and covert kinds) one finds within school settings imply notions of power and of economic resources and control. The very choice of school knowledge, the act of designing school environments, though they may not be done consciously, are often based on ideological and economic presuppositions which provide commonsense rules for educators' thought and action. Perhaps the links between meaning and control in schools will become clearer if we reflect on a relatively abbreviated account of the history of curriculum.

Meaning and Control in Curriculum History

The British sociologist Bill Williamson argues that men and women "have to contend with the institutional and ideological forms of earlier times as the basic constraints on what they can achieve."[9] If this notion is to be taken seriously, then one must understand what is provided and taught in schools in historical terms. As Williamson notes, "Earlier educational attitudes of dominant groups in society still carry historical weight and are exemplified even in the bricks and mortar of the school buildings themselves."[10]

If we are to be honest with ourselves, we must acknowledge that the curriculum field has its roots in the soil of social control. Its intellectual paradigm first took shape in the early part of this century, and became an identifiable set of procedures for the selection and organization of school knowledge—procedures to be taught to teachers and other educators. At that time, the fundamental concern of the people in the curriculum field was that of social control. Part of this concern is understandable. Many of the important figures who influenced the curriculum field (such as Charles C. Peters, Ross Finney, and especially David Snedden) had interests that spanned both the field of educational sociology and the more general problems of what should actually happen in schools. The idea of social control was of growing importance in the American Sociological Society at that time, and was an idea which seemed to capture both the imagination and energy of many of the nation's intelligentsia, as well as of powerful segments of the business community. It is, therefore, not difficult to see how it also captured those figures who wore two hats, who were both sociologists and curriculum workers.[11]

But an interest in schooling as a mechanism for social control was not merely borrowed from sociology. The individuals who first called themselves curriculists (men like Franklin Bobbitt and W. W. Charters) were vitally concerned with social control for ideological reasons as well. These men were strongly influenced by the scientific management movement and by the work of social measurement specialists;[12] they were also guided by beliefs that found the popular eugenics movement a "progressive" social force. Thus, they brought social control into the very heart of the field whose task it was to develop criteria for selecting those meanings with which students would come into contact in our schools.

This is not, of course, to say that social control in and of itself is always undesirable. Social life without some element of control is nearly impossible to envisage, if only because of the fact that institutions, *qua* institutions, tend to respond to the *regularities* of human interaction. Rather, there was historically a specific set of assumptions—of commonsense rules—about school meanings and control that strongly influenced early curriculum workers. They not only assumed that organized society must maintain itself through the preservation of some of its valued forms of interaction and meaning (a quite general and wholly understandable "weak" sense of social control). They also had, deeply embedded in their ideological perspective, a "strong" sense of control. Here, education in general, and the everyday meanings of the curriculum in schools in particular, were seen as essential elements in the preservation of existing social privilege, interests, and knowledge, which were the prerogatives of one element of the population, maintained at the expense of less powerful groups.[13] As we shall see in considerably more detail in Chapter 4, more often this took the form of attempting to guarantee expert and scientific control in society, to eliminate or "socialize" unwanted racial or ethnic groups or their characteristics, or to produce an economically efficient group of citizens, in order to, as C. C. Peters put it, reduce the maladjustment of workers to their jobs. This latter interest, the economic substratum of everyday school life, becomes of particular importance when, later in this chapter, we look at what schools teach about work and play.

Of course, social control as an idea or interest did not originate with the early curriculum movement's attempts to use school knowledge for rather conservative social ends. Social control was an implied aim of a large number of ameliorative social and political programs carried out during the nineteenth century by both state and private agencies. It had been their intention, too, that order, stability, and the imperative of industrial growth might be maintained in the face of a variety of social and economic changes.[14] As Feinberg's analysis of the ideological roots of liberal educational policy demonstrates, even in this century many of the proposed "reforms," both in schools and elsewhere, have latently served the conservative social interests of stability and social stratification.[15]

The argument presented so far is not meant to debunk the efforts of educators and social reformers. Instead, it is an attempt to place the current debate concerning the lack of humaneness in schools, the tacit teaching of social norms, values, and so forth, within a larger historical context. Without such a context, we cannot fully understand the relationship between what schools actually do and an advanced industrial economy like our own. The best example of this context can be found in the changing ideological functions of schooling in general and curricular meanings in particular. Behind much of the debate about the role of formal education in the USA during the nineteenth century lay a variety of concerns about the standardization of educational environments, about the teaching, through day-to-day school interaction, of moral, normative, and dispositional values, and about economic functionalism. Today these concerns have been given the name of the "hidden curriculum" by Philip Jackson[16] and others. But it is the very question of its hiddenness that may help us uncover the historical relationship between what is taught in schools and the larger context of the institutions that surround them.

We should be aware that, historically, the hidden curriculum was *not* hidden at all, but was instead the overt function of schools during much of their careers as institutions. During the nineteenth century, the increasing diversity of political, social, and cultural attributes and structures "pushed educators to resume with renewed vigor the language of social control and homogenization that had dominated educational rhetoric from the earliest colonial period."[17] As the century progressed, the rhetoric of reform—of justifying one's ideological position against other interest groups—did not merely focus on the critical need for social homogeneity. Using schools as a primary agency for inculcating values and for creating an "American community" was not enough. The growing pressures of modernization and industrialization also created certain expectations of efficiency and functionalism among some classes and in an industrial elite in society as well. As Vallance puts it, "to assertive socialization was added a focus on organizational efficiency." Thus, the reforms having the greatest effect on school organization, and ultimately on the procedures and principles which governed life in classrooms, were dominated by the language of and an interest in production, well-adjusted economic functioning, and bureaucratic skills. In this process, the underlying reasons for reform slowly changed from an active concern for consensus of values to an economic functionalism.[18] But this could occur only if the prior period, with its search for a standardized national character, built in large part through the characteristics of schools, had both been accepted and perceived as successful. Thus, the institutional outlines of schools with their relatively standardized day-to-day forms of interaction provided the mechanisms by which a normative consensus could be "taught." And within these broad outlines, these behavioral regularities of the institution, if you will, an ideological set of commonsense rules for curriculum selection and for organizing school experience based on efficiency, economic functionalism, and bureaucratic exigencies took hold. The former became the deep structure, the first hidden curriculum, which encased the latter. Once the hidden curriculum had become hidden, when a uniform and standardized learning context had become established, and when social selection and control were taken as given in schooling, only then could attention be paid to the needs of the individual or other more "ethereal" concerns.[19]

Thus, historically, a core of commonsense meanings, combining normative consensus and economic adjustment, was built into the very structure of formal education. This is not to say that there have been no significant educational movements toward, say, education for self-development. But rather, behind these preferential choices about individual needs there was a more powerful set of expectations surrounding schooling which provided the constitutive structure of school experience. As a number of economists have recently noted, the most economically important "latent function" of school life seems to be the selection and generation of personality attributes and normative meanings that enable one to have a supposed chance at economic rewards.[20] As we saw, this is closely linked, as well, to the school's cultural role in maximizing the production of technical knowledge. Since the school is the only major institution that stands between the family and the labor market, it is not odd that, both historically and currently, certain social meanings which have differential benefits are distributed in schools.

But what are these particular social meanings? How are they organized and displayed in everyday school life? It is these questions to which we now turn.

Ideology and Curriculum in Use

The larger concerns of the prior section with the relationship between ideology and school knowledge, between meanings and control, tend to be altogether too vague unless one can see them as forces in the activities of school people and students, as they go about their particular lives in classrooms. As investigators of the hidden curriculum and others have noted, the concrete modes by which knowledge is distributed in classrooms and the commonsense practices of teachers and students can illuminate the connections between school life and the structures of ideology, power, and economic resources of which schools are a part.[21]

Just as there is a social distribution of cultural capital in society, so too is there a social distribution of knowledge within classrooms. For example, different "kinds" of students get different "kinds" of knowledge. Keddie documents this well in her study of the knowledge teachers have of their students and the curricular knowledge then made available to them.[22] However, although the differential distribution of classroom knowledge does exist and although it is intimately linked to the process of social labeling that goes on in schools,[23] (something I will document more clearly in Chapter 7), it is less important to my analysis than what might be called the "deep structure" of school experience. What underlying meanings are negotiated and transmitted in schools behind the actual formal "stuff" of curriculum content? What happens when knowledge is filtered through teachers? Through what categories of normality and deviance is it filtered? What is the basic and organizing framework of the normative and conceptual knowledge that students actually get? In short, what is the *curriculum in use*? It is only by seeing this deep structure that we can begin pointing out how social norms, institutions, and ideological rules are continually sustained and mediated by the day-to-day interaction of commonsense actors, as they go about their normal practices.[24] This is especially true in classrooms. Social definitions about school knowledge—definitions that are both dialectically related to and rest within the larger context of the surrounding social and economic institutions—are maintained and recreated by the commonsense practices of teaching and evaluation in classrooms.[25]

I shall focus on kindergarten here because it occupies a critical moment in the process by which students become competent in the rules, norms, values, and dispositions "necessary" to function within institutional life as it now exists. Learning the role of student is a complex activity, one that takes time and continual interaction with institutional expectations. By focusing on how this occurs and on the content of the dispositions that are, both overtly and covertly, part of kindergarten knowledge, we can begin to illuminate the background knowledge children use as organizing principles for much of the rest of their school career.

In short, the social definitions internalized during one's initial school life provide the constitutive rules for later life in classrooms. Thus, the elements needing examination are what is construed as work or play, "school knowledge" or merely "my knowledge," normality or deviance. As we shall see, the use of praise, the rules of access to materials, and the control of time and emotions all make significant contributions to the teaching of social meanings in school. But, as we shall also see, it is the meanings attached to the category of *work* which most clearly illuminate the possible place of schools in the complex nexus of economic and social institutions which surrounds us all.

Kindergarten experience serves as a foundation for the years of schooling to follow. Children who have attended kindergarten tend to demonstrate a general superiority in achievement in the elementary grades compared with children who have not attended kindergarten. However, attempts to determine exactly which teaching techniques and learning experiences contribute most directly to the "intellectual and emotional growth" of kindergarten children have produced inconclusive results. Kindergarten training appears to exert its most powerful and lasting influence on the attitudes and the behavior of the children by acclimating them to a classroom environment. Children are introduced to their roles as elementary school pupils in kindergarten classrooms; it is understanding and mastery of this *role* which makes for the greater success of kindergarten-trained children in elementary school.

Socialization in kindergarten classrooms includes the learning of norms and definitions of social interactions. It is the ongoing development of a working definition of the situation by the participants. In order to function adequately in a social situation, those involved must reach a common understanding of the meanings, limitations, and potential the setting affords for their interaction. During the first few weeks of the school year, the children and the teacher forge a common definition of the situation out of repeated interaction in the classroom. When one common set of social meanings is accepted, classroom activities will proceed smoothly. Most often these common meanings remain relatively stable unless the flow of events in the setting ceases to be orderly.

We should understand that just as in our earlier discussion of the metaphor of cultural distribution, socialization is not a one-way process either.[26] To some extent, the children in a classroom socialize the teacher as well as becoming socialized themselves. However, the children and the teacher do not have equal influence in determining the working definition of the situation. On the first day of school in a kindergarten classroom, the teacher has a more highly organized set of commonsense rules than the children. Since he or she also holds most of the power to control the events and resources in the classroom, it is his or her set of meanings that is dominant. Of course, even teachers are not free to define the classroom situation in any way they choose. As we saw earlier in this chapter, the school is a well-established institution, and it may be that neither the teacher nor the children can perceive more than marginal ways to deviate to any significant extent from the commonsense rules and expectations that distinguish schools from other institutions.

The negotiation of meanings in a kindergarten classroom is a critical phase in the socialization of the children. The meanings of classroom objects and events are not intrinsic to them, but are formed through social interaction. These meanings, as with other aspects of the definition of the situation, may shift for a time. At some point, however, they become stable and are not likely to be renegotiated unless the orderly flow of events in the classroom is disrupted.

Meanings of objects and events become clear to children as they participate in the social setting. The *use* of materials, the nature of authority, the quality of personal relationships, the spontaneous remarks, as well as other aspects of daily classroom life, all contribute to the child's growing awareness of his or her role in the classroom and to his or her understanding of the social setting. Therefore, as was argued in Chapter 1, to understand the social reality of schooling, it is necessary to study it in actual classroom settings. Each concept, role, and object is a social creation bound to the situation in which it is produced. The meanings of classroom interaction cannot be assumed; they must be discovered. The abstraction of these meanings, together with the generalizations and insights drawn from them, may be applicable to other contexts, but the researcher's initial descriptions, understandings, and interpretations require that the social phenomena be encountered where they are produced, that is, in the classroom.[27]

Observation and interviewing of the participants in one particular public school kindergarten classroom, one that was considered by many other school people to be a model, revealed that the social meanings of events and materials were established remarkably early in the school year. As with most classroom settings, the socialization of the children was an overt priority during the opening weeks of school. The four most important skills that the teacher expected the children to learn during those opening weeks were to share, to listen, to put things away, and to follow the classroom routine. Thus, her statement of her goals for the children's early school experiences also constitutes her definition of socialized behavior in the classroom.

The children had no part in organizing the classroom materials and were relatively impotent to affect the course of daily events. The teacher made no special effort to make the children comfortable in the room, nor to reduce their uncertainty about the schedule of activities. Rather than mediating intrusive aspects of the environment, she chose to require that the children accommodate themselves to the materials as presented. When the ongoing noise of another class in the hallway distracted the children, for example, the teacher called for their attention; however, she did not close the door. Similarly, the cubby-holes where the children kept their crayons, smocks, and tennis shoes were not labeled although the children had considerable difficulty remembering which cubby-hole they had been assigned. In spite of many instances of lost crayons and crying children, the teacher refused to permit a student teacher to label the cubby-holes. She told the student teacher that the children must learn to remember their assigned cubby-holes because "that is their job." When one girl forgot where her cubby-hole was on the day after they had been assigned, the teacher pointed her out to the class as an example of a "girl who was not listening yesterday."

The objects in the classroom were attractively displayed in an apparent invitation for the class to interact with them. Most of the materials were placed on the floor or on shelves within easy reach of the children. However, the opportunities to interact with materials in the classroom were severely circumscribed. The teacher's organization of time in the classroom contradicted the apparent availability of materials in the physical setting. During most of the kindergarten session, the children were not permitted to handle objects. The materials, then, were organized so that the children learned restraint; they learned to handle things within easy reach only when permitted to do so by the teacher. The children were "punished" for touching things when the time was not right and praised at moments when they showed restraint. For example, the teacher praised the children for their prompt obedience when, on being told to do so, they quickly stopped bouncing basketballs in the gym; she made no mention of their ball-handling skills.

The teacher made it clear to the children that good kindergarteners were quiet and cooperative. One morning, a child brought two large stuffed dolls to school and sat them in her assigned seat. During the first period of large group instruction, the teacher referred to them, saying, "Raggedy Ann and Raggedy Andy are such good helpers! They haven't said a thing all morning."

As part of learning to exhibit socialized behavior the children learned to tolerate the ambiguity and discomfort of the classroom and to accept a considerable degree of arbitrariness in their school activities. They were required to adjust their emotional responses to conform to those considered appropriate by the teacher. They learned to respond to her personally and to the manner in which she organized the classroom environment.

After some two weeks of kindergarten experience, the children had established a category system for defining and organizing their social reality in the classroom. Their interview responses indicated that the activities in the classroom did not have intrinsic meanings; the children assigned meanings depending on the context in which each was carried on. The teacher presented the classroom materials either as a part of instruction or, more overtly, she discussed and demonstrated their uses to the class. This is critical. The use of a particular object—that is the manner in which we are predisposed to act toward it—constitutes its meaning for us. In defining the meanings of the things in the classroom, then, the teacher defined the relationships between the children and the materials in terms of contextual meanings bound to the classroom environment.

When asked about classroom objects, the children responded with remarkable agreement and uniformity. The children divided the materials into two categories: things to work with and things to play with. No child organized any material in violation of what seemed to be their guiding principle. Those materials that the children used at the direction of the teacher were work materials. These included books, paper, paste, crayons, glue, and other materials traditionally associated with school tasks. No child chose to use these materials during "play" time, early in the school year. The materials which the children chose during free time were labeled play materials or toys. These included, among other things, games, small manipulatives, the play house, dolls, and the wagon.

The meaning of classroom materials, then, is derived from the nature of the activity in which they are used. The categories of work and play emerged as powerful organizers of the classroom reality early in the school year. Both the teacher and the children considered work activities more important than play activities. Information which the children said they learned in school were all things that the teacher had told them during activities they called "work." "Play" activities were permitted only if time allowed and if the children had finished their assigned work activities. Observation data revealed that the category of work had several well-defined parameters sharply separating it from the category of play. First, work includes any and all teacher-directed activities; only free-time activities were called "play" by the children. Activities such as coloring, drawing, waiting in line, listening to stories, watching movies, cleaning up, and singing were called work. To work, then, is to do what one is *told* to do, no matter the nature of the activity involved.

Second, all work activities, and only work activities, were compulsory. For example, the children were required to draw pictures about specific topics on numerous occasions. During singing, the teacher often interrupted to encourage or exhort the children who were not singing or who were singing too softly. Any choices permitted during work periods were circumscribed to fit the limits of accepted uniform procedure. During an Indian dance, for example, the teacher allowed the "sleeping" children to snore if they wanted. After a trip to the fire station, all the children were required to draw a picture, but each child was permitted to choose whatever part of the tour he or she liked best as the subject of his or her picture. (Of course, it is also true that each child was *required* to illustrate his or her favorite part of the trip.) When introducing another art project the teacher said, "Today you will make a cowboy horse. You can make your horse any color you want, black or grey or brown." At another time, she announced, with great emphasis, that the children could choose three colors for the flowers they were making from cupcake liners. The children gasped with excitement and applauded. These choices did not change the principle that the children were required to use the same materials in the same manner during work periods. If anything, the nature of the choices emphasized the general principle.

Not only was every work activity required, but every child had to start at the designated time. The entire class worked on all assigned tasks simultaneously. Further, all the children were required to complete the assigned tasks during the designated work period. In a typical incident, on the second day of school, many children complained that they either could not or did not want to finish a lengthy art project. The teacher said that everyone must finish. One child, on asking if she could finish "next time," was told, "You must finish now."

In addition to requiring that all the children do the same thing at the same time, work activities also involved the children with the same materials and produced similar or identical products or attainments. During work periods the same materials were presented to the entire class simultaneously, and the same product was expected of each child. All the children were expected to use work materials in the same way. Even seemingly inconsequential procedures had to be followed by every child. For example, after large-group instruction on the second day of school, the teacher told the children, "Get a piece of paper and your crayons, and go back to your seats." One child, who got her crayons first, was reminded to get her paper first.

The products or skills, which the children exhibited at the completion of a period of work, were intended to be identical or, at least, similar. The teacher demonstrated most art projects to the entire class before the children got their materials. The children then tried to produce a product as similar to the one the teacher had made as possible. Only those pieces of artwork which were nearly identical to the product the teacher made as demonstration were saved and displayed in the classroom.

Work periods, as defined by the children, then, involved every child working simultaneously, at the same activity, with the same materials, and directed to the same ends. The point of work activities was to *do* them, not necessarily to do them well. By the second day of school, many children hastily finished their assigned tasks in order to join their friends playing with toys. During music, for example, the teacher exhorted the children to sing loudly. Neither tunefulness, rhythm, purity of tone nor mood were mentioned to the children or expected of them. It was their enthusiastic and lusty participation which was required. Similarly, the teacher accepted any child's art project on which sufficient time had been spent. The assigned tasks were compulsory and identical, and, in accepting all finished products, the teacher often accepted poor or shoddy work. The acceptance of such work nullified any notion of excellence as an evaluative category. Diligence, perseverance, obedience, and participation were rewarded. These are characteristics of the children, not of their work. In this way, the notion of excellence was separated from that of successful or acceptable work and replaced by the criterion of adequate participation.

The children, interviewed in September and again in October, used the categories of work and play to create and describe their social reality. Their responses indicate that the first few weeks of school are an important time for learning about the nature of work in the classroom. In September, no child said "work" when asked what children do in kindergarten. In October, half of those interviewed responded with the word "work." All the children talked more about working and less about playing in October than they had in September. The teacher was pleased with the progress of the class during the first weeks of school and repeatedly referred to the children as "my good workers."

The teacher often justified her presentation of work activities in the classroom in terms of the preparation of the children for elementary school and for adulthood. For example, she believed that work activities should be compulsory because the children needed practice following directions, without their exercising of options, as preparation for the reality of adult work. The children were expected to view kindergarten as a year of preparation for the first grade. In stressing the importance of coloring neatly or sequencing pictures properly, the teacher spoke of the necessity of these skills in first grade, and of the difficulty that children who were inattentive in kindergarten would have the following year.

The children were relatively powerless to influence the flow of daily events, and obedience was more highly valued than ingenuity. Again, this atmosphere was seen as an important bridge between home and future work situations. The teacher expected the children to adjust to the classroom setting and to tolerate whatever level of discomfort that adjustment included.

Thus, as part of their initiation into the kindergarten community, young children also receive their first initiation into the social dimension of the world of work. The content of specific lessons is relatively less important than the experience of being a worker. Personal attributes of obedience, enthusiasm, adaptability, and perseverance are more highly valued than academic competence. Unquestioning acceptance of authority and of the vicissitudes of life in institutional settings are among a kindergartener's first lessons. It is in the progressive acceptance, as natural, as the work *tout court,* of meanings of important and unimportant knowledge, of work and play, of normality and deviance, that these lessons reside.

Beyond a Rhetorical Humanism

As Gramsci argued, the control of the knowledge preserving and producing sectors of a society is a critical factor in enhancing the ideological dominance of one group of people or one class over less powerful groups of people or classes.[28] In this regard, the role of the school in selecting, preserving, and passing on conceptions of competence, ideological norms, and values (and often only certain social groups' "knowledge")—all of which are embedded within both the overt and hidden curricula in schools—is of no small moment.

At least two aspects of school life serve distributive, social, and economic functions. As the growing literature on the hidden curriculum shows, and as I have supported with historical and empirical evidence here, the forms of interaction in school life may serve as mechanisms for communicating normative and dispositional meanings to students. Yet, the body of the school knowledge itself—what is included and excluded, what is important and what is unimportant—also often serves an ideological purpose.

As will be demonstrated in Chapter 5, much of the formal content of curricular knowledge is dominated by a consensus ideology. Conflict, either intellectual or normative, is seen as a negative attribute in social life. Thus, there is a peculiar kind of redundancy in school knowledge. Both the everyday experience and the curriculum knowledge itself display messages of normative and cognitive consensus. The deep structure of school life, the basic and organizing framework of commonsense rules that is negotiated, internalized, and ultimately seems to give meaning to our experience in educational institutions, seems closely linked to the normative and communicative structures of industrial life.[29] How could it be otherwise?

Perhaps we can expect little more from the school experience than what I have portrayed here, given the distribution of resources in the USA, and given the wishes of a large portion of its citizenry. One hypothesis that should not be dismissed too readily is that, in fact, schools do work. In an odd way, they may succeed in reproducing a population that is roughly equivalent to the economic and social stratification in society. Thus, when one asks of schools, "Where is their humaneness?" perhaps the question may be more difficult to grapple with than the questioner expects.

For example, one could interpret this chapter as a statement against a particular community's commitment to education, or as a negative statement about particular kinds of teachers who are "less able than they might be." This would be basically incorrect, I believe. The city where this study was conducted is educationally oriented. It spends a large amount of its resources on schooling and feels that it deserves its reputation as having one of the best school systems in the area, if not the nation.

Just as important, we should be careful not to view this kind of teacher as poorly trained, unsuccessful, or uncaring. Exactly the opposite is often the case. The classroom teacher who was observed is, in fact, perceived as a competent teacher by administrators, colleagues, and parents. Given this, the teacher's activities must be understood, not merely in terms of the patterns of social interaction that dominate classrooms, but in terms of the wider patterning of social and economic relationships in the social structure of which he or she and the school itself are a part.[30]

When teachers distribute normative interpretations of, say, work and play like the historical and contemporary ones I have documented here, one must ask, with Sharp and Green, "to what problems are these viable solutions for the teachers?"[31] "What is the commonsense interpretive framework of teachers and to what set of ideological presuppositions does it respond?" In this way, we can situate classroom knowledge and activity within the larger framework of structural relationships which—either through teacher and parent expectations, the classroom material environment, what are considered important problems for teachers to focus on, or the relationship between schools and, say, the economic sector of a society—often determines what goes on in classrooms.

This chapter cannot by itself entirely support the argument that schools seem to act latently to enhance an already unequal and stratified social order. With the other chapters in this book, it does confirm, however, a number of recent analyses that point out how schools, through their distribution of social and ideological categories, contribute to the promotion of a rather static framework of institutions.[32] Thus, my argument should not be seen as a statement against an individual school or any particular groups of teachers. Rather, I want to suggest that educators need to see teachers as "encapsulated" within a social and economic context that by necessity often produces the problems teachers are confronted with and the material limitations on their responses. This very "external" context provides substantial legitimation for the allocation of teachers' time and energies and for the kinds of cultural capital embodied in the school itself.[33]

If this is the case, as I strongly suggest it is, the questions we ask must go beyond the humanistic level (without losing their humanistic and emancipatory intent) to a more relational approach. While educators continue to ask what is wrong in schools and what can be done—can our problems be "solved" with more humanistic teachers, more openness, better content, and so on—it is of immense import that we begin to take seriously the questions of "In whose interest do schools often function today?" and "What is the relation between the distribution of cultural capital and economic capital?" and finally, "Can we deal with the political and economic realities of creating institutions which enhance meaning and lessen control?"

Sharp and Green summarize this concern about a rhetorical humanism rather well:[34]

> [We] want to stress that a humanist concern for the child necessitates a greater awareness of the limits within which teacher autonomy can operate, and to pose the questions. "What interests do schools serve, those of the parents and children, or those of the teachers and headmaster?" and "What wider interests are served by the school?" and, possibly more importantly, "How do we conceptualize 'interests' in social reality?" Therefore instead of seeing the classroom as a social system and as such insulated from wider structural processes, we suggest that the teacher who has developed an understanding of his [or her] location in the wider process may well be in a better position to understand where and how it is possible to alter that situation. The educator who is of necessity a moralist must preoccupy himself with the social and [economic] preconditions for the achievement of his ideals. Rather than affirming the separation of politics and education, as is done with commonsense liberal assumptions, the authors assume all education to be in its implications a political process.

Thus, to isolate school experience from the complex totality of which it is a constitutive part is to be a bit too limited in one's analysis. In fact, the study of the relationship between ideology and school knowledge is especially important for our understanding of the larger social collectivity of which we are all a part. It enables us to begin to see how a society reproduces itself, how it perpetuates its conditions of existence through the selection and transmission of certain kinds of cultural capital on which a complex yet unequal industrial society depends, and how it maintains cohesion among its classes and individuals by propagating ideologies that ultimately sanction the existing institutional arrangements which may cause the unnecessary stratification and inequality in the first place. Can we afford not to understand these things?

Yet, as I noted in Chapter 1, a full understanding that seeks to go beyond the positivistic models which now dominate our consciousness must combine an analysis of what actually happens in schools with an appraisal of its growth, of its *history.* Only by combining these two can we see why these everyday experiences are what they are. And it is to this expanded history that we shall now turn.

CHAPTER 4

Curricular History and Social Control

(with BARRY FRANKLIN)

It should be getting clearer by now that one of the ways schools are used for hegemonic purposes is in their teaching of cultural and economic values and dispositions that are supposedly "shared by all," while at the same time "guaranteeing" that only a specified number of students are selected for higher levels of education because of their "ability" to contribute to the maximization of the production of the technical knowledge also needed by the economy. This focus on valuative consensus in the everyday regularities of school life and the concomitant teaching of economic dispositions to children, did not spring up overnight, however. It has had a long history in American education. Both this chapter and the next will focus on that problem. First, we shall examine in considerably more detail than in Chapter 3 how it came about historically through the school's response to ideological and economic conflicts among classes at a time of rapid change from an economy based on agricultural capital to one rooted in industrial capital in the beginnings of this century. As we shall see, schools were not necessarily built to enhance or preserve the cultural capital of classes or communities other than the most powerful segments of the population. The *hegemonic role of the intellectual,* of the professional educator, in this development is quite clear.

Then, to show that the emphasis on ideological hegemony is not "merely" of historical interest but still dominates the very core of classroom life, we shall return in Chapter 5 to the current formal corpus of school knowledge and investigate the emphasis on consensus again.

Toward a Sense of the Present as History

Imagine yourself as living in one of the larger ghettos of an American city. Another community member comes up to you and says, "You know, schools work." You look at him somewhat incredulously. After all, your children are doing relatively poorly on intelligence and achievement tests. Most of the community's young go on to lower paying jobs than their white counterparts. Many are rather disheartened about their futures. The school has increasing violence and vandalism. The curriculum seems out of touch with the reality and the history of your people. The community, rightly, feels it has little say in what goes on in the institution that is supposed to educate its young.

You lay this all out for him, explaining each of these issues and trying to show him that he is either just plain wrong or one of the least perceptive people you have seen in a long time. Then he says, "I agree with all you have told me. All these things you have just mentioned occur, not only here but throughout the United States in communities where people live who are poor, politically and culturally disenfranchised, or oppressed." Yet he begins documenting an important set of facts. Carefully, yet somehow passionately, he shows that these "community" schools are doing what they were in fact historically built to do. They were not built to give you control; quite the opposite is the case. As he talks, it slowly begins to make sense to you. A few more pieces of a larger picture begin to come together. What if he is correct? What if schools and the curriculum within them evolved in such a way that the interests of my community were to be subsumed under the interests of more powerful people? What if existing social and economic arrangements *require* that some people are relatively poor and unskilled and others are not? Then you begin to get a tacit understanding of how schools may help to maintain this set of institutional arrangements. You begin to agree, but you add something important he forgot to verbalize. You say, "Yes, schools work . . . for them." And you both nod.

Now this little vignette was meant to be more than simply an exercise in imagining. Rather, it was meant to reiterate points that lie at the heart of this book: both that schools have a history and that they are linked through their everyday practices to other powerful institutions in ways that are often hidden and complex. This history and these linkages need to be understood if we are to know the real possibilities for our own action on schools in that hypothetical community.

The curriculum field has played a major part in this history of the relationship between school and community. Because of this, it can also serve as an excellent exemplar for an analysis of the linkages schools have had with other institutions. By focusing on some of the past moments of the curriculum field here, I hope to show that the conclusions of the people in the imaginary story we started out with are not that imaginary at all. They provide, unfortunately, quite an accurate description of the hopes, plans, and conservative vision of community of a significant portion of a group of educators who had a large impact on how and what knowledge was chosen for, and ultimately got into, schools.

In order to illuminate these things, there are a number of questions we need to ask here. What did "community" mean for the educators and intellectuals who had the strongest influence on the early curriculum field? What social and ideological interests guided their work? These questions are critically important for a number of reasons. As has been repeatedly argued here, the knowledge that got into schools in the past and gets into schools now is not random.

It is selected and organized around sets of principles and values that come from somewhere, that represent particular views of normality and deviance, of good and bad, and of what "good people act like." Thus, if we are to understand why the knowledge of only certain groups has been primarily represented in schools, we need to see the social interests which often guided curriculum selection and organization.

As I shall demonstrate here, the social and economic interests that served as the foundation upon which the most influential curriculum workers acted were not neutral; nor were they random. They embodied commitments to specific economic structures and educational policies, which, when put into practice, contributed to inequality. The educational and cultural policies, and the vision of how communities should operate and who should have power in them, served as mechanisms of social control. These mechanisms did little to increase the relative economic or cultural efficacy of these groups of people who still have little power today. But before examining the roots the curriculum field has in the soil of social control, let us look briefly at the general perspective which underpins this chapter's critical analysis.

Power and Culture

Social and economic control occurs in schools not merely in the forms of discipline schools have or in the dispositions they teach—the rules and routines to keep order, the hidden curriculum that reinforces norms of work, obedience, punctuality, and so on. Control is exercised as well through the forms of meaning the school distributes. That is, the "formal corpus of school knowledge" can become a form of social and economic control.[1]

Schools do not only control people; they also help control meaning. Since they preserve and distribute what is perceived to be "legitimate knowledge"—the knowledge that "we all must have," schools confer cultural legitimacy on the knowledge of specific groups.[2] But this is not all, for the ability of a group to make its knowledge into "knowledge for all" is related to that group's power in the larger political and economic arena. Power and culture, then, need to be seen, not as static entities with no connection to each other, but as attributes of existing economic relations in a society. They are dialectically interwoven so that economic power and control is interconnected with cultural power and control. This very sense of the connectedness between knowledge or cultural control and economic power once again serves as the basis for our historical analysis here.

Two things have been central to this approach, so far. First, it sees schools as caught up in a nexus of other institutions—political, economic, and cultural—that are basically unequal. That is, schools exist through their relations to other more powerful institutions, institutions that are combined in such a way as to generate structural inequalities of power and access to resources. Second, these inequalities are reinforced and reproduced by schools (though not by them alone, of course). Through their curricular, pedagogical, and evaluative activities in day-to-day life in classrooms, schools play a significant role in preserving if not generating these inequalities. Along with other mechanisms for cultural preservation and distribution, schools contribute to what has elsewhere been called the *cultural reproduction of class relations* in advanced industrial societies.[3]

These two central concerns—the problem of schools being caught in a powerful set of institutions and the role of the school in reproducing inequalities—mean that one interprets schools in a different way than is usually done by educators. Rather than interpreting them as "the great engines of democracy" (though there is an element of truth in that), one looks at schools as institutions which are not necessarily or always progressive forces. They may perform economic and cultural functions and embody ideological rules that both preserve and enhance an existing set of structural relations. These relations operate at a fundamental level to help some groups and serve as a barrier to others.

This is not to imply that all school people are racist (though some may in fact be) or that they are part of a conscious conspiracy to "keep the lower classes in their place." In fact, many of the arguments for "community" and about curriculum put forth by some of the early educators, curriculum workers, and intellectuals whom I shall examine were based on the best liberal intentions of "helping people." Rather the argument being presented here is that "naturally" generated out of many of educators' commonsense assumptions and practices about teaching and learning, normal and abnormal behavior, important and unimportant knowledge, and so forth are conditions and forms of interaction that have latent functions. And these latent functions include some things that many educators are not usually aware of.

As has been pointed out elsewhere, for example, one important tacit function of schooling seems to be the teaching of different dispositions and values to different school populations. If a set of students is seen as being prospective members of a professional and managerial class of people, then their schools and curriculum seem to be organized around flexibility, choice, inquiry, etc. If, on the other hand, students' probable destinations are seen as that of semiskilled or unskilled workers, the school experience tends to stress punctuality, neatness, habit formation, and so on. These expectations are reinforced by the kinds of curricula and tests schools give and by the labels affixed to different kinds of students.[4] Thus, the formal and informal knowledge that is taught in schools, the evaluative procedures, and so forth, need to be looked at connectedly or we shall miss much of their real significance. For these everyday school practices are linked to economic, social, and ideological structures outside of the school buildings. These linkages need to be uncovered both today and in the past. It will be just this past that will concern us here.

Urbanization and the Historical Function of Schooling

Any serious attempt at understanding whose knowlege gets into schools must be, by its very nature, historical. It must begin by seeing current arguments about curriculum, pedagogy, and institutional control as outgrowths of specific historical conditions, as arguments that were and are generated by the role schools have played in our social order. Thus, if we can begin to comprehend the economic and ideological purposes schools have served in the past, then we can also begin to see the reasons why progressive social movements which aim at certain kinds of school reforms—such as community participation and control of institutions—are often less successful than their proponents would like them to be. We can also begin to illuminate some of the reasons *why* schools do what we saw them do in the last chapter.

To make this clear, I shall briefly focus on some historical purposes of urban schooling (the model from which most public schooling was generated), on what its "community" role was seen to be and how it functioned. Then I shall turn to a more extensive historical examination of the part of schooling that dealt with the knowledge students would "receive" in schools—the curriculum field.

Because of the ahistorical nature of education, we are in danger of forgetting many of the roots of schools in cities in the USA. This is unfortunate for these roots might help explain why many working class, Black, Latino, and other communities find little of their own culture and language in schools. Recent investigations of the growth of education in the urban centers of the East are quite helpful in this regard. In New York City in the 1850s, for example, when the public school system became increasingly solidified, schools were seen as institutions that could preserve the cultural hegemony of an embattled "native" population. Education was the way in which the community life, values, norms, and economic advantages of the powerful were to be protected. Schools could be the great engines of a moral crusade to make the children of the immigrants and the Blacks like "us." Thus, for many people who were important in the growth of schooling as we know it, cultural differences were not at all legitimate. Instead, these differences were seen as the tip of an iceberg made up of waters containing mostly impurities and immorality. The urban historian Carl Kaestle catches this attitude exceptionally well when he quotes from a New York State Assembly report which warned that, "Like the vast Atlantic, we must decompose and cleanse the impurities which rush into our midst, or like the inland lake, we shall receive their poison into our whole national system."[5]

Kaestle goes on to note that:[6]

> *Putman's Monthly* used the same metaphor and indicated the same solution to the pollution problem: "Our readers will agree with us that for the effectual defecation of the stream of life in a great city, there is but one rectifying agent—one infallible filter—the *school*." . . .

Most schoolmen were probably not adverse to the success of limited numbers of the poor through education, but the schools' mission—and most promoters were quite frank about it—was to inculcate cooperative attitudes among the city's children whatever the vicissitudes of urban life might bring them. Acculturation is thus a more accurate term for the school's intention than assimilation, although the terms are often used synonymously. The schools reflected the attitude of the general native public, who wished to Americanize the habits, not the status, of the immigrant.

This moral mission of the school had a major impact on the kinds of curricular selections made and on general school policy as you can well imagine. But this was not all. The crusade to eliminate diversity was heightened by another set of factors. The scale of city problems increased as the population increased. Something had to be done about the rapid growth in the numbers upon numbers of "different" children to be acculturated. The answer was bureaucratization—the seemingly commonsensical consolidation of schools and standardization of procedures and curriculum, both of which would promote economy and efficiency. Thus, the emphases on acculturation and standardization, issues community members still confront today, were intimately intertwined. In essence, "the bureaucratic ethic and the moral mission of the schoolmen arose from the same problem—the rapid expansion and diversification of the population—and they tended toward the same result—a vigorously conformist system."[7]

This moral mission with its emphasis on cultural conformity was not simply found in New York; nor was it limited to the early and middle parts of the nineteenth century. The moral values became increasingly coupled with economic ideologies and purposes as the country expanded its industrial base. Schools in New York, Massachusetts, and elsewhere, were looked at more and more as a set of institutions that would "produce" people who would have the traditional values of community life (a life that may never really have existed in this ideal form) and, as well, the norms and dispositions required of industrious, thrifty, and efficient workers for this industrial base. Not just in 1850, but even more between 1870–1920, the school was pronounced as the fundamental institution that would solve the problems of the city, the impoverishment and moral decay of the masses, and, increasingly, would adjust individuals to their respective places in an industrial economy.[8]

Marvin Lazerson's portrayal of the growth of schooling in the urban centers of Massachusetts makes these points in a rather telling fashion.[9]

By 1915 two central themes have thus become apparent in Massachusetts' city schools. One drew upon the reform ferments of the decades between 1870 and 1900 and saw education as the basis of social amelioration. The school would reach out and uplift the poor, *particularly through new techniques to teach traditional moral values.* The second theme, increasingly prominent after 1900, involved acceptance of the industrial order and a concern that schools mirror that order. It made the school's major function the fitting of the individual into the economy. By the teaching of specific skills and behavior patterns, schools would produce better and more efficient workers and citizens, and they would do this through a process of selection [testing], and guidance. These developments would transform the idea of equality of educational opportunity in America *for they made segregation—by curriculum, social class, projected vocational role— fundamental to the workings of the school.* [my italics]

Thus, at the base of schooling was a set of concerns which, when put together, embodied a conservative ideology. "We" must preserve "our" community by teaching the immigrants our values and adjusting them to existing economic roles.

This account gives us a general picture of the ideological climate of the times, particularly in the urban areas of the East, when the curriculum field began to define itself. It was a climate that pervaded the perceptions of more than just the public at large. It also affected many articulate intellectuals and educators, even those whose own roots were outside of the urban centers. As we shall see, neither the members of the rising intelligentsia nor the early members of the curriculum field were immune from these perceptions. Both the school's role in the moral crusade or in economic adjustment and stratification were things with which they felt more comfortable than not. In fact, the notion of immunity is something of an inaccurate one. A large portion of the early leaders of the movement to make curriculum selection and determination into a field of professional specialization wholeheartedly embraced both the moral crusade and the ethic of economic adjustment as overt functions of schooling. They saw the standardized procedures for selecting and organizing school knowledge as contributing to both of these purposes.

By examining the work of some of the most forceful and influential of these intellectuals and curriculum workers, we can begin to see the ideological commitments that have guided a good deal of curriculum decision-making in the past. For just as the vision of schooling as an institution of acculturation was slowly combined with the vision of schooling for economic adjustment in the minds of the public, so too did a generation of educators and social scientists begin to combine the two. We can also begin to understand, hence, how an economically and culturally conservative curricular model took shape and became the paradigm that still dominates the field today. It will be clear that, historically, curriculum theory and development have been strongly connected to and influenced by economic needs and changes, and, as we shall see, by a rather interesting notion of what the ideal "community" should be.

The Social Function of the Curriculum

The curriculum field's most important early members—Franklin Bobbitt, W. W. Charters, Edward L. Thorndike, Ross L. Finney, Charles C. Peters, and David Snedden—defined what the relationship should be between curriculum construction and community control and power that continues to influence the contemporary curriculum field.[10]

In delimiting the basic social role the school curriculum should play, the critical social and economic issue that concerned these formative theorists of the field was that of industrialization and its accompanying division of labor. Such a division, according to Bobbitt, had replaced the craftsman with the specialized worker. The small shop was replaced by the large corporation. In this situation the individual was no longer responsible for the design and production of a single product. Instead he or she was responsible for the production of only a portion of a product, the nature and specifications of which were provided to him or her by a supervisor. Beyond this narrow task in the production of one segment of a larger product, the individual worker was also dependent on other individuals, particularly the supervisor, for direction and guidance in his or her work. Furthermore, the individual was now almost totally dependent on other specialists in other lines of work for his or her food, shelter, and all the additional requirements needed for physical survival. Such a situation brought forth new needs, needs unknown in nineteenth century rural, agrarian America. On the one hand, this new corporate working class, which Bobbitt referred to as "group or associated workers," needed to be able to perform their specialized function in the hierarchical mode of organization that dominated the corporation.[11] And on the other hand, they needed enough knowledge of their economic and social tasks to allow them to work together toward the completion of a product which they had little role in designing.[12]

Bobbitt and Charters responded to this new economic need for specialized training by adopting the procedures of job analysis. They borrowed from the scientific management movement and built a theory of curriculum construction that was based on the differentiation of educational objectives in terms of the particular and narrow functions of adult life.[13] This is of no small moment, for it was the need in adult life for unity, cooperation, and an accepting attitude among these specialized workers that led the formative theorists of the field to define one of the major roles of the curriculum as developing "community." The curriculum would be used to foster "social integration."[14] Bobbitt, for instance, saw the curiculum as one means to develop what he called "large group consciousness," his term for the individual's feeling of belonging to his or her social and economic group or community and his or her commitment to its ends, values, and standards of behavior.[15] Yet it was the very definition of a person's community that made this model of curriculum selection and determination an exceptionally conservative one.

Social Homogeneity and the Problem of Community

Two features of this social function that people such as Bobbitt and Charters gave to the curriculum are important here. First, oddly, in defining the purpose of the curriculum, these educators were concerned to identify that function with the needs of the community. Bobbitt in fact made a special point of stating that the task of the curriculum worker was to be determined by the local community in which the school resided.[16] This does sound progressive. However, the second feature may make us a bit more cautious, for these theorists also viewed the social role of the curriculum as that of developing a high degree of normative and cognitive consensus among the elements of society. It was this that Bobbitt referred to as "large group consciousness:"[17]

> How does one develop a genuine feeling of membership in a social group, whether large or small? There seems to be but one method and that is, *To think and feel and ACT with the group as a part of it as it performs its activities and strives to attain its ends.* Individuals are fused into coherent small groups, discordant small groups are fused into the large internally-cooperating group, when they *act together* for common ends, with common vision, and with united judgment. [Bobbitt's italics]

These two aspects of the social task of the curriculum are rather significant. Both issues, community and "like-mindedness," were common themes in American social thought, particularly in the newly emerging fields of sociology, psychology, and education, during the late nineteenth and early twentieth centuries. Looking at these themes and how they were employed during this period will, I believe, go a long way in telling us about the nature of the curriculum field and its past and present response to the relationship between school and community, about its response to the problem of whose knowledge shall be construed as legitimate knowledge.

Like the author of the *Putnam's Monthly* piece I quoted earlier, the formative members of the curriculum field, as well as most of the early leaders in sociology, psychology, and education, were by birth and upbringing members of a native and rural middle class, Protestant in religion, and Anglo-Saxon in descent. In defining the nature, boundaries and interests of their fields of study, these intellectual leaders, along with other social scientists, reflected and spoke to the concerns of the middle class. Specifically, they reflected what they believed was the declining power and influence of the middle class in the wake of America's transition in the late nineteenth and early twentieth centuries from a rural, agrarian society to an urban, industrialized one.[18] They defined the issues in a particular way, as a problem of the *loss* of community.

As we saw, in the discussion of the growth of urban education, the period during which these future leaders came to maturity, 1865 to 1900, was a time of doubt and fear for the small farmers, merchants, and professionals who made up the nation's middle class. They felt their social order, which they viewed as being rooted in the small rural town with its deep, face to face personal relationships, was endangered. They were afraid of the emerging dominance of a new economic unit, the corporation. They also felt that a new economic and social class of great wealth and power, composed of the owners of these corporations and their financial backers, would threaten the economic security and political influence of the small town, thus harming its economic base in agriculture and small-scale manufacturing. But the growth of a corporate economy also was tied to the growth of urban centers. The cities were increasingly being populated by immigrants from eastern and southern Europe and Blacks from the rural South. These diverse people were seen as a threat to a homogeneous American culture, a culture centered in the small town and rooted in beliefs and attitudes of the middle class. The "community" that the English and Protestant forebearers of this class had "carved from a wilderness" seemed to be crumbling before an expanding urban and industrial society.

Of these two concerns, the early spokespeople of the new social sciences focused most of their attention on the problem of immigration. They suspected that these immigrants, who seemed to have a higher birthrate than the native population, would soon outnumber the "native well bred population." Increasing numbers of immigrants, with their urban enclaves and different political, cultural, and religious traditions, were a threat to a homogeneous culture. This unitary culture was not only the source of America's stability and a key to progress, but was synonymous for these members of the intelligentsia with the idea of democracy itself.[19]

At first these intellectuals talked of the issue of community in terms of a threat to the existence of the rural town. For Edward A. Ross, one of the first American sociologists, the deep, intimate, face to face relationships of the small town provided a natural and spontaneous mechanism of social control.[20] For Ross and other early social scientists, the small town assumed almost mystical proportions as the guarantor of social order and stability. The small town, its politics, its religion, its values, came to be seen, as the sociologist Robert Nisbet puts it, as the very essence of the American community.[21]

Later and more importantly, the members of this new group of intellectuals (who in actuality owed the emergence of their professions and the opportunities it offered them to both urbanization and industrialization) took a different tack in defining the problem of community, one that did not require them to defend the small town as a physical entity.[22] Instead, they took what they thought constituted the basis of the small town's ability to provide for stability, its like-mindedness in beliefs, values, and standards of behavior, and idealized this feature of small town life as the basis of the order necessary for an emerging urban and industrialized society. For these intellectuals the notion of community became synonymous with the idea of homogeneity and cultural consensus. If their upbringing in the rural town taught these individuals anything, it taught them that order and progress were dependent on the degree to which beliefs and behavior were common and shared. Applying this view to the increasingly urban society in which they lived, they argued for the maintenance of a unitary culture (what they meant by a sense of community) rooted in the values, beliefs, and behavior of the middle class. When it seemed to them that cultural homogeneity was dissolving, because of urbanization, industrialization, and immigration, and that their sense of community was being eclipsed, they acted by "striking out at whatever enemies their view of the world allowed them to see."[23]

Social Control and the Problem of Community

In the name of cultural conformity, these early social scientists "struck out" with a particular passion at the Eastern and Southern European immigrant. Adopting for the most part an hereditarian perspective, they viewed the immigrants and workers as being inferior to the native population. Given the high birthrate, they were concerned that these immigrants would come to threaten the existence of the more economically advantaged classes with what Ross called "race suicide."[24] More immediately, however, these immigrants were perceived as a threat to the existence of democracy itself. Charles A. Ellwood, another early American sociologist, argued that genetically immigrants did not seem to have "the capacity for self government and free institutions which the peoples of Northern and Western Europe have shown."[25]

To deal with this supposed threat, the intellectuals joined the growing movement during the late nineteenth and early twentieth centuries for immigration restriction.[26] However, to insure cultural homogeneity in the face of the immigration that had already occurred, they saw a need for a second line of defense. In essence, they perceived that the imposition of meaning could be an instrument of social control. The immigrant could be increasingly acculturated into middle class values, beliefs and standards of behavior. One such instrument, according to Ross, was the school. Ross argues in a manner strikingly similiar to the attitudes seen in our treatment of the ideological climate surrounding the growth of urban schools.[27]

> To nationalize a multitudinous people calls for institutions to disseminate certain ideas and ideals. The Tsars relied on the blue-domed Orthodox church in every peasant village to Russify their heterogeneous subjects, while we Americans rely for unity on the "little red school house."

It was in this vein that Bobbitt and the other formative leaders of the curriculum field would use the curriculum to serve the cause of community. The *curriculum* could restore what was being lost.

The Curriculum Field and the Problem of Community

The most influential early members of the curriculum field seemed for the most part to share these views about the declining position of the middle class and the threat posed by immigrants and other diverse peoples. Ross L. Finney, not only an early curriculum theorist but one of the first educational sociologists, like earlier social scientists and educators viewed the middle class as being threatened from above by a class of corporate capitalists and from below by an immigrant working class, who were entering the population in growing numbers to meet the demands of industrialization for a cheap labor supply. Writing in the post World War I period, he reflected the national paranoia known as the Red Scare. He argued that the Eastern and Southern European immigrants, whom he believed had carried with them to America a Bolshevik ideology, would attempt to overthrow the nation and with it the middle class in a revolution similar to the Russian Revolution of 1917.[28]

In making his defense of the middle class, Finney bemoaned the loss of community. He spoke longingly of what he viewed as a more serene time in the history of the nation, a time when industrialization had not taken the ownership of the nation's wealth out of the hands of those who had produced it and in the process had created conflicting economic and social classes and interests.[29]

Finney's solution to this problem was familiar. The nation must instill the immigrants with specific values and standards of behavior. The immigrant working class had to hold the same firm commitments to their work which he attributed to people from his own class. It was this commitment, he believed, that would reduce their potential revolutionary threat by making them happy performing the "humbler" economic functions that he saw as the future lot of the mass of the American population in an industrialized society.[30] Along with the other intellectuals of his day, he argued that "if a democratic people's conduct is to be dependable and harmonious, they must think and feel alike."[31]

Other major curriculum workers had a similar commitment to like-mindedness. Charles C. Peters, who like Finney was both an influential curriculum theorist and educational sociologist, viewed the immigrants as a threat to American civilization until they came "to think about, and act on, political, social, economic, sanitary, and other matters in the approved American way."[32] Just as importantly, Edward L. Thorndike, who did more than any other individual to articulate the behavioristic psychology that has dominated the curriculum field since its earliest times, viewed Blacks in the same way as these other educators viewed the immigrant. He not only doubted their ability to adjust to democratic institutions, but he saw them as an undesirable element within the population of most American cities.[33] But how were we to cope with these undesirable elements? Since the people were already here, how could we make them to be like us? How could we restore community?

Just as in earlier periods, these individuals looked to the schools. The school curriculum could create the valuative consensus that was the goal of their economic and social policies. Finney in this respect argued that "a far wiser propaganda for the workers is one that will ally and amalgamate them with the middle class. And such an alliance and amalgamation should be forced upon the lower classes, whether their agitators like it or not by compulsory attendance laws that make high school graduation practically universal."[34]

But when these social scientists and educators actually came to deal with the practicalities of the nature and design of the curriculum, an important change in their argument occurred, a change which proved important for both the future development of the field and those people whom these developments would affect. Instead of talking about the need for homogeneity in terms of ethnic, class and racial differences, they began to talk about the question in terms of differences in intelligence. "Science" became the rhetorical, though often unconscious, cloak to cover conservative social and educational decisions, a fact that will become of increasing importance when we turn to the uses of scientific and technical language in education today in Chapters 6, 7 and 8 and examine its use to disguise ideological and ethical assumptions.

Finney, for example, seemed to alter his view about what constituted the principal problem facing American society. The primary threat to the middle class was no longer the growing, immigrant, working class. More important was the fact "that half the people have brains of just average quality or less, of whom a very considerable percentage have very poor brains indeed."[35] Joining him in this view of the problem was Thorndike who argued that individuals of low intelligence within the population constituted a threat to the very existence of "civilization."[36] Bobbitt and others increasingly codified their arguments in scientific terms. In fact, they even warned against extreme nationalism and the hatred of European peoples which it engendered.[37] Now when these individuals came to deal directly with the issue of curriculum construction, it does appear that they altered their view of the problem of community. The problem was no longer that of maintaining the hegemony of the more advantaged members of the community, the problem that most of the early leaders in the social sciences identified, but that of maintaining the hegemony of those of high intelligence in a society in which the mass of the population was believed to be at best of average intelligence. As we shall see, this is less of a change than one might think.

Curriculum Differentiation and the Issue of Community

The central feature of the view of curriculum construction that dominated the thinking of these early educators, and in fact still dominates the thinking of contemporary curriculum theorists, was that the curriculum needed to be differentiated to prepare individuals of differing intelligence and ability for a variety of different but specific adult life functions.[38] This is a critical point. These varying adult functions were seen to involve *unequal* social responsibilities yielding unequal social power and privilege. These educators believed that individuals of high intelligence were more moral, more dedicated to their work, and more willing to apply their talents to the benefit of the larger society than were the majority of the population. As a consequence Thorndike and others argued that the views of these individuals were of more social import than those of the majority. Therefore, these individuals deserved a position of social and political preeminence.[39]

This view of the unequal distribution of responsibility and power was reflected when they talked about how curriculum differentiation would fulfill two social purposes—education for leadership and education for what they called "followership." Those of high intelligence were to be educated to lead the nation by being taught to understand the needs of the society. They would also learn to define appropriate beliefs and standards of behavior to meet those needs. The mass of the population was to be taught to accept these beliefs and standards whether or not they understood them or agreed with them.[40] As Finney argued, "instead of trying to teach dullards to think for themselves, the intellectual leaders must think for them, and drill the results, memoriter, into their synapses."[41] In this way, curriculum differentiation based on "intelligence" would create cultural homogeneity and thereby stability within American society.[42]

In short, what these early curriculum workers were concerned about was the preservation of cultural consensus while at the same time allocating individuals to their "proper" place in an interdependent industrialized society. Bobbitt alluded to this concern in his identification of the two principal functions of modern, industrial life. There was the "specialist" worker whom I mentioned earlier in the paper. His or her function was to be skilled in one narrow task within a given organization. Beyond that he needed a limited knowledge of the total organization to allow him to see the importance of his narrow function within the larger process of production and distribution and for his "willing and intelligent acquiescence" in the purposes of the organization.[43] The "specialist" worker only needed a thorough understanding of his particular task. Outside of that task, according to Thorndike, he or she only needed to "know when not to think and where to buy the thinking he needs."[44] And there was the "generalist," Bobbitt's term for the manager or supervisor. He did not need to be skilled in any one task, but rather he needed a complete understanding of and commitment to the purposes of the organization to allow him to direct the activities of the "specialists" and to gain their acquiescence.[45] Thus, some people of greater wisdom would direct others. What could be wrong with that? It is who these people would be that makes this vision less than neutral.

Ethnicity, Intelligence, and Community

As we just saw, in defining the function of the curriculum many of the most influential members of the field, although they seemed to fear and dislike the immigrants, increasingly talked of the issue of maintaining community as a problem of widespread low intelligence within the population. But there is evidence to suggest that this redefinition was not indicative of a change from the viewpoint they shared with the earlier leaders in the social sciences. Although they talked about differentiating the curriculum in terms of intelligence, both Bobbitt and David Snedden, another individual who was both a curriculist and an educational sociologist, suggested that the differentiation should also be made in terms of differences in social class and ethnic background respectively.[46] When Thorndike identified those within American society whom he believed possessed greater natural capacity and high intelligence, he pointed to the businessman, scientist, and lawyer.[47] These were occupations that during his day were almost totally monopolized by members of the native, middle class. The highly intelligent, hence, were to be predominantly found within this class and not the lower ones. The unintelligent masses were the elements of diversity within the population, primarily the eastern and southern European immigrant and to a lesser degree the Black population. Thus, what was originally seen by American intellectuals as a cultural problem of ethnic and class differences was redefined in the seemingly neutral language of science as a problem of differences in intelligence, as a problem in differing "abilities" to contribute to the maximization and control of "expert" moral and technical knowledge, in this way divesting the problem of its economic and social content. Social control, hence, became covered by the language of science, something that continues to this day.[48] By controlling and differentiating school curricula, so could people and classes be controlled and differentiated as well.

But why did they do this? The formative theorists of the curriculum field, despite their identification with the middle class, increasingly viewed industrialization and the emergence of the corporation with favor. They were particularly enamored of the seeming efficiency and productivity of industrial processes and thus incorporated into their conception of curriculum construction the principles of scientific management that were thought to be responsible for it.[49] But beyond this faith in corporate procedures, they were committed to its hierarchical mode of organization as *a model for society itself.* We can see this most clearly in Finney's vision for American society:[50]

> This conception of leadership and followship—leads us again to the notion of a graduated hierarchy of intelligence and enlightenment. . . . At the apex of such a system must be the experts, who are pushing forward research in highly specialized sectors of the front. Behind them are such men and women as the colleges should produce, who are familiar with the findings of the experts and are able to relate part with part. By these relatively independent leaders of thought, progressive change and constant readjustment will be provided for. Back of these are the high school graduates, who are somewhat familiar with the vocabulary of those above them, have some feeling of acquaintance with the various fields, and a respect for expert knowledge. Finally, there are the duller masses, who mouth the catchwords of those in front of them, imagine that they understand, and follow by imitation.

Notice that this view of social organization does not attempt to eliminate all diversity but rather to control it by narrowing its scope and channeling it toward areas that do not seem to threaten the imperatives of social stability, the production of "expert knowledge," and economic growth. Industrialists, for example, from the 1880s to the early 1920s, the period in which these formative theorists grew to maturity and carried on their work, resisted the growing national movement for immigration restriction. Instead they attempted to diminish the immigrants' supposed threat to American society by instilling them with middle-class attitudes, beliefs, and standards of behavior. At the same time, they employed their seeming "willingness" to work for low wages to meet the demands of industrialization for a cheap source of labor.[51] Here, the formative members of the curriculum field, unlike some of the early social scientists, seemed to share this view held by the industrialists.[52] They may have believed that, given the growing nativistic sentiments of the post First World War period, they would be more successful in promoting the integration of diverse elements of the population into a hierarchically organized society if they conceptualized that diversity in terms of intelligence and not ethnicity. In the context of the time, they no doubt believed that American society was more willing to deal with diversity in intelligence than diversity in ethnicity or race.[53] But they undoubtedly felt secure in their belief that a "real" community could be built through education, one with "natural" leaders and "natural" followers, and one in which people like "us" could define what "they" should be like.

But this does not explain all of it. To this must be added the role of "science" as once again providing the "ultimately right principles" about which there must be consensus. As the scientific justification of stratification increased, as it became more systematic, it provided the ideal solution to the ideological problem of justifying one's power over other competing and ultimately threatening groups. And it provided it in two ways: giving an "adequate" definition of these individuals' situation and in serving the interests of these classes in the competition over economic and cultural capital. By treating science as a form of technology, as a neutral method that could be applied to the economic and cultural dilemmas these people faced in their attempt to recreate and create hegemony, the role (the scope and function) of their ideological vision is obvious.

For these "reformers" were faced with an interesting dilemma. Generally speaking, with the breakdown of a once accepted economic and moral order—caused in part by rapid industrialization, the shift from the accumulation of agricultural to industrial capital, the growth of technology, immigration, the perceived disintegration of community life, the increasing "need" to divide and control labor to increase profits, and so on—bonds of affiliation became shaky. The meanings that provided ties among people had to be reconstituted, often on a new foundation. The language form of science and technology provided these ties in a number of ways for educators by giving a whole new range of meanings around which they could affiliate.[54] First, it offered a mode of description that seemed more powerful than previous ways of talking about educational events and policy, a way of describing both the relationship between schools and the problems of society and for describing what went on or should go on in classrooms. Second, it was an explanatory language that seemed as if it could establish causes and infer reasons as to why things occurred or didn't occur in and out of schools. Third, and quite important, the language of science and technology held forth the promise of better control, giving educators a greater ease of prediction and manipulation. It would help us in our goal to get different students from point A to point B quickly and efficiently (though whether the ends and means of getting from A to B were themselves ethically and economically "just" is one of the critical questions that was not adequately raised by these people), thereby going a long way toward creating the categories and procedures that have maintained the abstract individual, the unconnected educator and student, to this day.

These kinds of meanings generated by such a linguistic system were overt and probably helped provide these educators with a sense of the rightness of their endeavors. After all, who could quarrel with being better able to describe, explain, or control events? However, the latent ideological functions of science and technology as a linguistic system were as and perhaps even more important than the overt ones of providing a useful "definition of the situation." Science, with its inferred logic of efficiency and control, performed a legitimating or justificatory function. As Huebner notes, legitimating language serves to establish a person's claim that he or she knows what he or she is doing, or that he "has the right, responsibility, authority or legitimacy to do it."[55] In short, it reassures a number of groups and people, not the least of whom is the educator himself, that he or she knows and has a right to continue doing what he or she has been doing all along. Given the increasing faith in industrial and efficiency models at the time by powerful classes in the economic sector of the society, science and technology combined to create a form of language that linked these educators and intellectuals to the value system of the larger economic order.

Furthermore, not only did it justify educators' activity—after all, it did create group cohesion among educators and rested easily within a growing economy with its need for efficiency, technical knowledge, industrial growth, and socialization to "democracy"—but it also helped attract recruits, committed individuals who would labor for the cause. Finally, it acted as a hortatory device that could prescribe action that should be taken by various individuals and groups. This was primarily a political use of language in which science and technology carried a logical imperative and an ideological commitment needed to convince people to join a movement for what seemed to be ameliorative institutional reform.[56]

In all of these ways—descriptive, explanatory, prescriptive, legitimating or justificatory, and hortatory—the rationality of science and technology was an ideal device to create a new set of meanings, a new vision of the "sacred," if you will, that would rebuild the affiliative bonds that had become so fragile, that could recreate "community." But this was not merely the case for educators. Science, progress, efficiency, industrial growth, and expansion, all within the bounds of social stability, became an integral part of the ideological world view of most of the more powerful sectors of the nation as well. Its historical residue still provides the constitutive social rules for the day-to-day classroom life I examined in Chapter 3, (the roots of schooling as preparing children for "work" are obviously quite deep) and for the kinds of formal knowledge considered essential to a corporate economy that I analyzed in Chapter 2.

Conclusion

It is this commitment to maintaining a sense of community, one based on cultural homogeneity and valuative consensus, that has been and remains one of the primary, though tacit, legacies of the curriculum field. It is a function that is embedded in the historic reliance of the field on procedures and techniques borrowed from corporate enterprises. As we shall see in Chapter 6, oddly (though perhaps not, given what we have seen of the field's past) this reliance remains as strong today (with the dominance within the field of things, for example, like systems management procedures) as it did almost sixty years ago when the leaders of the field turned to the scientific management movement for direction in articulating the nature of curriculum construction. Since the historic tendency of this commitment is to build "community" (and curricula) that reflects the values of those with economic and cultural power, it is a commitment that may pose the same threat to contemporary workers, women, Blacks, Latinos, and American Indians as it did to early twentieth century Blacks and immigrants from Eastern and Southern Europe. Given the tendency of many curriculum theorists since the earliest days of the field to articulate their rather conservative commitments in the scientific and seemingly neutral language of intelligence and ability, it is also a threat that historically has remained unrecognized. Only by seeing how the curriculum field often served the rather conservative interests of homogeneity and social control, can we begin to see how it functions today. We may still find, unfortunately, that the rhetoric of science and neutrality covers more than it reveals. At the very least, though it may be unfortunate, we should not expect the curriculum field to totally overthrow its past. After all, as in our imaginary vignette at the beginning of this analysis, schools do work . . . for "them." In education, as in the unequal distribution of economic goods and services, "them" that has, gets.[57] If we are indeed serious about making our institutions responsive to communities in ways they are not now, the first step is in recognizing the historical connections between groups that have had power and the culture that is preserved and distributed by our schools. This recognition may do something else. It may cause us to ask similar questions today. Perhaps we could start by returning to our initial vignette and asking again, "For *whom* do schools work?" Some educators may be quite discomfited by the answer. But whoever said that an awareness of one's tacit political stance was supposed to make one comfortable?

CHAPTER 5

The Hidden Curriculum
and the Nature of Conflict

I argued in Chapter 1 that in order to understand the relationship between curriculum and cultural and economic reproduction we would have to grapple more completely with the maintenance and control of particular forms of ideology, with hegemony. We have now seen how both historically and currently certain normative conceptions of legitimate culture and values enter into curriculum. Yet we need to stress that hegemony is created and recreated by the formal corpus of school knowledge, as well as by the covert teaching that has and does go on. As the quotes from Williams indicated earlier, selective tradition and incorporation function at the level of overt knowledge so that certain meanings and practices are chosen for emphasis (usually by a segment of the middle class[1]), and others are neglected, excluded, diluted, or reinterpreted. For just as many educators and members of the curriculum field have often lost a serious sense of their historical rootedness in past interests of maintaining consensus through the selection of knowledge based on a vision of a society stratified by class and "ability," so too has the selective tradition operated today to deny the importance of both conflict and serious ideological difference. What was often in the past a conscious attempt by the bourgeoisie to *create* a consensus that was not there, has now become the only possible interpretation of social and intellectual possibilities. What was at first an ideology in the form of class interest has now become *the* definition of the situation in most school curricula. We shall look at this by examining some aspects of that formal corpus of school knowledge and see how what goes on within the black box can create the outcomes the economic reproduction theorists have sought to describe. Once more our view of science will play an interesting, and in this case rather direct role.

Before proceeding, however, it is important to note that in order for the school to continue to perform in a relatively smooth manner its complex historical roles in the maximization of the production of technical knowledge and in the socialization of students into the normative structure required by our society, it has to do something else which is related to and helps underpin both roles. It has to make legitimate a basically technical perspective, a tension of consciousness that responds to the social and intellectual world in an acritical fashion. That is, the school needs to make all this seem natural. A society based on technical cultural capital and individual accumulation of economic capital needs to seem as if it were the only possible world. Part of the school's role, in other words, is to contribute to the distribution of what the critical theorists of the Frankfurt School might call purposive-rational patterns of rationality and action.

This is an important element in ideological hegemony, for, as was noted in Chapter 3, in order for students' definitions of situations (like those taught in their initial school experience) to be maintained, these definitions must be ongoingly confirmed. This confirmation must entail a continuation of the patterns of interaction that dominated kindergarten, of course. But, since students, as they get older, now verbally reason with some facility, and can think through aspects of their social and cultural conditions, the curriculum content itself becomes even more important. There needs to be continuous and increasingly sophisticated *justification* for acceptance of the distinctions and social rules they learned earlier. This justification needs to *set the ideological limits* of such thinking by embodying "appropriate" ways in which students can begin to reason through the logic of why the institutions and the culture they interact with everyday are in fact legitimate. This requires that institutions, commonsense rules, and knowledge be seen as relatively pregiven, neutral, and basically unchanging because they all continue to exist by "consensus." Thus, the curriculum should stress hegemonic assumptions, ones which ignore the actual working of power in cultural and social life and which point to the naturalness of acceptance, institutional beneficence, and a positivistic vision in which knowledge is divorced from the real human actors who created it. The key to uncovering this, I believe, is the treatment *of conflict* in the curriculum.

Conflict and the Hidden Curriculum

The fact that schools normally seem neutral and are usually *overtly* insulated from political processes and ideological argumentation has both positive and negative qualities. The insulation has served to defend the school against whims and fads that can often have a destructive effect upon educational practice. It also, however, can make the school rather unresponsive to the needs of local communities and a changing social order. The pros and cons of the schools as a "conservative" institution have been argued fervently for the last ten years or so, at least. Among the most articulate of the spokespeople have been Edgar Z. Friedenberg and the late Jules Henry. Aside from the discussions of the teaching of work related norms, the covert teaching of an achievement and marketplace ethic and the probable substitution of a "middle class" and often "schizophrenic" value system for a student's own biographical meanings have been some of the topics most usually subject to analysis. As we saw, a good deal of the focus has been on what Jackson has so felicitously labeled the "hidden curriculum"—that is, on the norms and values that are implicitly, but effectively, taught in schools and that are not usually talked about in teachers' statements of end or goals. In a manner similar, though not as politically oriented, to that found in Chapter 3 here, for instance, Jackson deals extensively with the way students learn to cope with the systems of crowds, praise, and power in classrooms: with the large amount of waiting children are called upon to experience, with the teacher as a child's first "boss," and how children learn to falsify certain aspects of their behavior to conform to the reward system extant in most classrooms.[2]

These critiques of the ideological world-view being legitimated in the schools have been incisive, yet they have failed to focus on a prevailing characteristic of current schooling that significantly contributes to the maintenance of hegemony. There has been, so far, little examination of how the treatment of conflict in the school curriculum can lead to political quiescence and the acceptance by students of a perspective on social and intellectual conflict that acts to maintain the existing distribution of power and rationality in a society. Besides its support for the production and socialization functions of schooling, the topic of conflict is crucial for two reasons. How it is dealt with helps to posit a student's sense of the legitimate means of gaining recourse within unequal societies. This is particularly important, and will become more so, in urban and working class areas. It may be rather imperative that urban and working class, among other, students develop positive perspectives toward conflict and change, ones that will enable them to deal with the complex and often repressive political realities and dynamics of power of their society in a manner less apt to preserve current institutional modes of interaction.[3] Also, there may well be specific programmatic suggestions that can be made and instituted fairly readily in ongoing school programs that may alleviate some of the problems (and which might be attempted for tactical reasons as well).

We can learn a bit about the importance of tacit or hidden teaching from the literature on political socialization. It is beginning to be clear that "incidental learning" contributes more to the political socialization of a student than do, say, civics classes or other forms of deliberate teaching of specific value orientations.[4] Children are taught how to deal with and relate to the structure of authority of the collectivity to which they belong by the patterns of interaction they are exposed to to a certain extent in schools.

Obviously, it is not only the school that contributes to a student's "adjustment to authority." For instance, peer groups and especially the family, through its child-rearing practices and its style of interpersonal interaction, can profoundly affect a child's general orientation to authority.[5] However, there is a strong suggestion in recent research that schools are rather close rivals to the family as significant agents of political socialization. As Sigel puts it:[6]

> [There] is probably little doubt that the public schools are a choice transmission belt for the traditional rather than the innovative, much less the radical. As a result, they facilitate the political socialization of the mainstream young and tend

to equip them with the tools necessary for the particular roles they are expected to play in a given society. One may wish to quarrel with the differential roles the government and the schools assign to students, but it would probably be considerably more difficult to deny the school's effectiveness.

It should be stated that the negative treatment given to the uses of conflict goes far beyond the way with which it is overtly dealt in any one subject, say, social studies, the area in which one usually finds material on and teaching about conflict situations. Rather, the negative and quite unrealistic approach seems endemic to many areas, and especially to science, the area usually associated with objectivity and non-interpersonal conflict.

It has become increasingly evident that the formal corpus of school knowledge found in, say, most history books and social studies texts and materials has, over the years, presented a somewhat biased view of the true nature of the amount and possible use of internecine strife in which groups in this country and others have engaged. Our side is good; their side is bad. "We" are peace loving and want an end to strife; "they" are warlike and aim to dominate. The list could be extended considerably especially in racial and class matters.[7] Yet, we must go beyond this type of analysis, often even beyond the work of the revisionist historians, political scientists, students of political socialization, and educators to get at many of the roots of the teaching of this dominant orientation. I shall examine here two specific areas—social studies and science. In so doing, I shall point out that the presentation of these two areas (among others) in schools both mirrors and fosters an ideology that is oriented to a static perspective: in the social studies, on the positive and even essential functions of social conflict; and in science, on the nature of scientific work and argumentation and on what has been called "revolutionary" science. The view presented of science, especially, in the schools is particularly interesting since it is essentially an archetype of the ideological position on conflict I wish to illuminate.

Two tacit assumptions seem to be prominent in teaching and in curricular materials. The first centers around a negative position on the nature and uses of conflict. The second focuses on men and women as recipients of values and institutions, not on men and women as creators and recreators of values and institutions. These assumptions act as basic guidelines that order experiences.

Basic Rules and Tacit Assumptions

The concept of hegemony implies that fundamental patterns in society are held together by tacit ideological assumptions, rules if you will, which are not usually conscious, as well as economic control and power. These rules serve to organize and legitimate the activity of the many individuals whose interaction makes up a social order. Analytically it is helpful to distinguish two types of rules—constitutive or basic rules and preference rules.[8] Basic rules are like the rules of a game; they are broad parameters in which action takes place. Preference rules, as the name suggests, are the choices one has within the rules of the game. Take chess, for instance. There are basic ground rules (which are not usually brought to a level of awareness) that make chess different from, say, checkers or other board games or even nonboard games. And within the game of chess, one has choices of the moves to make within this constitutive framework. Pawn's choices involve moving forward (except in "taking" an opponent), rooks move forward or side to side, and so forth. If an opponent's pawn were to jump over three men to put you in check, then he or she obviously would not be following the "rules of the game;" nor would he be following the tacitly accepted rules if he, say, swept all your men from the board and shouted "I win!"

On the very broadest level, one of the constitutive rules most predominant in our society involves the notion of trust. When we drive down the street, we trust that the car approaching from the opposite direction will stay in its lane. Unless there is some outward manifestation of deviance from this rule, we never even bring to a level of conscious awareness how this basic rule of activity organizes our lives.[9] A similar rule is the one that posits the legitimate bounds of conflict. The rules of the game implicitly set out the boundaries of the activities people are to engage or not to engage in, the types of questions to ask, and the acceptance or rejection of other people's activities.[10] Within these boundaries, there are choices among a range of activities. We can use the courts, but not bomb; we can argue, but not duel; and so forth. A basic assumption seems to be that conflict among groups of people is *inherently* and fundamentally bad and we should strive to eliminate it *within* the established framework of institutions, rather than seeing conflict and contradiction as the basic "driving forces" in society.

While some of the better schools and classrooms are alive with issues and controversy, the controversies usually exhibited in schools concern choices *within* the parameters of implicitly held rules of activity. Little attempt is made to focus on the parameters themselves.

The hidden curriculum in schools serves to reinforce basic rules surrounding the nature of conflict and its uses. It posits a network of assumptions that, when internalized by students, establishes the boundaries of legitimacy. This process is accomplished not so much by explicit instances showing the negative value of conflict, but by nearly the total absence of instances showing the importance of intellectual and normative conflict in subject areas. The fact is that these assumptions are obligatory for the students, since at no time are the assumptions articulated or questioned. By the very fact that they are tacit, that they reside not at the roof but the root of our brains, their potency as aspects of hegemony is enlarged.

Some of the potent relationship between basic assumptions dominant in a collectivity and the hidden curriculum of school is examined by Dreeben. He argues that students tacitly learn certain identifiable social norms mainly by coping with the day to day encounters and tasks of classroom life. The fact that these norms that students learn penetrate many areas of later life is critical since it helps document how schooling contributes to individual adjustment to an ongoing social, economic, and political order. While his analysis is rather conservative, as we saw in Chapter 2, still schooling, occupation, and politics in the USA are well integrated for Dreeben. The former acts as a distributor of a form of rationality that, when internalized by the student, enables him or her to function in and, often, accept "the occupational and political institutions which contribute to the stability of an industrial society."[11]

Social studies and science as they are taught in the large majority of schools provide some of the most explicit instances of the hidden teaching. I have chosen these areas for two reasons. First, there has been built up a rather extensive and important literature concerned with the sociology of the disciplines of scientific endeavor. This literature deals rather insightfully with the "logic in use" of scientists (that is, what scientists seem actually to do) as opposed to the "reconstructed logic" of scientists (that is, what philosophers of science and other observers say scientists do) that is normally taught in schools.[12] Second, in social studies the problems we discuss can be illuminated rather clearly by drawing upon selected Marxian notions to show that the commonsense views of social life often found in the teaching of social studies are not inevitable. Let us examine science initially. In so doing, I also want to propose, as one of the suggestions I noted in Chapter 1 that I would make, an alternate or, rather, a broader view of scientific endeavor that should be considered by educators and, especially, curriculum workers, if they are, at the very least, to focus on the ideological assumptions inherent in much that is taught in our educational institutions.

Conflict in Scientific Communities

One of my basic theses is that science, as it is presented in most elementary and a large proportion of secondary classrooms, contributes to the learning by students of a basically unrealistic and essentially conservative perspective on the usefulness of conflict. Scientific domains are presented as bodies of knowledge ("thats" and "hows"), at best organized around certain fundamental regularities as in the many discipline and inquiry-centered curricula that evolved after the "Brunerian revolution," at worst as fairly isolated data one masters for tests. Almost never is it seriously examined as a personal construction of human beings. Let us examine this situation rather closely.

A science is not "just" a domain of knowledge or techniques of discovery and formulating justifications; it is a *group* (or rather, groups) of individuals, a *community* of scholars in Polanyi's terms, pursuing projects in the world.[13] Like all communities, it is governed by norms, values, and principles that are both overtly seen and covertly felt. By being made up of individuals and groups of scholars, it also has had a significant history of both intellectual and interpersonal struggle. Often the conflict is generated by the introduction of a new and usually quite revolutionary paradigm that challenges the basic meaning structures that were previously accepted by the particular body of scientists, often, thereby, effectively dividing the scholarly community. These struggles have been concerned with the modes of gaining warranted knowledge, with what is to be considered properly scientific, with the very basic foundations upon which science is based. They have also been concerned with such situations as conflicting interpretations of data, with who discovered what first, and many more issues.

What can be found in schools, however, is a perspective that is akin to what has been called the *positivist ideal*.[14] In our schools, scientific work is tacitly always linked with accepted standards of validity and is seen (and taught) as always subject to empirical verification with no outside influences, either personal or political. "Schools of thought" in science do not exist or, if they do, "objective" criteria are used to persuade scientists that one side is correct and the other wrong. Just as will be evident in our discussion of social studies instruction, children are presented with a *consensus theory of science,* one that underemphasizes the serious disagreements over methodology, goals, and other elements that make up the paradigms of activity of scientists. By the fact that scientific consensus is continually exhibited, students are not permitted to see that without disagreement and controversy science would not progress or would progress at a much slower pace. Not only does controversy stimulate discovery by drawing the attention of scientists to critical problems,[15] but it serves to clarify conflicting intellectual positions. More will be mentioned about this point later in our discussion.

A point that is also quite potent is that it is very possible that the standard of "objectivity" (one is tempted to say "vulgar objectivity") being exhibited and taught in school may often lead to a detachment from political commitment. That is, it may not be neutrality as it is overtly expressed, but it may mirror a rather deep fear of intellectual, moral, and political conflict.[16] The focus in educational institutions on the student/scientist (who is often a passive observer in many classrooms despite the emphasis being placed on inquiry by theorists and curriculum specialists) as an individual who objectively and rationally tests or deduces warranted assumptions or makes and checks hypotheses or what have you, critically misrepresents the nature of the conflicts so often found between proponents of alternative solutions, interpretations, or modes of procedure in scientific communities. It cannot enable students to see the political dimensions of the process by which one alternative theory's proponents win out over their competitors. Nor can such a presentation of science do more than systematically neglect the power dimension involved in scientific argumentation.

Not only is the historical and continuing conflict between competing theories in scientific domains ignored, but little or no thought has evidently been given to the fact that hypothesis-testing and the application of *existing* scientific criteria are *not sufficient* to explain how and why a choice is made between competing theories. There have been too many counter-instances that belie this view of science.[17] It is much more perceptive to note that science itself is not necessarily fully cumulative, nor does it proceed according to a basic criterion of consensus, but that it is driven by conceptual revolutions that cause groups of scientists to reorganize and reconceptualize the models by which they attempt to understand and manipulate the world.[18]

> The history of science has been and should be [seen] as a history of competing research programs (or, if you wish, "paradigms"), but it has not been and must not become a succession of periods of normal science: the sooner competition starts the better for progress.

Now I am not trying to make a case here for a view of science that states that "objectivity" and "neutrality," hypothesis-testing and inquiry procedures are not of paramount importance. What I am saying is that scientific argumentation and counter-argumentation are a major part of the scientific enterprise and that the theories and modes of procedure ("structures of disciplines," if you will) act as norms or psychological commitments that lead to intense controversy between groups of scientists.[19] This controversy is central to progress in science, and it is this continuing conflict that is hidden from students.

Perhaps this point can be made clearer by delving a bit more deeply into some of the realistic characteristics of scientific disciplines often hidden from public view and almost never taught in schools. While the discussion has focused on conflict in scientific domains, it is sometimes difficult to separate conflict from competition. One of the more important oversights in schools is the lack of treatment whatsoever of the "problem" of competition in science. Competition over priority and recognition in new discoveries is a characteristic of *all* established sciences.[20] One need only read Watson's lively account of his race with Linus Pauling for the Nobel Prize for the discovery of the structure of DNA, in *The Double Helix,* to realize how intense the competitiveness can be and how very human are scientists as individuals and in groups.

Competition also can be seen quite clearly between specialties in a discipline, not necessarily on the "frontiers" of knowledge as in Watson's case. Here, as in football, the "commodity" (if I may speak metaphorically) is topnotch students who can be recruited to expand the power and prestige of an emerging specialty. There is continuous, but usually covert, competition among subdisciplines in science for what seem to be limited amounts of prestige available. The conflict here is crucial. Areas whose prestige is relatively high tend to recruit members with the most talent. Relatively lower prestige areas can have quite a difficult time gaining adherents to their particular interests. Realistically a prime factor, if not *the* most important factor, in high quality scientific research is the quality of student and scientific "labor" a specialty can recruit. Prestige has a strong influence in enticing students and the competition over relative prestige can be intense, therefore, because of these consequences.[21] This is, obviously, connected to the cultural and economic role of the school in identifying those "laborers" who can contribute to the maximization of expert knowledge.

My point here is not necessarily to denigrate competition in science (though as the Rose's have noted in their recent volumes, scientific activity can and needs to progress through a shared progressive ideological position as well),[22] nor is it to present a demonic view of the scientific enterprise in all its ramifications. Rather it is to espouse a more realistic perspective on this enterprise and the *uses of conflict among its practitioners.* Conflict here is quite "functional." It induces scientists in each area to try to establish a domain of competence in their subjects that is specifically theirs. "Competitive" pressures also sometimes help to assure that less popular research areas are not neglected. Furthermore, the strong competitive element in the scientific community can encourage members to take risks, to outdistance their competitors, in effect, thereby increasing the possibility of new and exciting discoveries[23] (though it may also have been a factor in ignoring the contributions of women in science as Olby's discussion of the neglected contributions of Rosalind Franklin to the discovery of the structure of DNA demonstrates).[24]

Conflict is also heightened by the very normative structure of the scientific community itself. In fact, it may be a significant contributing agent in both conflict and competition. Among the many norms that guide the behavior of scientists, perhaps the most important for our discussion here is that of organized skepticism. Storer defines it as follows:[25]

> This norm is directive, embodying the principle that each scientist should be held individually responsible for making sure that previous research by others on which he bases his work is valid. He cannot be excused if he has accepted a false idea and then pleads innocence "because Dr. X told me it was true," even if privately we cannot accuse him of willfully substituting error for truth; he should have been properly skeptical of Dr. X's work in the first place . . .
>
> The scientist is obligated also by this norm to make public his criticisms of the work of others when he believes it to be in error . . . It follows that no scientist's contribution to knowledge can be accepted without careful scrutiny, and the scientist must doubt his own findings as well as those of others.

It is not difficult to see how the norm of organized skepticism has contributed to the controversies within scientific communities.

Other examples of conflict abound. Perhaps the one most important for our own topic is the existence of "rebellious" subgroups in scientific communities. Specialties that revolt against the goals and/or means of a larger discipline are quite common within the scientific tradition. These rebellious groups of researchers are alienated from the main body of current scientific discourse in their particular areas and sparks may very well fly because of the argumentation between the rebels and the traditionalists. Here, often added to this situation, even the usual arguments that we associate with science—that is, arguments among groups and individuals over substantive issues such as warranted knowledge and the like—blend with arguments over goals and policies. Even more importantly today, it is becoming quite common (and in my view, happily so) for there to be heated discussion and dissension over the political stance a discipline should take and over the social uses of its knowledge.[26]

So far I have been documenting the rather important dimension of conflict in scientific communities. I have been making the point that scientific knowledge as it is taught in schools has, in effect, been divorced from the structure of the community from which it evolved and which acts to criticize it. Students are "forced," because of the very absence of a realistic picture of how communities in science apportion power and economic resources, to internalize a view that has little potency for questioning the legitimacy of the tacit assumptions about interpersonal conflict that govern their lives and their own educational, economic, and political situations. Not only are they presented with a view of science that is patently unrealistic, but, what is more important for my own position, they are not shown how critical interpersonal intergroup (and, hence, class) argumentation and conflict have been for the progress of science. When this situation is generalized into a basic perspective on one's relation to the economic and political paradigms of activity in a society, it is not difficult to see how it can serve to reinforce the quiescence of students, lead them into "proper channels" for changing these structures, or help justify this structural arrangement by providing the constitutive rules of thought that make any other perspective on knowledge seem unnatural.

Conflict in Society

The second area of schooling in which one finds hidden curricular encounters with and tacit teaching of constitutive assumptions about conflict, and that I have chosen to explicitly focus upon, is that of social studies. As in our discussion of science, in delving into this area I shall propose an alternative or broader view on conflict in society. I want also to document some of the social uses of intellectual and normative conflict, uses that are ignored in most of the curricular encounters found in schools.

An examination of much of the literature in social studies points to an acceptance of society as basically a cooperative system. Observations in classrooms, like these reported in Chapter 3, over an extended period of time reveal a similar perspective. The orientation stems in large part from the (perhaps necessarily unconscious) basic ideological assumption that conflict, and especially social conflict, is *not an essential* feature of the network of social relations we call society.[27]

More often than not, a social reality is pictured that tacitly accepts "happy cooperation" as the normal if not the best way of life. Now it must be made clear that the truth value of the statement that society is a cooperative system (if only everyone would cooperate) *cannot* be determined empirically. It is essentially a value orientation that helps determine the questions that one asks or the educational experiences one designs for students. And the educational experiences seem to emphasize what is fundamentally a conservative perspective.

The perspective found in schools leans heavily upon how all elements of a society, from the postal worker and fire fighter in first grade to the partial institutions in civics courses in high school, are linked to each other in a functional relationship, each contributing to the ongoing *maintenance* of society. Internal dissension and conflict in a society are viewed as inherently antithetical to the smooth functioning of the social order. *Consensus* is once more a pronounced feature. This orientation is also evident in the implicit emphasis upon students (and "man" in general) as value-transmitting and value-receiving persons rather than as value-creating persons in much of their school experience.[28]

The fact that there are a number of paradigmatic ways one can perceive the social world has long been noted. However, it is also important to note that each posits a certain logic of organization upon social activity and each has certain, often strikingly different, valuative assumptions that underlie it. The differences between the Durkheimian and the more subjectivistic Weberian perspectives offer a case in point. Though less economically sophisticated than some of his very new work, the recent analysis of structural-functional social theories, especially those of Parsons, by Gouldner offers a more current example. His examination, one that has a long intellectual history in the sociology of knowledge, raises intriguing questions about the social and political consequences of contemporary social thought—that much of its background of assumptions is determined by the personal and class existence of the thinker, that it presents a "very selective, one-sided picture of American society," one geared to "the avoidance of political tensions" and aimed at a notion that political stability, say, "would be achieved if efforts at social change prudently stopped short of changing established ways of allocating and justifying power."[29] In short the underlying basis of such a social "paradigm" used to order and guide our perceptions is fundamentally oriented to the legitimation of the existing social order. By the very fact that it seeks to treat such topics as social *equilibrium* and system *maintenance,* for example, there is a strong tendency toward conformity and a denial that there need be conflict.[30] Like the socialization tradition of curriculum research we discussed in Chapter 2 (which stems from a structural-functional framework) it assumes the existence of the societal values, a perfect match between the ideological consciousness of intellectuals and the requirements of the recreation of hegemonic categories in children.

Opposed to the structural-functional type of reasoning, Gouldner advocates a different "paradigm," one that is rooted in the individual's search to transform herself and her activity, and one that sets not existing society as measure but rather the possibility of basic structural change through an individual's passionate commitment and social involvement. The question of legitimation, hence, becomes less a process of studying how institutional tensions evolve and can be "settled," and more an attempt to link institutions with their historical development and their need for transformation according to explicitly chosen principles based on political, economic, and ethical argumentation. The perspective on conflict of the latter position is quite different from that of the school of thought Gouldner criticizes.

In its analysis of the background assumptions of Parsonian social thought, for example, Gouldner's examination documents the place of moral argumentation and value conflict, which are at the heart of the human sciences and their understanding of society. He thereby considerably expands the boundaries of possible conflict. This situation is perhaps most evident in his criticism of the inordinate place Parsons gives to a socialization process that implicitly defines "man" as primarily a recipient of values.[31] He censures functionalist social theories for being incapable of dealing with "those who oppose social establishments actively and who struggle to change its rules and membership requirements." Gouldner opposes this view with a focus upon human beings as engaged in a dialectical process of receiving, creating, and recreating values and institutions.[32] The continual recreation of values in a society is a difficult process and often involves conflict among those of disparate valuative frameworks. It is this type of conflict, among others, to which Gouldner attempts to give a place.

By their very nature, social "paradigms" themselves are constantly changing, often "driven" by class conflict and social and economic contradictions. In fact, Gouldner's recent work can be seen to mirror and be a part of this change. However, they leave behind reifications of themselves found in both elementary and high school curricula. This may be particularly true in the case of the models of understanding of social life we find in schools today. These models bear a rather striking resemblance to the ideological positions first articulated by early educators and curriculists that I analyzed in the last chapter.

There is, perhaps, no better example of the emphasis upon consensus, order, and the absence of any conflict in social studies curricula than that found in one of the more popular sets of educational materials, Science Research Associates' economics "kit," *Our Working World*. It is designed to teach basic concepts of disciplined economics to elementary school students. The primary grade course of study subtitled "Families at Work" is organized around everyday social interaction, the likes of which children would be familiar with. Statements such as the following pervade the materials.[33]

> When we follow the rules, we are rewarded; but if we break the rules, we will be punished. So you see, dear, that is why everyone does care. That is why we *learn* customs and rules, and why we *follow* them. Because if we do, we are all rewarded by a nicer and more orderly world.

The attitude exhibited toward the *creation* of new values and customs and the value placed on an orderly, nonconflicting world seem to be indicative of a more constitutive set of assumptions concerning consensus and social life. When one realizes that students are inundated with examples of this type throughout the day, ones in which it is rather difficult to find any value placed upon disorder of any significant sort, it makes one pause.

Even most of the inquiry-oriented curricula, though fruitful in other ways to be sure, show a signal neglect of the efficacy of conflict and the rather long and deep-seated history it has held in social relationships. For example, the basic assumptions that conflicts are to be "resolved" within accepted boundaries and that continuing change in the framework and texture of institutional arrangements is less than desirable can be seen in the relatively sophisticated discipline-centered social science curricula that are being developed currently. One of these curricula was put out by the Center for the Study of Instruction in 1970. It overtly offers a "conceptual schemes" approach that puts forward a hierarchy of generalizations that, ideally, are to be internalized by the student through his or her other active participation in role-playing and inquiry. These levels of generalizations range from rather simple to fairly complex and are subsumed under a broad "descriptive" generalization or "cognitive scheme." For example, subsumed under the organizing generalization "Political organization (government) resolves conflicts and makes interactions easier among people" are the following sub-generalizations. They are listed in ascending complexity.[34]

1. The behavior of individuals is governed by commonly accepted rules.
2. Members of family groups are governed by rules and law.
3. Community groups are governed through leadership and authority.
4. Man's peaceful interaction depends on social controls.
5. The pattern of government depends upon control by participation in the political system.
6. Stable political organization improves the quality of life shared by its citizens.

Coupled with these "descriptive" generalizations, which the students are to be led up to, are such "supporting concepts" as "Rules help to maintain order" and "Rules help protect health and safety."[35] Now, few will quarrel with these statements. After all, rules do help. But, like the assumptions prevalent in the economics materials, children are confronted with a tacit emphasis once again on a stable set of structures and on the maintenance of order.

What is intriguing is the nearly complete lack of treatment of or even reference to conflict as a social concern or as a category of thought in most available social studies curricula or in most classrooms observed. Of the more popular materials, only those developed under the aegis of the late Hilda Taba refer to it as a key concept. However, while the Taba Social Studies Curriculum overtly focuses on conflict, and while this focus in itself is a welcome sight, its orientation is on the serious consequences of sustained conflict rather than on the many positive aspects also associated with conflict itself. Conflict again is viewed as "dysfunctional," even though it is pictured as being ever present.[36]

As was noted previously, to a large extent society as it exists, in *both* its positive and negative aspects, is held together by implicit commonsense rules and paradigms of thought, by hegemony as well as by overt power. Social studies materials such as this (and there are many others to which I have not referred) can contribute to the reinforcing and tacit teaching of certain dominant basic assumptions and, hence, a pro-consensus and anti-dissension belief structure.

This view is being countered somewhat by a portion of the content now being taught under the rubric of Black and Women's Studies. Here, struggle and conflict on a communal basis are often explicitly and positively focused upon.[37] While many curriculists may find such overt espousal of community goals somewhat antithetical to their own inclinations, the fact that there has been an attempt to present a comparatively realistic outlook on the significant history and uses of conflict in the progress of social classes and groups, through the civil rights and black power movements for instance, must be recognized. Even those who would not applaud or would applaud only a rather safe or conservative view on this subject should realize the potency and positive value of just such a perspective for developing a group consciousness and a cohesiveness not heretofore possible. This point will be made again in my more general discussion of the uses of conflict in social groups.

To say, however, that most Black Studies curricula exhibit this same perspective would be less than accurate. One could also point to the by now apparent presentation of Black historical material where those Blacks are presented who stayed within what were considered to be the legitimate boundaries (constitutive rules) of protest or progressed in accepted economic, athletic, scholarly, or artistic fields. Usually, one does not find reference to Malcolm X, Marcus Garvey, or others who offered a potent critique of existing modes of economic and cultural control and activity. However, it is the *massiveness* of the tacit presentation of the consensus perspective that must be stressed, as well as its occurrence in the two areas examined in this chapter.

It is not sufficient, though, for our purposes to "merely" illuminate how the hidden currriculum obligates students to experience certain encounters with basic rules. It is essential that an alternative view be posited and that the uses of social conflict that I have been mentioning be documented.

It is possible to counter the consensus orientation with a somewhat less consensus bound set of assumptions, assumptions that seem to be as empirically warranted, if not more so, as those to which I have raised objections. For instance, some social theorists have taken the position that "society is not primarily a smoothly functioning order of the form of a social organism, a social system, or a static social fabric." Rather, continuous change in the elements *and* basic structural form of society is a dominant characteristic. Conflicts are the systematic products of the changing structure of a society and by their very nature tend to lead to progress. The "order" of society, hence, becomes the regularity of change. The "reality" of society is conflict and flux, not a "closed functional system."[38] It has been stated that the most significant contribution to the understanding of society made by Marx was his insight that a major source of change and innovation is internal conflict.[39] In essence, therefore, conflicts must be looked at as a basic and often beneficial dimension of the dialectic of activity we label society.

An examination of positions within and closely allied with this general orientation can help to illuminate the importance of conflict. One of the more interesting perspectives points to its utility in preventing the reification of existing social institutions by exerting pressure upon individuals and groups to be innovative and creative in bringing about changes in institutional activities. Coser puts it well:[40]

> Conflict within and between groups in a society can prevent accommodations and habitual relations from progressively impoverishing creativity. The clash of values and interests, the tension between what is and what some groups feel ought to be, the conflict between vested interests and new strata and groups demanding their share of power, have been productive of vitality.

Yet one is hard pressed to find anything akin to this orientation in most of the materials and teaching exhibited in schools. The basic rules of activity that govern our perception tend to cause us to picture conflict as primarily a negative quality in a collectivity. However, "happy cooperation" and conflict are the two sides of the societal coin, neither of which is wholly positive or negative. Though he does speak here from within something of a functionalist perspective, this outlook is still forcefully put by Coser in one of his earlier treatments of the topic.[41]

> No group can be entirely harmonious for it would then be devoid of process and structure. Groups require disharmony as well as harmony, dissociation as well as association; and conflicts within them are by no means altogether disruptive factors. Group formation is the result of both types of processes. The belief that one process tears down what the other builds up, so that what finally remains is the result of subtracting the one from the other, is based on a misconception. On the contrary, both "positive" and "negative" factors build group relations. Far from being necessarily dysfunctional, a certain degree of conflict is an essential element in group formation and the persistence of group life.

The basic rule of activity that constitutes the unconscious negative value associated with conflict tends to lead to the designing of experiences that focus on the "law or rule breaking" dimension of conflict, yet it should be made clear that conflict leads not "merely" to law breaking but is, in effect, law *creating* as well.[42] It performs the considerable task of pointing to areas of needed redress.

Furthermore, it brings into conscious awareness the more basic rules that govern the particular activity over which there is conflict but that were hidden from view. That is, it performs the unique function of enabling individuals to see the hidden imperatives built into situations that act to structure their actions, thereby partially freeing individuals to create relevant patterns of actions to an extent not usually possible. These law-creating and expanding-awareness properties of conflict situations offer, in combination, a rather positive effect. Since conflict brings about inherently new situations that to a large degree are undefined by previous assumptions, it acts as a stimulus for the establishment of new and possibly more flexible or situationally pertinent norms of activity. By literally forcing conscious attention, issues are defined and new dimensions can be explored and made clear.[43]

Documentation of the positive effects of conflict would not be even nearly adequate if a major use were to go unmentioned, especially given my own commitment to making education, in particular, more responsive to the needs of the communities and classes it serves. Here I am speaking of the importance of conflict for both creating and legitimating a conscious and specifically class, ethnic and sexual experience. It is now well known that one of the primary ways groups define themselves is by perceiving themselves as struggling with other groups and that such struggle both increases members' participation in group activities and makes them more conscious of the bonds that tie them together.[44] That the Black, other ethnic, and women's communities have, to a significant extent, defined themselves along these in-group/out-group lines, is of no small moment since it enables a greater cohesiveness among the various elements within their respective communities. By drawing upon "primordial sentiments" such as class, race and sex, a communal meaning structure is created that makes plausible an individual's and a group's continued and separate existence.[45] Just as conflict seems to be a primary means for the establishment of individual autonomy and for the full differentiation of personality from the outside world,[46] so too is it effective for the full differentiation of community autonomy. In essence, it can create a "strain toward the articulation of assumptions which mark that group alone, in order to reinforce solidarity and agreement among its members," a point that we saw in Chapter 1 is an important element in a potent ideology.

I have been proposing an alternative outlook on the presence and uses of conflict in social groups. It is feasible for it to be used as a more objective foundation for designing curricula and guiding teaching so that the more static hidden curriculum students encounter can be counterbalanced to some extent. The explicit focusing on conflict as a legitimate category of conceptualization and as a valid and essential dimension of collective life could enable the development by students of a more viable and potent political and intellectual perspective from which to perceive their relation to existing economic and political institutions. At the least, such a perspective gives them a better understanding of the tacit ideological assumptions that act to structure their own activity.

Programmatic Considerations

There are a number of programmatic suggestions that can be made that could at least partially serve to counterbalance the hidden curriculum and selective tradition most evident in science and social studies as representatives of the formal corpus of school knowledge. While these are by their very nature still rather tentative and only partial, they may prove important.

A more balanced presentation of some of the espoused values of science is essential, especially that relating to organized skepticism. The historical importance to the scientific communities of the overriding skeptical outlook needs to be recognized and focused upon.

The history of science can be seen as a continuing dialectic of controversy and conflict between advocates of competing research programs and paradigms, between accepted answers and challenges to these "truths." As such, science itself could be presented with a greater historical orientation documenting the conceptual revolutions necessary for significant breakthroughs to occur.

Rather than adhering to a view of science as truth, the balanced presentation of science as truth-until-further-notice, as a process of continual change, could prevent the crystallization of attitude. In this connection also, the study of how conceptual revolutions in science have proceeded would contribute to a less positive perspective on consensus as the only mode of progress.

To this point can be added a focus upon the moral uses and dilemmas of science. For example, personalizing the history of science through cases such as Oppenheimer, Watson, and, intriguingly, the controversy surrounding the Velikovsky case, would indeed be helpful.[47] When taken together with a serious analysis of, say, the role of women in science and medicine, these suggestions would help to eliminate the bias of present curricula by introducing the idea of personal and interpersonal controversy and conflict.[48]

In the social studies, a number of suggestions can be made. The comparative study of revolution, say the American, French, Russian, Portuguese, and Chinese, would serve to focus upon the properties of the human condition that cause and are ameliorated by interpersonal conflict. This suggestion is made more appropriate when coupled with the fact that in many countries revolution is the legitimate (in a quite real sense of the word) mode of procedure for redressing grievances. To this could be added studies of economic and cultural imperialism.[49]

A more realistic appraisal and presentation of the uses of conflict in the legal and economic rights movement of Blacks, Indians, women, workers, and others would no doubt assist in the formation of a perspective that perceives these and similar activities as legitimate models of action. The fact that laws *had* to be broken and were then struck down by the courts later is not usually focused upon in social studies curricula. Yet, it was through these types of activities that a good deal of progress was and is made. Here community and "movement" studies of how changes have been effected is an interesting process, one that should prove of considerable moment. This points to how critical it is that things like serious labor history be taught in schools. All too often we minimize the history of the concrete struggles workers had to engage in and the sacrifices they made. At the same time, students can be led to ground their own family and personal experiences in the history of class and ethnic group as well. Numerous bibliographies on topics such as labor history, the struggles of women, Blacks, and others are available to assist us in countering the selective tradition here.[50]

Beyond these suggestions for specific programmatic changes, one further area should be noted. Sociological "paradigms" also attempt to account for the commonsense reality in which students and teachers dwell. Schools are integrally involved in this reality and its internalization. It might be wise to consider engaging students in the articulation and development of paradigms of activity within their everyday lives at school. Such involvement could enable students to come to grips with and amplify crucial insights into their own conditionedness and freedom. Such insights could potentially alter the original paradigm and the commonsense reality itself. It would also make possible to a greater degree a concrete and meaningful educational encounter for students with the process of value and institutional recreation. Social action curricula and student rights struggles, though limited in their usefulness because of the serious danger of "incorporation," could be quite helpful here in giving students a sense of their own possible competence in challenging hegemonic conditions in certain areas.[51]

Conclusions

Research on political socialization of children seems to indicate the importance of the president and the police as points of contact between children and the structures of authority and legitimacy in a society.[52] For instance, there is a strongly personal initial bond between the child and these representatives of the structures of authority. As the child matures, these very personal ties are transferred to more anonymous institutions such as Congress or to political activities such as voting. The tendency to lift impersonal institutions to high esteem may be quite an important source of the relative stability and durability of the structures of authority in industrial societies.[53]

Yet it is not quite certain that this formulation really answers the questions one could raise concerning political and social stability. The foundation of political (broadly conceived) leanings and relations to political and social structures is in a belief system that itself rests upon basic patterns of assumptions "determined" by social and economic activity. Such rules for activity (and thought as a fundamental form of this activity) are probably more important to a person's relation to his or her life-world than we realize. We have been examining one of these constitutive ideological assumptions.

It has been my contention that the schools systematically distort the functions of social conflict in collectivities. The social, intellectual, and political manifestations of this distortion are manifold. They may contribute significantly to the ideological underpinnings that serve to fundamentally orient individuals toward an unequal society.

Students in most schools and in urban centers in particular are presented with a view that serves to legitimate the existing social order since change, conflict, and men and women as creators as well as receivers of values and institutions are systematically neglected. I have pointed to the massiveness of the presentation. Now something else must be stressed once again—the fact that these meaning structures are obligatory. Students receive them from persons who are "significant others" in their lives, through their teachers, other role models in books and elsewhere. To change this situation, students' perceptions of to whom they are to look as holders of "expert knowledge" must be radically altered. In ghetto areas, a partial answer is, perhaps, instituting a more radical perspective in the schools. This change can be carried out only by political activity. As has been mentioned before, it may very well be that to divorce an educator's educational existence from his or her other political existence is to forget that as an act of influence, education is also an inherently political act. Yet with this political sensitivity must also come a fair measure of economic and cultural understanding that speaks to the power of these ideological meanings, that situates them back into the actual social processes which generated them.

Thus, that these assumptions exist should not surprise us given the argument about the "inner logic" of a particular economic and ideological form. The selective tradition I have analyzed in this chapter is a "natural" outgrowth of the relations between our extant cultural and economic institutions. When a society "requires," at both an economic and a cultural level, the maximization (not distribution) of the production of technical knowledge, then the science that is taught will be divorced from the concrete human practices that sustain it. When a society "requires," at an economic level, the "production" of agents who have internalized norms which stress engaging in often personally meaningless work, acceptance of our basic political and economic institutions as stable and always beneficient, a belief structure resting on consensus, and a positivistic and technical logic, then we would expect that the formal and informal curricula, the cultural capital, in schools will become aspects of hegemony. The inner logic of these tensions and expectations will set the limits, the constitutive rules, that will become our common sense. Any other response will seem unnatural, which is exactly the point both Williams and Gramsci have maintained.

The overt and covert teaching of these views of science and social life combine with and justify earlier socialization. Both make it quite difficult for one to be at all aware of the ideological saturation that goes on. For if the "facts" of the world do rest on our theories of them, then the world people see, the economic and cultural meanings they give to it, will be defined in such a way as to be self-justifying. Meanings are given about the way the world "really is" and the economic and cultural interests that determine *why* it is this way are legitimated as well. The ideological function is circular. Power and knowledge are here again intimately and subtly linked through the roots of our common sense, through hegemony.

One of the primary tasks of this chapter has been to present lenses that are alternative to those that normally legitimate many of the activities and encounters curriculists design for students. It will become clearer as this volume progresses that the curriculum field itself has limited its own forms of consciousness so that the political and ideological assumptions that undergird a good deal of its normal patterns of activity are as hidden as those that students encounter in schools.[54] I have pointed to the possibilities inherent in a more realistic approach to the nature of conflict as one alternative "form of consciousness." Yet when all has been said, it is still possible to raise the question of whether such theoretical investigations are either heuristically, politically, or programmatically helpful.

One of the difficulties in seeking to develop new perspectives is the obvious and oft pointed to distinction between theory and practice or, to put it in commonsense language, between "merely" understanding the world and changing it. This distinction is rooted in our very language. Yet it is crucial to remind ourselves that while, say, Marx felt that the ultimate task of philosophy and theory was not merely to "comprehend reality" but to change it, it is also true that according to Marx revolutionizing the world has as its very foundation an adequate understanding of it. (After all, Marx spent a good deal of his lifetime writing *Das Kapital* while he also engaged in political and economic action which served to help clarify the correctness of that understanding. Action and reflection merged into *praxis*.)[55]

The significant danger is not that "theory" offers no mode of critiquing and changing reality, but that it can lead to quietism or a perspective that, like Hamlet, necessitates a continuing monologue on the complexity of it all, while the world tumbles down around us. It would seem important to note that not only is an understanding of existing reality a necessary condition for changing it, but it is a major step in actually effecting an ethically, aesthetically and economically adequate reconstruction.[56] However, with this understanding of the social milieu in which curriculists operate, there must also be a continual attempt to bring to a conscious level and act against those hidden epistemological and ideological assumptions that help to structure the decisions they make, the environments they design, and the traditions they select. These fundamental assumptions can have a significant impact on the hidden curriculum which students tacitly experience and which helps recreate hegemony.

Without an analysis and greater understanding of these latent assumptions, educators run the very real risk of continuing to let ideological values work through them. A conscious advocacy of a more realistic outlook on and teaching of the dialectic of social change would, no doubt, contribute to preparing students with the political and conceptual tools necessary to deal with the dense reality they must face. However, can we accomplish the same for curriculists and other educators? Can we illuminate the political and conceptual tools needed to face the unequal society in which they also live? The most fruitful way to begin this task is to document what their conceptual and political tools do *now*: Do they again maintain a false consensus? How do they act as aspects of hegemony? What are their latent ideological functions? With a firmer grasp on the way schools assist in the creation of hegemony through the "socialization" of students, it is this task—how hegemony operates in the heads of educators—to which we shall now turn.

CHAPTER 6

Systems Management
and the Ideology of Control

In Chapter 4, we saw how, historically, "science" provided the rhetorical justification that covered the fact that curriculum thinking was increasingly based on ideological presuppositions. This process has not stopped, either in the way that, as I just disclosed, certain views of science and social life are selected as the most legitimate knowledge in the overt curriculum in schools or in the ideological functions of science as justification for conservative research and decision making. Thus, we shall have to inquire into how the vision of education as a science functions ideologically today. For just as hegemony is maintained within schools through the tacit teaching that goes on, so too is an acritical view of institutions and an overly technical and positivistic view of science made an aspect of an effective and dominant culture by the "intellectuals" whose action makes it legitimate, who make it seem like a set of neutral categories that gives meaning so that we may act appropriately to help children.

We shall have to ask a number of questions about the ideological saturation of *educators'* consciousness, in the same way as we asked how the students' life within the black box contributed to economic and cultural reproduction before. What is the latent role of the linguistic and logical structure of technical, efficiency, and "scientific" perspectives in curriculum and in education in general? Who benefits from such perspectives? How do these categories and forms of consciousness serve as mechanisms of social and economic interest, when they are so clearly guided by the liberal urge to help? Are real, or abstracted, individuals "helped" by these interests?

The current exemplars of such approaches, ones that fit into the long lineage of "scientific" curriculum work based on the achievement and socialization traditions, are systems management and behavioral objectives, technically and positivistically oriented educational evaluation done by "experts," and clinical terminology and research. Each of these has found its way to the very roots of the brains of educators. The next two chapters of the book will turn our focus to these areas. The analysis will begin with one of the most rapidly growing "technologies" in the rhetorical arsenal of education, that of systems management. "Science" will play an important part by providing the "ultimately right principles" upon which there must be consensus, once again. Yet this time the ideological consensus will be less in the heads of students and more within the heads of intellectuals like educators. Because of its very nature, this set of ideological "principles" has a major impact on the fundamental perspectives educators themselves employ to order, guide and give meaning to their own activity, on the principles used to organize and structure the knowledge and symbols schools select and distribute. For they comprise the filter through which the knowledge and symbols are chosen and organized. And, as in our earlier discussions, they seem self-justifying. They have become part of our common sense.

On the State of the Field

A few years ago, a well-known curriculum worker began his arguments for behavioral objectives—one of the precursors and usually a basic tenet of "systems management procedures" in education—with some rather interesting comments. Even though pointing to the necessity of dialogue for examining the respective worths of different positions on the controversial subject of designing educational activities in terms of "measurable learner behaviors," he had a few remarks to say that are quite pertinent to this chapter's analysis of the ideological place of "science" in curriculum. With your permission, I would like to quote these remarks.[1]

> Within the last few years a rather intense debate has developed in the field of curriculum and instruction regarding the merits of stating instructional objectives in terms of measurable learner behaviors. Because I am thoroughly committed, both rationally and viscerally, to the proposition that instructional goals should be stated behaviorally, I view this debate with some ambivalence. On the one hand, it is probably desirable to have a dialogue of this sort among specialists in our field. We get to know each other better—between attacks. We test the respective worths of opposing positions. We can have hopefully stimulating symposia such as this one. Yet as a partisan in the controversy, I would prefer unanimous support of the position to which I subscribe. You see, the other people are wrong. Adhering to a philosophic tenet that error is evil, I hate to see my friends wallowing in sin.

He then goes on to say:

> Moreover, their particular form of sin is more dangerous than some of the time-honored perversions of civilized societies. For example, it will probably harm more people than the most exotic forms of pornography. I believe that those who discourage educators from precisely explicating their instructional objectives are often permitting, if not promoting, the same kind of unclear thinking that has led in part to the generally abysmal quality of instruction in this country.

Now I find Popham's quote rather interesting. First, it documents the intellectual state of the curriculum field. While many of the specific criticisms of the curriculum field by individuals like Joseph Schwab are tautologous, I tend to agree with his suggestion that the imminent death of a discipline is seen in its increasing use of *ad hominem* arguments[2] such as the one we have just quoted. Second, and of more important concern, is the set of assumptions mirrored in the statement just quoted, assumptions that provide the ideological foundation for systems management in education. These assumptions are concerned with the tacit advocacy of a view once again negating the importance of intellectual and valuative conflict, a rather limited perspective on scientific endeavor, an inability to deal with ambiguity, and finally an outmoded separation of moral and technical questions. The increasing use of systems terminology in education rests on this set of beliefs which when examined is often unrealistic, and socially and politically conservative.

At the outset, let me make certain of my perspectives clear. Just as we saw in our treatment of how the hidden and overt knowledge found in schools cannot be considered apart from the other economic and social institutions of a collectivity—that such knowledge is intimately involved with, mirrors and helps reproduce the dominant institutions of a society—so too is it important to realize that our own thought about schooling and curriculum design is also fundamentally linked to the structure of the social order in which we exist.[3] While I would like to continue to avoid an overly deterministic interpretation of consciousness, I would take the position that the basic framework of most curriculum rationality is generally supportive and accepting of the *existing* economic, political, ideological, and intellectual framework that apportions opportunity and power in American society. I do not ask you to share all of my perceptions about exactly how this framework tends toward the sublimation of basic human sentiment and the repression of a large portion of people within it. What I do ask is that the perceptions not be dismissed offhandedly and that curriculists cease to act on tacit assumptions which prevent them from focusing upon the definite ideological and epistemological commitments they possess. Part of the task of curriculum scholarship is to bring to a level of awareness the latent results of our work, for values continually work through us and are sedimented within the very mind set we apply to our problems. It may very well be the case that the often unequal and problematic activities and consequences of schooling will not be fundamentally altered until we cease searching for simple solutions to our problems. Part of the answer, but only part, is to illuminate our political and conceptual orientations. It is possible that the two are considerably interwoven.

I would like to point to tendencies in systems management procedures that often have some interesting things to say about the curriculum field's social commitments, commitments that may be more hidden than those advocated by earlier curriculists, but commitments that are powerful nevertheless. They document the way the early ideological interests of the first curriculists have continued their transformation from overt class interests to "neutral" principles of helping. For example, I shall consider systems language as conservative social rhetoric and shall look behind it to portray its incorrect view of science. First, let us look at systems thought as a general intellectual framework in education. Let me state, however, that the points to be made here apply to the educational uses of systems logic and not necessarily to systems thought, *per se* (though this latter point does remain moot).

Systems and Technical Control

Usually, one engages in systems approaches to obtain a more exact and "scientific" analysis. However, the view of scientific activity underpinning the use of systems strategies in education and curriculum design is based less upon an accurate view of scientific processes than it is upon an after-the-fact examination of scientific products. A distinction that is helpful here is one between the *logic in use* of a science and its *reconstructed* logic.[4] The former connotes what scientists actually do; and that is *not* necessarily the linear progression of stating goals absolutely clearly, of hypothesis testing and verification or falsification through statistical or other analyses, and so forth. The latter connotes what observers, philosophers of science, and others say that the *logic* of scientific inquiry looks like. There has been an exceptionally long history in educational thought, from Snedden up to the present, of borrowing a reconstructed logic of scientific activity and expecting it to be sufficient for treating the complex problem of curriculum design, to say nothing of curriculum "research."

This has usually taken the form of the development of procedures to guarantee certainty and to rationalize and make explicit as many aspects of people's activity as possible, be it the researcher, the educational decision maker, or the student. Huebner has described this approach as "technological" in that it seeks to use strict forms of means-ends or process-product reasoning and is primarily interested in efficiency, thus tending to exclude other modes of valuing.[5] Examples include the aforementioned early work of Bobbitt on activity analysis, which seemed to crystallize the basic paradigm of the field of curriculum, and the latter emphasis on behavioral objectives. Each of these has sought to specify the operational boundaries of institutional interaction and has been motivated by a need for closure and, especially, surety. The behavioral objectives movement, for instance, in both its weak and strong senses, has sought to reduce student action to specifiable forms of overt behavior so that the educator can have certitude of outcome. While the need for certainty is understandable given the large sums of money spent on education, its superficiality is disturbing. The behavioral orientation itself (as well as many constitutive aspects of systems management approaches) has been effectively dealt with by such early treatments as Ryle's analysis of knowing in its dispositional vs. achievement senses, by Polanyi's exploration of forms of tacit knowing, and in Hannah Arendt's masterful examination of how the need for certainty often precludes the creation of personal meaning and effectively weakens the base of political action.[6] These analytic concerns aside, however, the perspective on systems as enabling a more "scientific" approach to educational problems requires further investigation.

Unlike the unceasing quest for surety among educators, scientific activity has been characterized less by a preference for certainty, for the slow and steady accumulation of technical data than we have supposed. What most members of the scientific community would label good science is a process that is constituted upon the leap of faith, an aesthetic sensitivity, a personal commitment, and of great importance, an ability to accept ambiguity and uncertainty.[7] Without such qualities, ones which maintain the scientific enterprise as an essentially human and changing artifact, science becomes mere technology. The view of science used to give legitimacy to a good deal of curriculum thought, especially that of systems approaches, is more reminiscent of a nineteenth century brand of positivism than it is of current scientific and philosophical discourse. While the trend toward naive reductionism, for example, in approaching human action was stemmed in philosophy by 1930 or so,[8] as we shall see much of curriculum rationality today has progressed no further.

The problem of drawing upon a reconstructed logic is further compounded by our belief in the inherent neutrality of systems management. There seems to be a tacit assumption that systems management procedures are merely "scientific" techniques; they are interest-free and can be applied to "engineer" nearly any problem one faces. A searching analysis discloses some provocative questions about this assumption, however.

To be accurate, systems management procedures are not interest-free. Their own constitutive interest lies primarily in, and has the social consequence of, effecting and maintaining *technical control* and *certainty*.[9] Like the reconstructed logic of the strict sciences, it is aimed, fundamentally and unalterably, at the regularities of human behavior, the language of "individual differences" to the contrary. It is, hence, essentially manipulative. The manipulative perspective is inherent in the quest for certainty. In fact it is difficult to envision how an unflinching requirement for exactitude in goals and behavioral specifications can be less than manipulative given the propensities of men and women to exist in a dialectical relationship with their social reality—that is to make meaning their own and go beyond the framework and texture of socially sedimented meanings and institutions.[10] It is here in the creation of an abstracted individual, one who bears a totally one-sided and acritical relationship to his or her social reality, that we find a primary example of the conservative orientation so deeply embedded in "technological" models of educational thought.

A similar point is made by Sennett in his discussion of the tendency of city planners to create systems whose ideal is that nothing "be out of control," for institutional life "to be manipulated on so tight a rein [that] all manner of diverse activities must be ruled by the lowest common denominator."[11] He summarizes his analysis of the propensity for systems planners to use technological and production models thus:[12]

> Their impulse has been to give way to that tendency . . . of men to control un-
> known threats by eliminating the possibility of experiencing surprise. By con-
> trolling the frame of what is available for social interaction, the subsequent path
> of social action is tamed. Social history is replaced by the passive "product" of so-
> cial planning. Buried in this hunger for preplanning along machine like lines is
> the desire to avoid pain, to create a transcendent order of living that is immune
> to the variety, and so the inevitable conflict, between men.

The philosophical naivete and the strikingly deterministic aspect of systems
management as it is applied in education is perhaps most evident in the dictum that requires of those building instructional systems, for instance, to "formulate specific learning objectives, clearly stating whatever the learner is
expected to be able to *do, know,* and *feel* as an outcome of his learning experiences."[13] (My italics.) Even a surface examination of the psychological and especially the philosophical analyses of the nature of dispositions, attainments,
and propensities, and how these are "taught" and linked with other types of
"knowledge," shows the lack of any significant amount of thought being given
to how human beings do, in fact, operate in real life.[14] Furthermore, the reductive mentality, one in which the components of cognition are divorced from
"feeling" and can be behaviorally specified, fundamentally misconstrues the
nature of human action.[15] The very idea that educators should specify all or
even the primary aspects of a person's action substitutes the slogan of manipulation for the awesome task of making moral choices.

It should be made clear that curriculum design, the creating of educative
environments in which students are to dwell, is inherently a political and
moral process. It involves competing ideological, political, and intensely personal conceptions of valuable educational activity. Furthermore, one of its primary components is the fact of influencing other people—namely students.
Our commonsense thought in education, however, tends to move in a direction quite the opposite from moral and political considerations. Instead
spheres of decision making are perceived as *technical problems* that only neces-
sitate instrumental strategies and information produced by technical experts,[16] hence both effectively removing the decisions from the realm of
political and ethical debate and covering the relationship between the status of
technical knowledge and economic and cultural reproduction. In other words,
even though rationales such as systems procedures cloak themselves in the language of "being realistic," there is a strong tendency in their use to flatten reality, to define the complex valuative issues out of existence by using a form of
thought that is amenable only to technical competence. In essence the employment of systems procedures *qua* formula tends to obscure for the educator the
fact that he or she is making profound ethical and economic decisions about a
group of other human beings.

Now the real issue is not that systems techniques yield information and
feedback that may be used *by* systems of social control. They themselves *are*

systems of control.[17] What is of equal importance is the fact that the belief system underlying them and a major portion of the curriculum field stems from and functions as a technocratic ideology which often can serve to legitimate the existing distribution of power and privilege in our society.[18] The very language used by a number of proponents of systems management in education conveys their assumptions. While change is viewed as important, it is usually dealt with by such notions as system *adjustment*.[19] The basis of the system itself remains unquestioned. The use of systems procedures assumes as its taken for granted foundation that the institutions of schooling are fundamentally sound. That is, while "the quality of instruction" is often poor, the same general pattern of human interaction is sufficient for education, if the institution can be "tuned up," so to speak. The problems of schooling are to be solved by "modest inputs of centralized administration, along with expert services, research and advice." The lack of quality in education is viewed in terms of only a lack of technical sophistication and can be effectively solved through engineering.[20] The increasing disaffection with much of the obligatory meaning structure of schooling by students and the growth of scholarship on the relationship between schooling and inequality belie this perception.

Like the Tyler Rationale in curriculum before it, systems management assumes that the effectiveness of a system can be evaluated by "how closely the output of the system satisfies the purpose for which it exists."[21] However, in the quest for orderliness, the political process by which often competing visions of purposes deal with each other and come to some sort of understanding is virtually ignored. Again, like Tyler, one—the manager of an institution perhaps—"engineers" in an unreal world. An understanding of the difficult ethical, ideological, and even aesthetic problems of who decides what and what these purposes should be that exist in the real world of education are advanced no further.

Now, systems design itself is an analytic procedure in its own right with its own history and, usually, its own modes of self-correction when kept *within* its tradition. However, the educational orientation labeled systems design does not approach this sophistication; nor does it borrow more than a veneer of terminology that is used to cover the dominant metaphor curriculists have used to look at schooling for over fifty years. As was evident in my earlier historical analysis, this metaphor or model pictures the school as a factory, and traces its roots back to the beginnings of curriculum as a field of study, especially to the work of Bobbitt and Charters.[22] In systems analysis in the field of computer design, inputs and outputs are *information*; in systems procedures in education, they are often children. The school is the processing plant and the "educated man" is the "product."[23] Given the fact that a field's language and metaphoric constructs often help determine its modes of operation, the use of the language of child *qua* product is apt to preserve and enhance the already strikingly manipulative ethos of schooling, an ethos that was so clear in the concrete experiences of the kindergarten children in Chapter 3. The ethos is also fostered by the relative lack of insight educators have into the domain of systems thought itself.

One is hard pressed to find more than occasional references in the literature on systems management procedures in the curriculum field, for example, to the most creative systems theorists. The structuralism of Von Bertalanffy is nearly absent as is the subtlety of the way he attempts to grapple with problems. While one does find a few references to him, it is quite obvious that the fundamental notions about systems procedures are not drawn from this school of thought. Rather, one sees a model that is actually taken from such fields as weapons technology and industry.[24] What is not found is of considerable moment given our attempt to be "scientific." What is found, though, is the encasing of the school-as-factory model in a layer of slogans to give a field intellectual and economic legitimacy and a sense of neutrality. Systems design as a field of scientific study has within itself self-correcting mechanisms. The continual criticism of research and thought, and the intellectual conflict within the systems field among members of varying persuasions, provide a context for keeping it vital. Educators have borrowed only the language, often only the surface language (what I have called the reconstructed logic) and have, hence, pulled the terminology out of its self-correcting context. Thus, they have little insight into the continuing critical dialogue in the field of systems design that enables it to remain potent. We have yet to learn the dangers of appropriating models from disparate fields and applying them to education. All too infrequently, the models are quickly outmoded, are intellectually inaccurate representations of those developed in the lending field,[25] and provide little in the way of the conceptual resources needed to grapple with the complex problem of designing environments and selecting and preserving "traditions" which mediate between a student's and concrete group's search for personal meaning and a society's need to preserve its socially sedimented fabric of institutions and knowledge.

Systems analysis began *not* as a management technique but as a mode by which the complex nature of problems could be illuminated. It sought to show how components of a field were interrelated and acted upon one another. Systems analysis was a mode of thought that sought to enhance our comprehension of change and stability—subsystem A is related in X fashion to subsystem B which in turn is related in Y fashion to subsystem C. The combination created a different relationship, Z. Any alteration of C, therefore, would have profound repercussions in A and B, and in all the linkages among them. Systems thought, then, was a model for understanding, not necessarily for control. However, many curriculists seem to be employing it to manage their problems without first understanding the complexity of the relationships themselves. This is one of the points in which Schwab is correct. Only when we begin to see the intricate nature of the relationships among the aspects of the educational environment can we begin to act as more than technicians.[26] As a model for disclosing possibilities, not as a picture of what should be, systems analysis has its place. As a management structure for making institutional meanings obligatory, for creating a false consensus, it is less than neutral to say the least.

While the advocates of systems procedures seek to enhance the scientific status of their work, as I have pointed out the systems thought they have borrowed is not from the scientific branch of systems logic. Rather, they have chosen to appropriate the models of operation of the business community.[27] This is not new by any means, of course.[28] While it would be just a bit unfair to point out that such "successful" concerns as Lockheed (which required major state economic intervention to keep from going bankrupt) are the major proponents of systems procedures for large scale endeavors, it would not be inaccurate to point out that the business and economic substructure of the USA continues to generate avenues that provide extremely limited means of equal power and control for a large part of the total population. One has to wonder if their models are indeed appropriate for dealing with students. This issue is made even more potent when one realizes that systems management was created originally to enhance the ability of owners to *control* labor more effectively, thereby increasing profits and weakening the burgeoning union movements early in this century [29]

There are other issues that could be raised about the idea that systems procedures are "scientific" and are neutral techniques for establishing better educational practices. As I have noted, it is one of the basic assumptions that must be examined rather closely. I would like to delve a bit further and raise a few questions about its possible latent conservatism. One question concerns itself with systems language as a social rhetoric; the other concerns a constitutive aspect of systems procedures as they are applied today in education—namely the specification of precise instructional and usually behavioral objectives as tacitly preserving in an unquestioning manner the dominant modes of institutional interaction in an unequal economy, as aspects of reproduction. I will then examine how the penchant for order in curriculum today serves a similar function. Let us examine the issue of systems as a language first.

Systems Procedures as Rhetoric

The Wittgensteinian principle that the meaning of language depends on its use is quite appropriate for analyzing systems language as it is applied in curriculum discourse. In a manner similar to the way the language of science and technology functioned for the early curriculists and educators we examined in Chapter 4, systems language performs a rhetorical and political function today. Without an understanding of this, we miss a major point. One of its primary, if latent, uses is to convince others of the sophisticated state of education. If a field can convince funding agencies, government, or the populace in general, that scientific procedures are being employed, whether or not they are in fact helpful, then the probability of increased monetary and political support is heightened. Given the high status of technical knowledge and the high esteem in which science is held in industrial nations, this is important. (Unfortunately, it is not science, *per se,* that is seen positively; rather it is technology and its concrete applicability.) Couching a field's problems in systems terminology evokes tacit meanings from a general audience, meanings that are supportive of a quasi-scientific belief system. More importantly, since funding is becoming increasingly centralized in governmental control and since educational experimentation almost always follows funding, systems language has as a primary function the political task of generating money from the federal government. Hence we can expect the "little science, big science" controversy that still rages in the physical sciences to rear its head in education as well.[30] Given the alternative pressure for decentralization, the question of funding and control *cannot* be ignored. Systems management procedures have a tendency toward centralization even without the issue of funding and rhetoric. In order to be most effective, as many variables as possible—interpersonal, economic, etc.—must be brought under and controlled by the system itself. Order and consensus become strikingly important; conflict and disorder are perceived as antithetical to the smooth functioning of the system. The fact that conflict and disorder are extraordinarily important to prevent the reification of institutional patterns of interaction is, thus, once again ignored.[31]

Now the *content* of systems procedures is empty. Systems thought is a formal set or methodology, if you will, that can be applied to educational problems. That is, its conceptual emptiness enables its application in a supposedly "neutral" manner to a range of problems requiring the precise formulation of goals, procedures, and feedback devices. Since systems methodology communicates this sense of neutrality, it is ideally suited to foster consensus around it. This process of consensus formation, and the avoidance of conflict, enables the interests of the administrative managers of institutions to direct the questions one asks about schooling (but always within the "determinations" of the actual linkages between economic and cultural institutions).[32]

This evocation of tacit meanings is crucial in examining systems management thought. Not only are supportive feelings generated, but political quiescence is also enhanced. For example, it may be the case that the common school and the ideological underpinnings that support it have *never* served to adequately educate, say, racial minorities in the USA.[33] It may also be the case that schools have served basically to apportion and distribute opportunities that are consistently unequal in terms of economic class. What the employment of sophisticated "scientific" rationales can do by evoking supportive sentiment, then, is to prevent a portion of the population from seeing that schools as they exist by and large simply cannot meet many of the needs of minority and other populations. The very institutional status of schools is caught up in a variety of other institutional forms—economic, for instance—that enhance the existing political and economic structures.

This quiescence is brought about in a two-pronged fashion and is aimed at two publics. First, systems management language is pronounced to critics of ongoing educational activity—again let us use the example of minority groups—and is often coupled with the notion of "accountability," thereby giving them the feeling that something is in fact being done.[34] After all, it does sound concise and straightforward. But this is not the essential prong. After all, ghetto dwellers, for example, may not be as enamored with technical terminology and have little political power, nor do they influence economic resources and funding as much as the second set of groups to which this language is aimed. The primary audience includes the members of the middle class and industry[35] whose sentiments often resonate strongly to technical expertise and industrial logic, who find such logic quite meaningful. Even when the members of minority and other groups may have determined over a period of time that school life has been made no less overtly repressive, as has been the case so often, the other more powerful public, due to the depth of the taken for granted acceptance of the benefits of technical rationality and technical expertise in solving human problems, will probably remain generally supportive. Thus, systems management provides meaning; it defines the situation. Yet, the definition it posits serves the interests of those classes who already "possess" economic and cultural capital.

To be accurate, one other public should be mentioned. These are the users of systems language themselves. Much of the history of curriculum discourse over the last fifty years or so has been indicative of a need on the part of curriculum workers to have their field become more like a science. I will not dwell upon the possibility of psychoanalyzing this need for prestige. However, a latent function of systems approaches is, no doubt, that it psychologically confirms curriculum workers' ties to a sought after reference group—here the scientific community, and, as I have and shall note, a misperceived scientific community at that.

It should be made clear, then, that systems approaches are not essentially neutral, nor are they only performing a "scientific" function. By tending to cause its users and the other publics involved to ignore certain possible fundamental problems with schools as institutions, systems management also acts to generate and channel political sentiments supportive of the existing modes of access to knowledge and power.[36]

Besides performing these political functions associated with funding and "affective" support, the rhetorical function of systems terminology and of technical methodologies tends to uphold the dominance of existing institutions in another way. Dealing with a type of systems thought in sociology, Gouldner makes the provocative statement that aside from serving "to defocalize the ideological dimensions of decision making, diverting attention from differences in ultimate values and from the more remote consequences of the social policies to which its research is harnessed," supposedly value-free technical perspectives provide the solution to an elite group of manager's problems,[37] not the complex and fundamental valuative issues that we face in, say, education concerning the proper ways to educate children, or the issues of education *v.* training, and freedom and authority. Gouldner summarizes this quite well by saying:[38]

> As ... funding becomes increasingly available, the emphasis on rigorous methodologies assumes a special rhetorical function. It serves to provide a framework for resolving limited differences among the managers of organizations and institutions, who have little conflict over basic values or social mappings, by lending the sanction of science to limited policy choices concerning ways and means. At the same time, its cognitive emphasis serves to defocalize the conflict of values that remain involved in political differences, and to focus contention on questions of fact, implying that the value conflict may be resolved apart from politics and without political conflict. Positivism [and perspectives such as systems management stemming partly from it, I would add] thus continue to serve as ways of avoiding conflicts about mapping. Yet despite this seemingly neutral, nonpartisan character, [these perspectives'] social impact is not random or neutral in regard to competing social mappings; because of [their] emphasis on the problem of social order, because of the social origins, education and character of [their] own personnel, and because of the dependencies generated by [their] funding requirements, [they] persistently tend to support the status quo.

Gouldner's argument is rather interesting and is one we all should reflect upon. Is systems management "merely" a mode by which an institutional and managerial elite avoids conflict over *basic* values and educational visions? By making choices about limited options within the framework of existing modes of interaction, are questions about the basis of the structure itself precluded? How, for instance, would systems management procedures deal with the clash of two competing ideologies about schooling where goals cannot be easily defined? These questions require much closer scrutiny if educational institutions are to be responsive to their varied publics.

I have made the point throughout this chapter so far that the consciousness of curriculum workers themselves as well as other educators can be seen as latently political and often somewhat conservative. That is, they use forms of thought that at least partially stem from and can tacitly act to maintain the existing social and economic substructure and distribution of power in a corporate society such as our own. Systems management procedures offer an intriguing example of this problem. I shall give one more example of this aspect of the role of the "intellectual" in enhancing hegemony.

A significant part of the framework of systems management is concerned with and is based upon the precise formulation of goals, on a microsystem level usually with the specification of behavioral goals. That is, a student's behavior is preselected *before* he or she engages in educational activity and this behavior is used as the end-product of the system so that feedback can be gained. Ultimately this will feed upwards on a macrosystem level for the management of large systems. Let us examine this. The process/product style of reasoning employed here, one that is most evident in the call for behavioral objectives, is quite functional to a society that requires a large proportion of its workers to engage in often boring assembly line labor or in personally unimportant white-collar work. By learning how to work for others' preordained goals using others' preselected behaviors, students also learn to function in an increasingly corporate and bureaucratized society in which the adult roles one is to play are already sedimented into the social fabric. Each role has its own brand of thinking *already* built into it,[39] and students will feel comfortable playing these often relatively alienating roles only in so far as they have been taught that this is the proper mode of existing. Curriculists, by internalizing and using an orientation that lends itself to such preordination, cannot help but contribute to the maintenance of a political and economic order that creates and maintains these roles and the meanings already distributed within them.[40] This problem is intricately involved with the perspective on disorder that most educators share.

Systems, Science, and Consensus

The view on order and conflict mirrored in a good deal of the way systems approaches are employed in education is striking. It is indicative of that constitutive rule of activity noted in Chapter 5 that causes most of us to see order as positive and conflict as negative.[41] Order becomes a psychological necessity and this is rather important. As I mentioned before, systems approaches attempt to bring about a technical solution to political and value problems. There is nothing odd about this occurrence. Most advanced corporate societies seem to transform their ethical, political, and aesthetic questions, for instance, into engineering problems.[42] Profound conflict between opposing ideological and moral positions is translated into puzzles to be solved by the technical expertise that is maximized by the cultural apparatus. Now, when questioned about the tendency to eliminate conflict, or redefine it, and search for consensus, proponents of systems management procedures in education could and do, in fact, take the position that they are merely trying to be scientific about their problems. This is where a basic difficulty lies. The perspective they have of science is notably inaccurate in ways other than those to which I referred earlier in my discussion.

In the quote on precise instructional objectives by Popham at the beginning of this chapter we saw a perspective that legitimated intellectual consensus, one that asked for total agreement on the "paradigm" to be used in curriculum thought so that we could be more scientific. In fact, those who looked askance at the accepted paradigm were, in effect, labeled as deviants. Such universe maintaining verbal activity is not wrong in itself nor is it unusual.[43] To link scientific rationality with consensus, however, is to do a disservice to science and shows a profound misunderstanding of the history of the scientific disciplines.

We need to reiterate that the history of science and the growth of individual disciplines, has *not* proceeded by consensus. In fact, most important progress in these fields has been occasioned by intense conflict, both intellectual and interpersonal, and by conceptual revolution.[44] It is primarily by such conflict that significant advancement is made, not primarily by the accumulation of factual data based on the solving of puzzles generated by a paradigm all must share. The very normative structure of scientific communities tends toward skepticism and not necessarily toward intellectual consensus.[45] The call for consensus, thus, is not a call for science.

One thing that the quote does make clear, however, is the intense personal commitment that accepted modes of thought generate. This is probably true in any field. It does put somewhat of a damper on our traditional concept of neutrality, though. Accepted thought becomes a psychological and valuative commitment, a norm of behavior. Scientists are intensely and personally committed[46] and this is one of the primary sources of conflict within disciplines. Hence, to call for consensus is to call for a *lack* of commitment and is to ignore the crucial value of the uncertain and of conceptual conflict in a field's progress. The covert request for a lack of commitment is of considerable moment. Systems management terminology, as was mentioned, tends to impose technical solutions on moral dilemmas—what is the proper way to influence another human being, for instance. If moral commitments are less firm, the task of flattening reality is made that much easier. When the "reality" is unequal, when classes with economic and cultural power control classes without such power, the flattening has severe consequences.

The Search for Alternatives

There are a number of ways of dealing with some of the possible difficulties associated with the use of systems management procedures in education, though. First, educators must engage in continuous and in-depth analysis of other forms of systems theory, ones not borrowed from industrial and corporate concerns. The lenses of open systems and biological systems could provide excellent disclosure models for further examination. Second, they can immerse themselves in the issues and controversies *within* the systems field so that they are aware of the concrete theoretic and practical difficulties facing systems analysis as a field. In this way, educators may prevent a further recapitulation of their history of borrowing knowledge that is taken out of its self-correcting context and, hence, is often surface or one-sided. While the use of systems approaches has an obvious immediate plausibility, we do not do justice to the intellectual complexity associated with systems thought itself or to the intricate nature of institutional relationships in education (which systems approaches can at least partially illuminate) if we base our analyses upon conceptions of systems that may be given only a weak warrant within the larger systems community. There are alternatives within systems discourse that educators have yet to explore in a rigorous fashion.

This rigorous exploration will not eliminate all of the difficulties, however, for there are a number of other questions one could raise concerning systems management procedures. Perhaps one of the more crucial ones centers around the very real possibility of increasing bureaucratization and social control through the total rationalization of education. This is not to raise the spectre of a bureaucratic machine overrunning human concerns. Rather it asks us to be realistic, if not tragic. Anyone familiar with the growth of urban schools knows that the history of rationalizing and centralizing decision making, no matter what the possibly humane or liberal sentiments behind it, has nearly invariably led to institutional crystalization and reification.[47] The fact that we are not familiar with our own history concerning "reforms" of this nature merely documents the simplicity with which we approach our problems.

There are no easy alternatives to a management and control ideology. One could easily show the epistemological and psychological problems associated with behavioral objectives,[48] for instance; or one could document the fact that the Tyler Rationale in curriculum is little more than an administrative document that does not adequately deal with the concrete reality of schools. Yet this type of activity treats such behavioristic rationales as if they were logically founded and scientifically arguable. It may very well be that they are not. As I have tried to show, what they do seem to be are expressions of a dominant industrialized consciousness that seeks certainty above all else. That is, they are social and ideological configurations stemming from and mirroring a set of basic rules of thought that are part of the taken for granted reality of curriculum workers and other educators. They are aspects of hegemony which help create a "reality," one which inclines us to search for relatively easy ways to eliminate the human dilemmas and social and economic contradictions involved in dealing with diversity and alternative conceptions of valued activity.

To ask, then, for *a* substitute or *one* alternative to systems management procedures is to confirm the assumption that utterly complex problems can be resolved easily within the accepted framework, and without the ambiguous and awesome necessity of engaging in the crucial task of challenging or at least illuminating the framework itself. The task is not to find the *one* acceptable alternative that will enable us "merely" to control our schools better. Rather, it is to begin to disclose the problems associated with our commonsense views of schooling and to begin to open up and explore conceptual and economic avenues that seem fruitful and may enable us to see and act on the complexity rather than define it out of existence.

Systems metaphors as *models of understanding* may prove helpful here. But there are prior questions with which we need to grapple. We must learn (perhaps relearn is more accurate) how to engage in serious ethical and political debate.[49] In this educators can be guided by the work in philosophical analysis dealing with modes of moral reasoning and valuative argumentation. Such investigations as Rawls's recent attempt at explicating warranted moral stands[50] take on an increasing importance as a beginning, given the intense controversy surrounding schools today. Yet this is not enough. For we must relearn our history. Where did systems management come from in industry? How did it function in the accumulation of economic capital? Who gained from its use? Once these questions are unpacked, then we can begin to envision the possibilities of different institutional alignments to prevent the reification of the present into the future. However, the field currently lacks the disciplined aesthetic, economic, and historical sense and imagination to envision the possibilities of alternative educative and economic environments. It is quite possible that the perceived need for operationally prespecified outcomes mitigates against the development of such imagination.[51]

Finally, a significant part of curriculum as a field must be devoted to the responsibility of becoming a "critical science" (a notion that will require more serious attention in Chapter 7). Its primary function is to be emancipatory in that it critically reflects upon the field's dominant interest in keeping most if not all aspects of human behavior in educational institutions under supposedly neutral technical control.[52] Such a responsibility is rooted in relational analysis, in seeking out and illuminating the ideological and epistemological presuppositions of curriculum thought. It seeks to make curriculum workers more self-aware. Only when this dialectic of critical awareness is begun can curriculists truthfully state that they are concerned with education and not merely cultural and economic reproduction. It is then that we may begin to explore in a rigorous fashion the complex problems of designing and valuing educational environments in a variety of ways,[53] ways which respond less to the economic and cultural requirements of hegemony and more to the needs of all of the concrete individuals, groups, and classes who make up this society.

A key word here in this last sentence, however, is *valuing,* for the very ways that we commonsensically value and reflect on our educational activity are a large part of the ideological problem that needs to be illuminated.

As we have seen, given the economic and cultural status of technical and positivistic forms—ones which are taught overtly and covertly quite early in one's school career—other forms of action and reflection are precluded from serious consideration by educators. In this way, just like the manner in which the selective tradition sets limits on the ways students may think through the ideological saturation they experience, so too do the kinds of commonsense sets of values and constitutive rules that educators employ to evaluate their and students' "success" or "failure" determine their own ideological position and the actual functioning of their theories, principles, and modes of organization. How the quite basic procedures of languaging and thinking that dominate education today give meaning (and latently prevent other forms of meaning from being seriously considered) on the one hand and on the other hand serve particular interests is the next area we shall need to investigate.

CHAPTER 7

Commonsense Categories and the Politics of Labeling

"There's the King's messenger," said the Queen. "He's in prison now, being punished; and the trial doesn't even begin 'til next Wednesday; and of course the crime comes last of all."

"Suppose he never commits the crime?" said Alice.

That would be all the better, wouldn't it?" the Queen said, as she turned the plaster round her finger with a bit of ribbon.

Alice felt there was no denying that. "Of course it would be all the better," she said, "but it wouldn't be all the better his being punished."

"You're wrong there, at any rate," said the Queen. "Were you ever punished?"

"Only for faults," said Alice.

"And you were all the better for it, I know!" the Queen said triumphantly.

"Yes, but then I had done the things I was punished for," said Alice, "That makes all the difference."

"But if you hadn't done them," the Queen said, "that would have been better still; better, and better, and better!"

Lewis Carroll, Through the Looking Glass

Ethics, Ideology, and Theory

Drawing upon the important work of both Williams and Gramsci, I argued at the very beginning of this book that control and domination are often vested in the commonsense practices and consciousness underlying our lives as well as by overt economic and political manipulation. Domination can be ideological as well as material

Systems management and behavioral objectives are not the only examples of the saturation of educational thought by ideological configurations. While such educational procedures do perform the dual roles of an effective ideology—by giving "adequate" definitions of situations and serving the interests of those who already possess economic and cultural capital today—they are linked to other aspects of our conceptual apparatus to form a larger taken for granted perspective that dominates education. For to challenge the use of systems management procedures and the like means that one must also raise questions about the very categories we employ to organize our thinking and action in cultural and economic institutions like schools. Therefore, in this chapter I shall examine how these commonsense categories we use to think through the very basis of what we are about and the modes of amelioration which stem from them are also aspects of the larger hegemonic configuration of an effective dominant culture.

The last chapter pointed to the importance of analyzing the ethical and ideological dimensions of our accepted ways of viewing students, noting that the two are considerably intertwined. This needs to be examined further. As I maintained, educational questions are, at least partly, moral questions. For one thing they assume choices as to the relevant realms of expertise educators should use to comprehend children and schools. As Blum puts it, "All inquiry [and especially educational inquiry I might add] displays a moral commitment in that it makes reference to an authoritative election concerning how a phenomenon ought to be understood."[1] Furthermore, if conceptions of "the moral" concern questions of oughtness or goodness, then it should be clear that educational questions are moral questions on this criterion as well. Finally, by the very fact that school people influence students, their acts cannot be interpreted fully without the use of an ethical rubric. However, there are a number of factors that cause educators to perceive their problems in ways significantly different from this. Because this causal nexus is exceptionally complex, this chapter cannot hope to explore all aspects of the difficulty. To do so would require an extensive investigation of the relationship between science, ideology, and educational thought[2] and a fuller analysis of the reduction of conceptions of humans and institutions to technical considerations in advanced industrial and especially corporate societies.[3] Hopefully, like the other chapters in this volume, this one will serve as a stimulus for further inquiry into these areas and especially into the ways by which school people pass over the ethical and, as we shall see, political and economic implications of their acts.

While part of my analysis will be more theoretic than, say, the earlier chapters on the hidden and overt curriculum in that it will continue the investigation of how hegemony operates in the heads of intellectuals like educators, its implications for the day to day density of classroom life are exceptionally important. I am using the idea of a theoretic investigation in a rather specific way in this particular aspect of my analysis, as a mode of standing back from the ideological categories and commonsense assumptions which underpin the curriculum field. Part of this type of orientation has been noted most clearly by Douglas in his statement concerning the differences between a naturalistic and a theoretical stance. He puts it this way:[4]

> There are different ways to make use of common-sense experience . . . There is, especially, a fundamental distinction between taking the *natural (or naturalistic)* stance and taking the *theoretic* stance, as the phenomenological philosophers have long called them. Taking the natural stance consists primarily in *taking the standpoint of common-sense,* of *acting within* common-sense, whereas taking the

theoretic stance consists in *standing back from* common-sense and *studying common-sense to determine its nature.*

That is, for Douglas and myself, one must bracket any commitment to the utility of employing our taken for granted perspectives so that these commonsense presuppositions themselves can become subject to investigation. In this way our commonsense presuppositions can be used as *data* to focus upon the latent significance of much that we unquestioningly do in schools. This is particularly important because they provide the basic logic which organizes our activity and often act as tacit guidelines for determining the success or failure of our educational procedures.

It is not the case, however, that these ideological configurations have been constructed consciously. The very fact that they are hegemonic, and are aspects of our "whole body of practices, expectations, and ordinary understanding," makes them even more difficult to deal with. They are difficult to question, that is, because they rest upon assumptions that are unarticulated and that seem essential in making some headway in education. But other things contribute to the lack of critical insight. In the field of education these configurations are academically and socially respectable and are supported by the prestige of a process that "shows every sign of being valid scholarship, complete with tables of numbers, copious footnotes, and scientific terminology." Furthermore, the altruistic and humanitarian elements of these positions are quite evident, so it is hard to conceive of them as principally functioning to detract from our ability to solve social or educational problems.[5]

However, an investigation into the history of many ameliorative reform movements that were supported by research and perspectives similar to those we will continue to consider here documents the rather interesting fact that often the ameliorative reforms had quite problematic results. Frequently they ultimately even ended up harming the individuals upon whom they focused. Platt's treatment of the reform of the juvenile justice system in the latter part of the last century is instructive here. In attempting to create more humane conditions for "wayward" youth, these reforms created a new category of deviance called "juvenile delinquency" and in the long run served to abridge the civil and constitutional rights of youth.[6] In many ways, we have yet to recover from these "reforms." As I shall argue in this chapter many of the seemingly ameliorative reforms school people propose in schools, and the assumptions that lie behind them, have the same effect—ultimately harming rather than helping, clouding over basic issues and value conflicts rather than contributing to our ability to face them honestly.

This is especially the case in the major topic of this chapter, the process of using expert (and "scientific") clinical, psychological, and therapeutic perspectives, evaluations, and labels in schools. These forms of language and the perspectives they embody may be interpreted not as liberal "helping" devices, but more critically as mechanisms by which schools engage in anonymizing and sorting out abstract individuals into preordained social, economic, and educational slots. The labeling process, thus, tends to function as a form of social control,[7] a "worthy" successor to that long line of mechanisms in schools that sought to homogenize social reality, to eliminate disparate perceptions, and to use supposedly therapeutic means to create moral, valuative, and intellectual consensus.[8] The fact that this process can be deadening, that the cultural capital of those in power is employed as if it were natural, thus enhancing both false consensus and economic and cultural control, that it results in the elimination of diversity, that it ignores the importance of conflict and surprise in human interaction is too often lost in the background in our rush to "help."

There is nothing very odd about the fact that we usually do not focus on the basic sets of assumptions which we use. First, they are normally known only tacitly, remain unspoken, and are very difficult to formulate explicitly. Second, these basic rules are so much a part of us that they do not have to be expressed. By the very fact that they are *shared* assumptions, the product of specific groups of people, and are commonly accepted by most educators (if not most people in general), they only become problematic when an individual violates them or else when a previously routine situation becomes significantly altered.[9] However, if we are to be true to the demands of rigorous analysis, it is a critical inquiry into just such things as the routine grounds of our day to day experience that is demanded.

On the Necessity of Critical Awareness

The curriculum field, and education as a whole, has been quite ameliorative in its orientation. This is understandable given the liberal ideology which guides most educational activity and given the pressures on and interest by the field to serve schools and their ongoing programs and concerns. The marked absorption in amelioration has had some rather detrimental effects, however. Not only has it caused us to ignore questions and research that might contribute in the long run to our basic understanding of the process of schooling,[10] but such an orientation neglects the crucial role critical reflection must play if a field is to remain vital. A critically reflective mode is important for a number of reasons. First, curriculists help establish and maintain institutions that affect students and others in a myriad of ways. Because of these effects, they must be aware of the reasons and intentions that guide them. This is especially true of ideological and political purposes, both manifest and latent.[11] As I have demonstrated throughout this volume, since schools as institutions are so interconnected with other political and economic institutions which dominate a collectivity and since schools often unquestioningly act to distribute knowledge and values through both the overt and hidden curriculum that often act to support these same institutions, it is a necessity for educators to engage in searching analyses of the ways in which they allow values and commitments to unconsciously work through them.

Second, it is important to argue that the very activity of rational investigation requires a critical style. The curriculum field has been much too accepting of forms of thought that do not do justice to the complexity of inquiry and thus it has not really changed its basic perspective for decades. It has been taken with the notions of systematicity, certainly, and control as the ideals of programmatic and conceptual activity, in its treatment of research and people. This is strongly mirrored in the behavioral objective movement and in the quest for taxonomies which codify "cognitive," "affective," and "psychomotor" behavior. These activities find their basis in a conception of rationality that is less than efficacious today. Not only is it somewhat limiting,[12] but it also is historically and empirically inaccurate.

Our taken for granted view posits a conception of rationality based upon ordering beliefs and concepts in tidy logical structures and upon the extant intellectual paradigms which seem to dominate the field of curriculum at a given time. Yet, any serious conception of rationality must be concerned not with the specific intellectual positions a professional group or individual employs at any given time, but instead *with the conditions on which and the manner in which this field of study is prepared to criticize and change those accepted doctrines*.[13] In this way, intellectual flux, not "intellectual immutability," is the expected and normal occurrence. What has to be explained is *not* why we should change our basic conceptual structure, but rather the stability or crystallization of the forms of thought a field has employed over time.[14]

The crystallization and lack of change of fundamental perspectives is not a new problem in the curriculum field by any means. In fact, a major effort was made in the 1940s to identify and deal with just such a concern.[15] The fact that many curriculum specialists are unaware of the very real traditions of grappling with the field's tendency toward hardening its positions obviously points to the necessity of greater attention being given to historical scholarship in the curriculum field.

This intellectual conservatism often coheres with a social conservatism as well. It is not the case that a critical perspective is "merely" important for illuminating the stagnation of the curriculum field. What is even more crucial is the fact that means must be found to illuminate the concrete ways in which the curriculum field supports the widespread interests in technical control of human activity, in rationalizing, manipulating, "incorporating," and bureaucratizing individual and collective action, and in eliminating personal style and political diversity. These are interests that dominate advanced corporate societies and they contribute quite a bit to the suffering of minorities and women, the alienation of youth, the malaise and meaninglessness of work for a large proportion of the population, and the increasing sense of powerlessness and cynicism that seem to dominate our society. Curriculists and other educators need to be aware of all of these outcomes, yet there is little in-depth analysis into the role our commonsense thought plays in causing us to be relatively impotent in the face of these problems.

While educators consistently attempt to portray themselves as being "scientific," by referring to the "scientific" (or technical) and therefore neutral status of their activity to give it legitimacy, they are ignoring the fact that a good deal of social science research is currently being strongly criticized for its support of bureaucratized assumptions and institutions that deny dignity and significant choice to individuals and groups of people. This criticism cannot be shunted aside easily by educators, for unlike many other people, their activity has a direct influence on the present and future of masses of children. By being the primary institution through which individuals pass to become "competent" adults, schools give children little choice about the means by which they are distributed into certain roles in society. As we have and shall see, "neutral scientific" terminology acts as a veneer to cover this fact, and, thus, becomes more ideological than helpful.[16]

Perhaps one of the fundamental reasons the field has stagnated both socially and intellectually involves our lack of concern for less positivistic scholarship, a lack of concern that mirrors the positivistic ideal taught to students. We have been less than open to forms of analysis that would effectively counterbalance our use of rubrics embodying the interests of technical and social control and certainty. This lack of openness has caused us to be inattentive to the functions of the very language systems we employ and has led us to disregard fields whose potency lies in their concern for a critical perspective. This will require a closer examination.

Are Things as They Seem?

Let us focus first on the linguistic tools we employ to talk about "students" in schools. My basic point will be that much of our language, while seemingly neutral, is not neutral in its impact nor is it unbiased in regard to existing institutions of schooling. An underlying thesis of this argument is that our accepted faith that the extension of "neutral techniques of science and technology" will provide solutions to all of the dilemmas we confront is misplaced and that such a faith tends to obscure the fact that much of educational research serves and justifies already existing technical, cultural, and economic control systems that accept the distribution of power in American society as given.[17] Much of the discussion here will be stimulated by insights derived from recent "critical theory" and neo-Marxist scholarship, particularly the potent notion that our basic perspectives often hide our "real" relationships with other persons with whom we have real and symbolic content. The analysis will employ arguments from research on the process of labeling to bring this initial point home.

An analysis of the process of labeling is of considerable import here for labeling is the end project of our modes of placing value on our own and students' actions. It is directly related to the principles which stand behind the practices we engage in to differentiate students according to their "ability" and their possession of particular kinds of cultural capital. Thus, as Ian Hextall has argued:[18]

> The differentiation, . . . grading [and evaluation] we accomplish in schools is articulated with the broader, more encompassing social division of labor. This is not to claim that there exists a direct one-to-one link between differentiation in education and, say, the occupational division of labor. Clearly, such an assumption would be mechanistic and facile. But by our [evaluation] activities we are helping to establish the general framework of the labor force which the market later refines into specific occupational categories. In this way the procedures that occur in schools are part of the political-economic context within which the schools are located. The differentiations, evaluations, and judgements of worth which are made in schools are tenaciously related to particular forms of the social division of labor.

Thus, since one quite significant means by which pupils are culturally and economically stratified is through the application of values and categories to them, it is critical that we examine these commonsense social principles and values. In order to do this, we need to remember that certain types of cultural capital—types of performance, knowledge, dispositions, achievements, and propensities—are not necessarily good in and of themselves. Rather, they are made so because of specific taken for granted assumptions. They are often historically and ideologically "conditioned." The categories that we employ to think through what we are doing with students, their and our success and failure, are involved in a process of social valuing. The guiding principles that we use to plan, order, and evaluate our activity—conceptions of achievement, of success and failure, of good and bad students—are *social and economic constructs.* They do not automatically inhere within individuals or groups. Instead, they are instances of the application of identifiable social *rules* about what is to be considered good or bad performance.[19] Hence, the very ways we talk about students provide excellent instances of the mechanisms through which dominant ideologies operate. And the recent investigations of the critical theorists, *when used critically,* can be quite helpful in unpacking these mechanisms.

The word "critically" is of considerable moment here. There are dangers in employing critical theory itself uncritically, especially since it has tended to become increasingly isolated from the study of political economy that so nicely complements it. With these dangers in mind, however, I do want to employ some aspects of the program of critical theory as modes of disclosing the ways the consciouness of intellectuals functions. At the same time, though, we need to remember that just as an overly deterministic and economistic position, by treating schools as black boxes, is too limited a program to understand how schools create what the political economists want to analyze, so too are there significant limitations in any totally "cultural" analysis.[20] Rather, the two must be integrated to fully explain the roles schools play in the cultural and economic reproduction of class relations. Thus, the combination of selected portions of the cultural program of the critical theorists (their focus on the control of language and consciousness, for example) with the more specific economic theories of recent Marxist interpretations of schools (the ways schools assist in the "allocation" of students to their proper positions in the larger society, for instance) may provide some insight into how educational institutions help create the conditions which support this system of economic allocations.

Before proceeding however, it would be wise to examine some possible explanations of why such critical Marxist understanding has had less than a major impact on our commonsense thought. This is odd since it is considered exceptionally powerful in other fields and on the European continent where it has made quite an impact on French and German philosophical and sociological thought, for example, and on the political and economic practice of large groups of people.[21]

There are a number of reasons why reconstructed Marxist scholarship has not found a serious place in Anglo-Western educational investigation. While, historically, orthodox Marxism had an effect in the 1930s on such educators as Counts and others, it lost its potency due to the political situation evolving later, especially the repressive political climate that we have not totally overcome.

To this problem, of course, can be added the overly deterministic and dogmatic interpretations of applying Marxist analysis by even many later "Marxists." Part of the problem of applying critical insights to advanced industrial societies like our own is to free these insights from their embeddedness in such dogmatism.[22] It should not have to be said, but unfortunately it must, that the rigidly controlled nature of a number of modern societies bears little relation to the uniquely cogent analyses found in the Marxist tradition itself. Our neglect of this scholarly tradition says more about the fear laden past of American society than it does about the merits of the (all too often unexplored) tradition of critical analysis. It also speaks eloquently to the point I mentioned early in this volume. The tradition itself has become an example of how the selective tradition operates. It has become a victim of the politics of knowledge distribution in that we have forgotten our past roots in these concerns.

Yet, there are other more basic and less overtly political explanations for the atrophy and lack of acceptance of a Marxist intellectual and political tradition in places like the USA. The atomistic, positivistic, and strict empiricist frame of mind so prevalent in our thought (and quite effectively taught, as we saw in Chapter 5) has difficulty with the critically oriented notion of the necessity of a plurality of, and conflict about, ways of looking at the world. On this, critical scholarship holds a position quite similar to that of phenomenology in that the "truth" of something can only be seen through the use of the totality of perspectives one can bring to bear upon it. (Though obviously some are more basic than

others in that subtle economic, class, and cultural interpretations take on an organizing function in the questions one asks in this critical tradition.)[23]

Also, the tendency in western industrialized societies to separate strictly
value from fact would make it difficult for there to be acceptance of a position
which holds that most social and intellectual categories are themselves *valuative* in nature and may reflect ideological commitments, a fact that will be of
exceptional import in this discussion. Furthermore, the long tradition of abstract individualism and a strongly utilitarian frame of mind would no doubt
cause one to look less than positively upon both a more social conception of
"man" and an ideal commitment that is less apt to be immediately ameliorative and more apt to raise basic questions about the very framework of social
and cultural life that is accepted as given by a society.[24]

In opposition to the atomistic assumptions that predominate in our commonsense thought, as we have seen a critical viewpoint usually sees any object
"relationally." This is an important key to understanding the type of analysis
one might engage in from such a perspective. This implies two things. First,
any subject matter under investigation must be seen in relation to its historical
roots—how it evolved, from what conditions it arose, etc.—and its latent contradictions and tendencies in the future. This is the case because in the highly
complicated world of critical analysis existing structures are actually in something like continual motion. Contradiction, change, and development are the
norm and any institutional structure is "merely" a stage in process.[25] Thus, institutional reification becomes problematic, as do the patterns of thought that
support this lack of institutional change. Second, anything being examined is
defined not only by its obvious characteristics, but by its less overt ties to other
factors. It *is* these ties or relationships that make the subject what it is and give
it its primary meanings.[26] In this way, our ability to illuminate the interdepen-
dence and interaction of factors is considerably expanded.

To accept this relational view is obviously to go against our traditional concept that what we see is as it appears. In fact, the argument is that our very
taken for granted perceptions mislead us here and that this is a rather grave
limitation on our thought and action. That is, anything is a good deal more
than it appears, especially when one is dealing with complex and interrelated
institutions including the school.[27] It is this very point that will enable us to
make progress in even further uncovering some of the ideological functions of
educational language.

One final point can be made. Historically, critical theory and a good deal of
neo-Marxist analysis have been reduced to variants of pragmatism, especially
by individuals like Sidney Hook and others. While I do not wish to debunk the
pragmatic tradition in American education (after all, we still have much to
learn from a serious treatment of Dewey's analysis of means and ends in education, for instance), I do want to caution against interpreting critical analysis
so that it easily fits within our taken for granted constitutive rules. To do so is

to lose the potential of a critical perspective in going beyond some of the very real conformist inclinations of pragmatism. The pragmatic position tends to ignore the possibility that some theories must contradict the present reality and, in fact, must consistently work against it.[28] These critical inquiries *stand in witness* of the negativity involved in all too many current institutional (economic, cultural, educational, political) arrangements and thus can illuminate the possibility of significant change. In this way, the act of criticism contributes to emancipation in that it shows the way linguistic or social institutions have been reified or thingified so that educators and the public at large have forgotten why they evolved, and that people made them and thus can change them.[29]

The intent of such a critique and of critical scholarship in general, then, is twofold. First, it aims at illuminating the tendencies for unwarranted and often unconscious domination, alienation, and repression within certain existing cultural, political, educational, and economic institutions. Second, through exploring the negative effects and contradictions of much that unquestioningly goes on in these institutions, it seeks to "promote conscious [individual and collective] emancipatory activity."[30] That is, it examines what is supposed to be happening in, say, schools if one takes the language and slogans of many school people seriously; and it then shows how these things *actually* work in a manner that is destructive of ethical rationality and personal political and institutional power. Once this actual functioning is held up to scrutiny, it attempts to point to concrete activity that will lead to challenging this taken for granted activity.

Institutional Language and Ethical Responsibility

One of the most potent issues raised by critical scholarship over the years is the tendency for us to hide what are profound interrelations between persons through the use of a "neutral" commodity language.[31] Williams's earlier discussion of the ideological function of the abstract individual obviously points to part of this problem. Educators are not immune to this tendency. That is, educators have developed categories and modes of perception which reify or thingify individuals so that they (the educators) can confront students as institutional abstractions rather than as concrete persons with whom they have real ties in the process of cultural and economic reproduction. Given the complexity of mass education this is understandable. However, the implications of the growth of this form of language are profound and must be examined in depth.

In order to accomplish this, one fact must be made clear. By the very fact that the categories that curriculum workers and other educators employ are themselves social constructs, they also imply the notion of the power of one group to "impose" these social constructions on others. For example, the categories by which we differentiate "smart" children from "stupid," "academic" areas from "non-academic," "play" activity from "learning" or "work" activity, and even "students" from "teachers," are all commonsense constructions *which grow out of the nature of existing institutions.*[32] As such they must be treated as historically conditioned data, not absolutes. This is not to say that they are necessarily always wrong; rather it points to the necessity of understanding them for what they are—categories that developed out of specific social and historical situations which conform to a specific framework of assumptions and institutions, the use of which categories brings with it the logic of the institutional assumptions as well.

As I mentioned, the field itself has a tendency to "disguise" relations between people as relations between things or abstractions.[33] Hence, ethical issues such as the profoundly difficult problem concerning the ways by which one person may seek to influence another are not usually treated as important considerations. It is here that the abstract categories that grow out of institutional life become quite serious. If an educator may define another as a "slow learner," a "discipline problem," or other general category, he or she may prescribe general "treatments" that are seemingly neutral and helpful. However, by the very fact that the categories themselves are based upon institutionally defined abstractions (the commonsense equivalent of statistical averages), the educator is freed from the more difficult task of examining the institutional and economic context that caused these abstract labels to be placed upon a concrete individual in the first place. Thus, the understandable attempt to reduce complexity leads to the use of "average treatments" applied to fillers of abstract roles. This preserves the anonymity of the intersubjective relationship between "educator" and "pupil" which is so essential if institutional definitions of situations are to prevail. It, thereby, protects both the existing institution and the educator from self-doubt and from the innocence and reality of the child.

This has important implications for educational scholarship. By using official categories and constructs such as those defined by and growing out of existing institutional practices—examples might be studies of the "slow learner," "discipline problems," and "remediation"—curriculum researchers may be lending the rhetorical prestige of science to what may be questionable practices of an educational bureaucracy[34] and a stratified economic system. That is, there is no rigorous attempt at examining *institutional* culpability. The notion of imputing culpability is of considerable moment to my analysis. Scott makes this point rather clearly in his discussion of the effects of labeling someone as different or deviant.[35]

> Another reaction that commonly occurs when a deviant label is applied is that within the community a feeling arises that "something ought to be done about *him*." Perhaps the most important fact about this reaction in our society is that almost all of the steps that are taken are *directed solely at the deviant*. Punishment, rehabilitation, therapy, coercion, and other common mechanisms of social control are things that are done to him, implying that the causes of deviance

reside within the person to whom the label has been attached, and that the solutions to the problems that he presents can be achieved by doing something to him. This is a curious fact, particularly when we examine it against the background of social science research on deviance that so clearly points to the crucial role played by ordinary people in determining who is labeled a deviant and how a deviant behaves. *This research suggests that none of the corrective measures that are taken can possibly succeed in the intended way unless they are directed at those who confer deviant labels as well as those to whom they are applied.* [my italics]

In clearer language, in the school students are the persons expressly focused upon. Attention is primarily paid to their specific behavioral, emotional, or educational "problems," and, thus, there is a strong inclination to divert attention both from the inadequacies of the educational institution itself[36] and what bureaucratic, cultural, and economic conditions caused the necessity of applying these constructs originally.

Let us now look a bit more deeply into the ideological and ethical configuration surrounding the idea of culpability. It is often the case that institutional labels, especially those that imply some sort of deviance, "slow learner," "discipline problem," "poor reader," etc., may again serve as types found in educational settings—confer an inferior status on those so labeled. This is shot through with moral meanings and significance. Usually the "deviant" label has an *essentializing* quality in that a person's (here, a student's) entire relationship to an institution is conditioned by the category applied to him. He or she *is* this and only this. The point is similar to Goffman's argument that the person to whom a deviant label is applied by others or by an institution is usually viewed as morally inferior, and his or her "condition" or behavior is quite often interpreted as evidence of *his or her* "moral culpability."[37] Thus, such labels are not neutral, at least not in their significance for the person. By the very fact that the labels are tinged with moral significance—not only is the child different but also inferior—their application has a profound impact. The fact that these labels once conferred are *lasting* due to the budgetary and bureaucratic reality of many schools—budgetary restrictions, the very real structural relations existing between schooling and economic and cultural control, lack of expertise in dealing with the "learning problems" of specific students, etc., all making it truly difficult to actually change the conditions which caused the child to be "a slow learner" or other category in the first place—gives even more weight to the points I have been illuminating. Since only rarely is a student reclassified,[38] the effect of these labels is immense for they call forth forms of "treatment" which tend to confirm the person in the institutionally applied category.

It is often argued that such rhetorical devices as the categories and labels to which I have been referring actually are used to help the child. After all, once so characterized the student can be given "proper treatment." However, just as plausible a case can be made that, given the reality of life in schools, and given the role of the school in maximizing the production both of certain kinds of cultural capital and of agents who are "required" by a society's economic apparatus, the very definition of a student as someone in need of this particular treatment harms him or her.[39] As I have pointed out, such definitions are essentializing; they tend to be generalized to all situations which the individual confronts. As Goffman so potently illustrates, in total institutions—and schools share many of their characteristics—the label and all that goes with it is likely to be used by the individual's peers and his or her custodians (e.g., other children, teachers, and administrators) to *define* him or her. It governs nearly all of the conduct toward the person, and, more importantly, the definition ultimately governs the student's conduct toward these others, thereby acting to support a self-fulfilling prophecy.[40]

My point is not to deny that within the existing institutional framework of schooling there are such "things" as "slow learners," "underachievers," or "poorly motivated students" which we can commonsensically identify, though as I have contended such language hides the more basic issue of inquiring into the conditions under which one group of people consistently labels others as deviant or applies some other taken for granted abstract category to them. Rather, I would like to argue that this linguistic system as it is commonly applied by school people does not serve a psychological or scientific function as much as they would like to suppose. To put it bluntly, it often serves to abase and degrade those individuals and classes of people to whom the designations are so quickly given.[41]

A fact that should bring this argument into even clearer focus—that is, that the process of classification as it functions in educational research and practice is a moral and political act, not a neutral helping act—is the evidence that those labels are *massively* applied to the children of the poor and ethnic minorities much more so than the children of the more economically advantaged and politically powerful.

Besides the historical documentation I offered in Chapter 4, there is powerful recent empirical evidence to support part of the argument offered here. For example, Mercer's analysis of the processes by which institutions like schools label individuals as, say, mentally retarded confirms this picture.[42] Children with "nonmodal" socio-cultural backgrounds and of minority groups predominate to a disproportionate degree in being so labeled. This is primarily due to diagnostic procedures in schools that were drawn almost totally from what she has called the dominance of "anglocentrism" in schools, a form of ethno-centrism that causes school people to act as if their own group's life style, language, history, and value and normative structure were the "proper" guidelines against which all other people's activity should be measured. Not only were students from low socio-economic and non-white backgrounds disproportionately labeled, but even more important, Mexican-American and Black students, for instance, who were assigned the label of mental retardate were actually less "deviant" than whites. That is, they had *higher* IQ's than the

"Anglos" who were so labeled. Given Bourdieu's arguments quoted in Chapter 2, this should not surprise us too much.

Yet another fact should be noted. The school was most often the only institution to label these nonmodal students as retarded, primarily because of the prevailing assumptions of normality that were held by school personnel. These students performed quite well once outside the boundaries of that institution.

Mercer is at least partly correct when she attributes this overdistribution of the mental retardate designation to the diagnostic, evaluative, and testing "machinery" of the school.[43] Based as it is on statistical formulations that conform to problematic institutional assumptions concerning normality and deviance drawn from existing and often biased economic and political structures, it plays a large part in the process of channeling certain types of students into preexisting categories. The painful fact that this supposedly helpful machinery of diagnosis and remediation does not meet the reality of the child is given further documentation by Mehan's important study of supposedly "normal" young children's reconstruction of the meaning of a testing situation and the evaluative instruments themselves.[44] In essence, what he found was that even in the most personally administered diagnostic testing, "testers" were apt to use speculative and inaccurate labels to summarize even more speculative and inaccurate results. The school tests actually *obscured* the children's real understanding of the materials and tasks, did not capture the children's varied abilities to reason adequately, and did not show "the negotiated, contextually bound measurement decisions that the tester makes while scoring children's behavior as 'correct' or 'incorrect'." While this was especially true of "nonmodal" children (in this case, Spanish-speaking) it was also strikingly true for all other students as well. If this research is correct, given the intense pressure for "accountability" today, the dominance of a process-product testing mentality, hence, will no doubt lead to even more problematic, anonymous, and culturally and economically biased institutions due to the labels that stem from the testing process itself. The importance given to testing in schools cannot be underestimated in other ways. The labels that come from these "diagnoses" and assessments are not easily shaken off, and are in fact used by other institutions to continue the definitional ascription given by the school.

That is, it should be quite clear that not only does the school perform a central function of assigning labels to children in the process of sorting them and then distributing different knowledge, dispositions, and views of self to each of these labeled groups, but, just as important, the school occupies *the* central position in a larger network of other institutions. The labels imputed by the public schools are borrowed by legal, economic, health, and community institutions to define the individual in his or her contact with them as well.[45]

Thus, as institutions that are heavily influenced by statistical and "scientific" models of operation to define normality and deviance, models that are consistently biased toward extant social regularities, schools seem to have a disproportionate effect on labeling students. Because public schools depend almost exclusively on a statistical model for their normative frame, they generate categories of deviance that are filled with individuals largely from lower socio-economic groups and ethnic minorities.[46] The ethical, political, and economic implications of this creation of deviant identities should be obvious.

This makes one notion very significant. The only serious way to make sense out of the imputation of labels in schools is to analyze the assumptions that underlie the definitions of competence these entail; and this can only be done in terms of an investigation of those who are in a position to *impose* these definitions.[47] Thus, the notion of *power* (what economic group or social class actually has it and how it is really being used) becomes a critical one if we are to understand why certain forms of social meanings—the authoritative election Blum talks of in the quote at the outset of this chapter—are used to select and organize the knowledge and perspectives educators employ to comprehend, order, value, and control activity in educational institutions.

Power and Labeling

How important a sense of the way power operates is to our understanding of the labeling process must not be underestimated for at least one particular reason. There has evolved over the past few years a large body of research on labeling. It has been strongly influenced by social phenomenology, symbolic interactionism, and other perspectives that tend to see, in part correctly, that labels, like "reality," are social constructions.[48] This rather phenomenological tradition has usually been less concerned with what I have called relational analysis, however. Because of this, we must be wary of some significant limitations in the usual analyses of categories and labels done by labeling theorists and others.

In fact, an unrelational focus on labeling, one that is not overtly concerned with the connections between economic and cultural power and schools, can lead us into the conceptual and political trap that has so often closed on the investigations done by the symbolic interactionists, labeling theorists, and phenomenological sociologists of the school.[49] By examining the labeling process (as an indicator of how ideological saturation in the heads of educators actually operates in day to day school life, here) we can forget that it *is* an indicator of something beyond itself as well. For as the quote from Whitty pointed out earlier in this volume, the mere fact that these categories and labels are social constructs does not explain why this particular set exists nor why it is so resistant to change.

Sharp and Green's discussion of the relationship between power and labeling in their ethnographic study of a working class British primary school provides a number of significant comments on this danger. For Sharp and Green, social phenomenology, symbolic interactionism, labeling theory, and so forth simply do not provide an adequate analytic framework for understanding *why* things such as the stratification and labeling of children go on in educational institutions. Not only is the framework conceptually weak, but it is inherently less political than it should be if we are to comprehend the complex relationship between common-sense meanings, practices, and decisions in schools and the ideological and institutional apparatus that surrounds these cultural institutions.

Sharp and Green are in strong agreement with other British sociologists who criticize phenomenologically oriented research as being onesided and ultimately apolitical. For example, most phenomenological studies want to focus on the social construction of classroom reality, how the commonsense interactions of both teachers and students create and maintain the sets of meanings and identities that enable classroom life to proceed in a relatively smooth manner. Here is where those of us influenced by Marxist and neo-Marxist perspectives want to go further, however. For the social world, with education as part of it, is not merely the result of the creative processes of interpretation that social actors engage in, a point so dear to the hearts of the social phenomenologists. It is partly this, of course. But, the everyday world that we all confront in our day to day lives as teachers, researchers, parents, children, and so forth "is structured not merely by language and meaning," by our face to face symbolic interactions and by our ongoing social constructions, "but by the modes and forces of material production and the system of domination which is related in some way to material reality and its control."[50]

Phenomenological description and analysis of social processes and labeling, while important to be sure, inclines us to forget that there *are* objective institutions and structures "out there" that have power, that can control our lives and our very perceptions. By focusing on how everyday social interaction sustains peoples' identities and their institutions, it can draw attention away from the fact that individual interaction and conception is constrained by material reality.

I do not mean that one should throw out social phenomenology or labeling theory here. Instead, one combines it with a more critical social interpretation that looks at the creation of identities and meanings in specific institutions like schools as taking place within a context that often determines the parameters of what is negotiable or meaningful. This context does not merely reside at the level of consciousness; it is the nexus of economic and political institutions, a nexus which defines what schools should be about, that sets limits on these parameters. These points have important implications for a serious analysis of classroom labeling, the use of "neutral" categories by educators, and the distribution of different kinds of knowledge to differently labeled children.

For example, much of the literature on the labeling of children in schools tends to rest upon a peculiar brand of "idealism." That is, it assumes that pupil identities are created almost wholly by teachers' perceptions of students in classrooms. However, this is not merely a question of teachers' consciousness making children's consciousness—e.g., a teacher conceives of a student as "really dumb" and, hence, the child becomes "really dumb," though there is some element of truth to that to be sure. Rather, it also deeply involves the objective material circumstances and expectations which both make up and surround the school environment. As Sharp and Green argue:[51]

> When considering the generation of pupil identities, for example, the pupil's opportunity structure for acquiring any particular identity relates not merely to the teacher's working conceptual categories in his or her consciousness, but also to the facets of the structure of classroom organization which has to be understood in relationship to a range of extra-classroom pressures which may be or may not be appreciated by the teacher or the pupils. It is important to attempt to understand classroom social structure as the product of both symbolic context *and* material circumstances. The latter factors tend to be underestimated in social interactionism and social phenomenology.

Thus, the modes of interaction in classrooms, the types of control, the generation and labeling of pupil identities, need to be understood as a dialectical relationship between ideology and material and economic environment. As I noted earlier, teachers' conceptions of competence, of what is "good student performance," of important *v.* unimportant knowledge, of "proper behavior" are not free-floating ideas. These mental productions come from somewhere. They are responses to what are perceived to be real problems caused, in part, by very real environmental conditions within schools and, often, economic and social conditions "outside" that building. Thus, to understand schools one must go beyond what educational practitioners and theorists think is going on, to see the connections between these thoughts and actions to the ideological and material conditions both in and outside the school that "determine" what we think are our "real" problems. The key to uncovering this is power.

Yet, as I have shown in this book, power is not always visible as economic manipulation and control. It is often manifest as forms of helping and as forms of "legitimate knowledge," forms which seem to provide their own justification by being interpreted as neutral. Thus, power is exercised through institutions which, by running their natural course, reproduce and legitimate the system of inequality. And all of this can in fact seem even more legitimate through the role of the intellectuals who make up the helping professions such as education.

This is obviously quite complex, yet even if we were to understand part of this, by the very fact of considering ourselves as a helping profession our prevailing liberal ideology would have us deal with the problems of labeling by instituting limited amelioration. We would introduce things like more openness in schools. The notion behind such reforms is that by opening up classrooms the labeling process would become less essential. Children would be able to excel wherever their individual talents lie. However, these kinds of ameliorative reforms must be examined quite carefully. They may be contradictory and may actually create more of a problem, in the same manner that "achievement problems" were naturally generated in Chapter 2.

Actually, as Sharp and Green show, what seems to happen is that the range of labels which can be applied is increased in more open settings, especially those in working class and culturally different areas, those areas where labeling is most intense. In the traditional classroom, what is considered as important overt knowledge tends to be limited to "academic areas"—mathematics, science, and so forth. Thus, students may tend to be labeled, when achievement criteria are used, on a fairly limited set of public knowledge forms. However, in more open settings that are part of the public school system (with its historical interest in social and "intellectual" stratification and ideological consensus) what is construed as specifically school knowledge is increased. One is now much more interested in the "whole child," if you will. Therefore, emotionality, dispositions, physicality, and other more general attributes are added to the usual academic curricula as overt areas one must be concerned with. The latent result seems to be to *increase the range of attributes* upon which students may be stratified. That is, by changing the definition of school knowledge so that it includes more personal and dispositional elements, one is also latently enabling a wider possibility of labeling to go on in more "open" environments. Student identities can be even more fixed than before. This probably occurs because the basic goals of the institution—e.g., sorting students according to "natural talent," maximizing the production of technical knowledge, etc.—are not really changed. At the same time, of course, open classrooms in middle class areas are ideally suited to teach decision-making, flexibility, and so on to students who will become managers and professionals. This finding is not trivial, for if, say, open classrooms within traditional institutions actually create a more powerful system of stratification, then their actual functioning has to be interpreted in reproductive, not only ameliorative, terms.

This ties in very closely to the discussion of the hidden curriculum in earlier chapters. As children learn to accept as natural the social distinctions schools both reinforce and teach between important and unimportant knowledge, between normality and deviance, between work and play, and the subtle ideological rules and norms that inhere in these distinctions, they also internalize visions of both the way institutions should be organized and their *appropriate* place in these institutions. These things are learned somewhat differently by different students, of course, and this is where the process of labeling becomes so important to social and economic class differentiation. The labeling of students, and the school's ameliorative ideology that surrounds its decision to use particular social labels, has a strong impact on which students accept which particular distinctions as natural.

Clinical Language, the Expert, and Social Control

As I argued in Chapters 2 and 3, one important latent function of schooling seems to be the distribution of forms of consciousness, often quite unequally,

to students. Sociologically, then, through their appropriation of these dispositions and outlooks, students are able to be sorted into the various roles sedimented throughout the fabric of an advanced corporate society. The process
of labeling occupies a subtle but essential place in this sorting. Because the designations, categories, and linguistic tools employed by educators, and especially by most members of the curriculum field of a behavioral persuasion, are
perceived by them to have both "scientific" status and to be geared to "helping"
students, there is little or no realization that the very language that they resort
to is ideally suited to maintain the bureaucratic rationality (and the concomitant effects of social control and consensus) that has dominated schooling for
so long a time.[52]

Edelman makes a similar point in discussing the way the distinctive language system of the "helping professions" is used to justify and marshal public
support for professional practices that have profound political and ethical
consequences.[53]

> Because the helping professions define other people's statuses (and their own),
> the special terms they employ to categorize clients and justify restrictions of
> their physical movements and of their moral and intellectual influence are espe-
> cially revealing of the political functions language performs and of the multiple
> realities it helps create. Language is both a sensitive indicator and a powerful cre-
> ator of background assumptions about people's levels of competence and merit.
> Just as any single numeral evokes the whole number scheme in our minds, so a
> term, a syntactic form, or a metaphor with political connotations can evoke and
> justify a power hierarchy in the person who used it and the groups that respond
> to it.

Edelman's basic argument is not merely that the language forms educators
and others use "arrange" their reality, but also that these forms covertly justify
status, power, and authority. In essence, they are ideological in both senses of
the term. In short, one must examine the contradiction between a liberal perspective that is there to help and at the same time actually serves the existing
distribution of power in institutions and society.[54] This contradiction is difficult to miss in the language employed by school people.

Perhaps this argument is best summarized by quoting again from Edelman.[55]

> In the symbolic worlds evoked by the language of the helping professions, specu-
> lations and verified fact readily merge with each other. Language dispels the un-
> certainty in speculation, changes facts to make them serve status distinctions
> and reinforce ideology. The names for forms of mental illness, forms of delin-
> quency, and for educational capacities are the basic terms. Each of them nor-
> mally involves a high degree of unreliability in diagnosis, in prognosis, and in the
> prescription of rehabilitative treatments; but also entail unambiguous con-
> straints upon clients, especially their confinement and subjection to the staff and
> the rules of a prison, school or hospital. *The confinement and constraints are con-*
> *verted into liberating and altruistic acts by defining them as education, therapy, or*
> *rehabilitation. The arbitrariness and speculation in the diagnosis and the prognosis,*

on the other hand, are converted into clear and specific perceptions of the need for control (by the "helping group"). Regardless of the arbitrariness or technical unreliability of professional terms, their political utility is manifest; they marshal popular support for professional discretion, concentrating public attention upon procedures and rationalizing in advance any failure of the procedures to achieve their formal objectives. [my italics]

That is, the supposedly neutral language of an institution, even though it rests upon highly speculative data and may be applied without actually being appropriate, provides a framework that legitimates control of major aspects of an individual's or group's behavior. At the same time, by sounding scientific and "expert," it contributes to the quiescence of the public by focusing attention on its "sophistication" not on its political or ethical results. Thus, historically outmoded, and socially and politically conservative (and often educationally disastrous) practices are not only continued, but are made to sound as if they were actually more enlightened and ethically responsive ways of dealing with children.

As in other institutions where there is little choice about whether an individual (student, patient, inmate) may come or go as he or she pleases, by defining students through the use of such a quasi-scientific and quasi-clinical and therapeutic terminology and hence "showing" that students are culpable and that they are indeed "different" (they are not adults; they have not reached a certain developmental stage; they have limited attention spans, they are "culturally and linguistically deprived," etc.), educators need not face the often coercive aspects of their own activity.[56] Therefore, the ethical and ideological questions of the nature of control in school settings do not have to be responded to. The liberal vision, the clinical perspectives, the treatment language, the "helping" labels, all define it out of existence.

It is possible to argue, then, that these criticisms are actually generic to clinical perspectives and helping labels themselves as they function in education since the assumptions in which they are grounded are themselves open to question.[57] These viewpoints are distinguished by a number of striking characteristics, each of which when combined with the others seem logically to lead to a conservative stance toward existing institutional arrangements. The first characteristic is that the researcher or practitioner studies or deals with those individuals who have already been labeled as different or deviant by the institution. In doing this, he or she adopts the values of the social system that defined the person as deviant. Furthermore, he or she assumes that the judgments made by the institution and based on these values are *the* valid measures of normality and competence without seriously questioning them.

Second, these clinical and helping perspectives have a strong tendency to perceive the difficulty as a problem with the individual, as something the individual rather than the institution lacks. Thus, combined with the assumption that the offficial definition is the only right definition, almost all action is focused on changing the individual rather than the defining agent, the larger institutional context. Third, researchers and practitioners who accept the institutional designations and definitions tend to assume that all of the people within these categories are the same. There is an assumption of homogeneity. In this way, individual complexity is automatically flattened. The actual process of creating an abstract individual is covered by the quasi-individualistic perspective.

But this is not all, for there seem to be strong motivations for use already built into these labels and the processes and expertise behind them. That is, the "professional helpers" who employ the supposedly diagnostic and therapeutic terminologies *must* find (and hence create) individuals who fit the categories, otherwise the expertise is useless. This is probably a general educational fact. Once a "new" (but always limited) tool or perspective for "helping" children is generated, it tends to expand beyond the "problem" for which it was initially developed. The tools (here diagnostic, therapeutic, and linguistic) also have the effect of redefining past issues in these other areas into problems the tool is capable of dealing with.[58] The best example is behavior modification. While applicable to a limited range of difficulties in schools, it becomes both a diagnostic language and a form of "treatment" for a wider range of "student problems." Thus, for instance, its increasing use and acceptance in ghetto and working class schools and elsewhere with "disruptive" children, or with entire school classes as is becoming more the case, really acts as a cloak to cover the political fact that the nature of the existing educational institutions is unresponsive to a large portion of students.[59] In addition, its treatment language acts to hide the alienating wage-product relationship that has been established and called education. Finally, the perspective, by defining itself clinically, covers the very real moral questions that must be raised concerning the appropriateness of the technique itself in dealing with students who have no choice about being in the institution.

One of the points that complements the foregoing discussion is that those people who are perceived as being different or deviant from normal institutional expectations are threatening to the day to day life of schools, to the normal pattern of operation that is constant and so often relatively sterile. In this regard, the labeling act can be seen as part of a complex avoidance process. It acts to preserve the tenuous nature of many interpersonal relationships within schools on which "adequate definitions of situations" depend. But even more important, it enables people like teachers, administrators, curriculum workers, and other school people to confront stereotypes rather than individuals since schools cannot deal with the distinctive characteristics of individuals to any significant degree. There is a good deal of research that supports the fact that differences from institutional expectations often result in avoidance reactions on the part of people who confront these individuals who are "deviant."[60] Thus, stereotyping and labeling are heightened and the comforting illusion that children are being helped is preserved.

Yet how is this illusion maintained? Schools are often evaluated. Both personnel and programs are repeatedly scrutinized, now even more so because of the dominance of the management perspectives I focused upon in the last chapter. A multitude of experts in research and evaluation expend a huge amount of time and effort investigating the effects of schooling. Even though these experts look at schools through the limited lenses of the achievement and socialization traditions, shouldn't the actual functioning of such day to day activity seem clear? Shouldn't the way a good deal of the work of schools and the expertise (clinical or otherwise) that stands behind its functions as an aspect of cultural and economic reproduction be recognized? Isn't the way "intellectuals" employ their commonsense expertise clear to them? After all, most schoolpeople and researchers truly care about both their work and the students who inhabit these institutions.

Unfortunately, this recognition is rather difficult to come by. First, as I have maintained, a major reason is the manner in which such expertise functions. It *is* ideological. It does provide a working definition of a complex situation (in much the same way as the material conditions of a teaching environment provided the justification for the teacher's time and energy in Chapter 3), while ongoingly recreating structurally based inequalities in knowledge and power at the same time. Second, there are barriers to such self-consciousness built into the very role and perspective of both the evaluative expert in corporate society and the receiver of such expertise as well.

We should not be surprised that the basic perspectives of "experts" are quite strongly influenced by the dominant values of the collectivity to which they belong and the social situation within that society which they fill. These dominant values necessarily affect their work.[61] In fact, as we have seen, these outlooks are already sedimented into the forms of language and the implicit perspectives found in the social roles intellectuals and technical experts fill. There are linguistic, programmatic, methodological, and conceptual tools, and expectations on how they are to be used, built into the job of the evaluator. It is not very common for these professionals to turn their backs on the institutionalized goals, procedures, and norms that already exist and the store-house of collected knowledge which serves these official goals that has been built up over the years in the field. In part, this is because this congerie of accepted wisdom and value is reinforced by the needs of institutional managers for special types of "expert" advice. This is an exceptionally important point.

Researchers and evaluators are "experts for hire." Here I do not mean to totally denigrate the important position they fill. Rather, the role of the expert in American society is rather unique and leads to certain expectations which are themselves problematic in educational settings.

Given the status of technical knowledge in corporate economies, "experts" are under a considerable amount of pressure to present their findings as scientific information, as knowledge that has to a significant degree a scientific warrant, and, therefore, an inherent plausibility.[62] As we saw in Chapter 2, this had a rather large impact on the rejection of the policy statements made by Jencks in *Inequality,* for instance. Not only are experts, especially educational research and evaluation experts, expected to couch their arguments in scientific terms, but because of their very position in the social system, their data and perspectives are perceived as authoritative. The weight and prestige given to their expertise is considerable.[63] However, our previous discussion of how educators have appropriated an inaccurate view of scientific activity makes this prestige problematic. This appropriation leads to considerable difficulty. It enables educators to practice poor research and, most importantly, it is a major component in their tendency to confirm the achievement and socialization paradigms under which educational researchers work, even though substantive progress may require a new disciplinary matrix to replace the current one.[64] The numerous findings of no significant difference might just point to this conclusion.

While there are considerable conceptual and technical (to say nothing of ideological) difficulties with the usual view of what important research looks like, one thing is obvious. Even given these difficulties, schoolpeople and decisionmakers do perceive the information they get from technical experts as "worthy," again because it comes from those who hold the title of expert.

One of the tasks of the expert is to furnish to the administrative leadership of an institution the special knowledge these persons require before decisions are made. The bureaucratic institution furnishes the problems to be investigated, not the expert. Hence, the type of knowledge that the expert is to supply is *determined in advance.* Since the expert bears no responsibility for the final outcome of a program, his or her activities can be guided by the practical interests of the administrative leaders, a point made so clearly earlier by Gouldner. And what administrators are *not* looking for are new hypotheses or new interpretations that are not immediately and noticeably relevant to the practical problems at hand—the teaching of reading, say. The fact that the expert is expected to work on the practical problems as defined by the institution and not offer advice outside of these boundaries is of considerable moment. It has become increasingly evident that, for whatever reasons (socialization into a position, timidity because of political pressure, a belief that engineering techniques will solve all of our problems, the ideological and material "determinations" affecting the institution, and so forth) the administrative leadership of a large organization seeks and is probably supposed to seek to reduce the new and uncertain of a complex situation with which it is confronted into a practically safe combination of "old and certain truths" about the processes of schooling.[65] However, there are very few things as conceptually, ethically, and politically complex as education, and educational scholarship has hardly scratched the surface of the intricacies involved. The fact that these "old and certain truths" may be less than efficacious given the questions being raised by the reproduction theorists and others about the complicated nature of educational problems in cities and elsewhere is not often perceived to be important to consider by practical decision-makers, for, after all, it is the role of the expert to deal with this complexity. But as we saw, the knowledge expected of the expert is already predetermined and, thus, we are caught in a double bind. The expert is expected to provide technical advice and services to help solve the institution's needs; however, the range of issues and the types of answers which are actually acceptable are ideologically limited by what the administrative apparatus has previously defined as "the problem." In this way the circle of inconsequential results is continued.

This is certainly not new. Expertise has been used by policymakers for quite a long time. It should be clear, though, that from the very beginnings of the assessment of social and educational programs, the kinds of help required were determined primarily by and in support of the political goals of officials, often at the expense of institutional responsiveness to its clientele.[66]

This raises a rather provocative question. Can one see the real functioning of one's work, can one study the real outcomes and processes of educational programs, when one's action and research employs categories and data derived from and serving the institution itself, without at the same time giving support to the cultural and economic apparatus which these categories and data themselves serve?[67] Because of this kind of question a crucial point should be noted at this time. Of particular import for curricular and other educational research and evaluation, then, is to argue *against* the temptation to uncritically use officially collected statistics based on these officially defined categories that are often readily available. Rather, the more critical question to ask is "What ideological assumptions underpin the constructs within which this data was generated?"[68] By raising questions of this type one may illuminate the very potent normative implications involved when educators designate students by some specific institutional abstraction.

I have argued that the distribution of labels among a student population is actually a process by which one social group makes value judgments about the appropriateness or inappropriateness of another group's action. If such a perspective is correct, then the points I have been articulating suggest that a good deal of investigation remains to be done showing how the ideologically hegemonic structures of dominant groups in American society when imposed upon schools have rather wide ethical, political, and social implications in that they may assist in sorting out individuals according to class, race, and sex quite early in life.

These are quite frankly difficult questions. Yet, in the very act of searching for relief from the all too real moral and political responsibilities and dilemmas of influencing others, educators have done what Szasz calls "mystifying and technicizing their problems of living." What this has to say about the dominance in educational thought of psychological models and metaphors based upon a neutral and "strict science" image is quite significant.[69]

The orientations which so predominate curriculum and educational theory, and indeed have consistently dominated it in the past, effectively obscure and often deny the profound ethical and economic issues educators face. As we have seen, they transform these dilemmas into engineering problems or puzzles that are amenable to technical "professional" solutions. Perhaps the best example is the field's nearly total reliance on perspectives drawn from the psychology of learning. The terminology drawn from this psychology and its allied fields is quite inadequate since it neglects or at base tends to draw attention from the basically political and moral character of social existence and human development. The language of reinforcement, learning, negative feedback, and so forth is a rather weak tool for dealing with the continual encroachment of contradiction upon order, with the issue of what counts as legitimate knowledge, with the creation and recreation of personal meaning and interpersonal institutions, with the reproductive nature of schooling and other institutions, and with notions such as responsibility and justice in conduct with others. In essence, like the language of systems management, the language of psychology as it is exercised in curriculum "de-ethicizes and depoliticizes human relations and personal conduct."[70]

For example, much of our busy endeavor to define operational objectives and to state student "outcomes" in behavioral terms may be interpreted as exactly that—busy work, if I may use commonsense terminology for the moment. That is, because of the field's preoccupation with the working of its goal statements and "output measures," attention is diverted from the crucial political and moral implications of our activity as educators. In this way means are turned into ends and children are transformed into manipulable and anonymous abstractions called "learners." Speaking of the field of sociology, though quite the same things could be said about a large portion of curricular language and research, Friedrich articulates part of the problem clearly.[71]

> What sociologists appear completely unaware of is the long-run impact of coming to *conceive* of one's fellows as manipulable. Language—and the choice among symbols it entails—pervades all meaningful social action, either overtly or covertly, consciously or unconsciously. The symbolic manipulation of man cannot be wholly isolated from the rest of a person's symbolically mediated relationships with others. As man's intellectual life more and more demands such symbolic manipulation, he runs the increasing risk of conceiving man in other areas of his life in terms that invite or are particularly amenable to a means-end relationship rather than those that support an attitude toward others as ends in themselves.

Thus, the manipulative ethos and the structures of ideological domination of a larger society are found within curriculum discourse in the basic behavioral and treatment language and categories used for even conceiving of educational relationships. It thereby creates and reinforces patterns of interaction that not only reflect but actually embody the interests in stratification, unequal power, certainty, and control that dominate the consciousness of advanced corporate societies.

Some Counterexamples

A number of alternative examples can be used to show that the conceptions, categories, and labels that I have been analyzing are, in fact, commonsensical and ideological not preordained or "natural." In our society, there is a high premium put on intelligence, especially in relation to the student's ability to enhance the production of economically important knowledge. Schools are obviously partly organized around and value such a concept. The fact that they limit it to quite constricted and mostly verbal versions of it, ones usually embodying the cultural capital of dominant groups, is important but not the point here. Rather, we should note that it is possible to describe other conceptions around which our educational and social institutions could be organized and our technology designed. For instance, envision a society in which physical *grace* not our overly constricted definitions of competence and intelligence was the most valued characteristic.[72] Those who were clumsy or reached merely lower categories of grace might then be discriminated against. The culture's educational structure would categorize individuals according to their "capacity for grace." The technology would be so designed that it would require elegance in motion for it to be employed.

Besides physical grace (which is really not too outlandish a concept) one could also point to the possibility of valuing, say, moral excellence or the collective commitment seen in students in many socialist countries. After all, these types of dispositional elements are some of the things that education is all about, aren't they? However, as the literature on the hidden curriculum strongly suggests, the basic regularities of schools excel in teaching the opposite. For example, because of the dominance of individualistic evaluation—both public and private, of oneself and one's peers—in school settings subterfuge, hiding one's real feelings, joy at someone else's failure, and so forth, are quite effectively taught. This occurs merely by the student living within an institution and having to cope with its density, power, and competitiveness.[73]

The implications of these counterexamples are rather significant for they indicate that a serious attempt at changing the accepted commonsense conceptions of competence *in practice* may need to change the basic regularities of the institutional structure of schooling itself. The regularities themselves are among the "teaching devices" that communicate lasting norms and dispositions to students, that instruct children in "how the world really is." It is important to notice the critical implications of each of these alternative conceptions for the business, advertising, and other institutions of the larger society as well. They act as potent reminders that criticism of many of the characteristics of schools and social, political, and cultural criticism must go hand in hand. Schools do not exist in a vacuum.

For instance, much of the labeling process that I have been examining here has at its roots a concern for efficiency. That is, schools as agents of both social control and cultural and economic reproduction in some sense need to operate as efficient organizations and labeling helps a good deal in this.[74] As much activity as possible must be rationalized and made goal specific so that cost effectiveness and smoothness of operation are heightened and "waste," inefficiency, and uncertainty are eliminated. Furthermore, conflict and argumentation over goals and procedures must be minimized so as not to jeopardize existing goals and procedures. After all, there is a good deal of economic and psychological investment in these basic institutional regularities. Techniques for the control and manipulation of difference must be developed, then, in order to prevent disorder of any significant sort from encroaching on institutional life. If significant difference (either intellectual, aesthetic, valuative or normative) is found, it must be incorporated, redefined into categories that can be handled by existing bureaucratic and ideological assumptions. The fact that these assumptions are relatively unexamined and are, in fact, *self-confirming* as long as educators employ categories that grow out of them is forgotten.

However, to point to the schools as the originators of this concern for efficiency above all else in education that I have analyzed in these last two chapters is too limited an appraisal. The roots of this perspective lie in an ideology that provides the constitutive framework for thought and action in all corporate societies, an instrumental ideology that places efficiency, standardized technique, profit, increasing division and control of labor, and consensus at its very heart. Consequently, the caughtness of schools and especially the curriculum field in what Kliebard has called a factory model[75] is part of a larger social problem concerning the lack of responsive of our major institutions to human needs and sentiment. To lose sight of this is to miss much of the real problem.

As we have seen, however, recognition of the dialectical relationship between schools and economic and cultural control is not something educators are used to looking for. This is really something of a problem of *misrecognition*, one that is compounded by the ideological saturation of educators' consciousness. Since educators employ the achievement and socialization traditions uncritically, the labels, categories, and legitimate knowledge generated from such perspectives are seen as natural. The real relations that these "differentiations, evaluations, and judgments of worth" have to the social division of labor and to economic and cultural control are obscured by the seemingly neutral scientific status of the perspectives themselves. Taken together, they provide an ideal agency of hegemony.

There is a complex combination of forces at work here. The selective tradition operates so that the cultural capital that has contributed to the rise of and continued domination by powerful groups and classes is transformed into legitimate knowledge and is used to create the categories by which students are dealt with. Because of the school's economic role in differentially distributing a hidden curriculum to different economic, cultural, racial, and sexual groups, linguistic, cultural, and class differences from the "normal" will be maximally focused upon and will be labeled as deviant. Technical knowledge will then be used as an intricate filter to stratify students according to their "ability" to contribute to its production. This, thereby, increases the sense of the neutrality of this process of economic and cultural stratification and both covers and makes more legitimate the actual workings of power and ideology in an unequal society. As Bourdieu and Passeron so forcefully put it, "Every power which manages to impose meanings and to impose them as legitimate by concealing the power relations which are the basis of its force, adds its own specifically symbolic force to those power relations."[76]

It is in the combination between the school's use of "neutral" perspectives embodying the interests of technical control and certainty, and the way schools serve the interests of economic and cultural reproduction, that schools carry out their varied functions. Technical perspectives, ones taught to and used by educators *as* mere procedures, complement the needs of an unequal society for the maximization of the production of technical knowledge, the distribution of an acritical and positivistic perspective, and the production of agents with the appropriate norms and values to roughly fill the requirements of the ongoing division of labor in society.[77] This is a dialectical process. Schools *make legitimate* the role of such technical and positivistic knowledge, as well. They, thereby, can employ it as a set of supposedly neutral procedures, ones based on "ultimately right principles," to stratify students according to their contribution to its maximization and to economic needs. Cultural forms, hence, residing at the very bottom of our brains, working in tandem with the nexus of relations the school has to the economic arena, help recreate the ideological and structural hegemony of the powerful.

The overt curriculum, the hidden curriculum, and the history of each, are tied to the categories we employ so easily to give meaning to our day to day activity, which are in turn tied to and justify social interests. It may be hard to see the results of our programmatic and intellectual labors as contributing to hegemony. Yet, by seeing how these elements fit together, relationally, with the actual structures of domination in a society, we can now begin to see the mechanisms through which cultural and economic reproduction operate in schools. In so doing, we get a clearer picture of why "Them that has, gets." Because of many of the "determinations" I have examined in this volume, in schools as in other institutions, they *do* get.

CHAPTER 8

Beyond Ideological Reproduction

Real Knowledge and Real Power

In his suggestive examination of the formation of ideological consciousness in corporate societies, Stanley Aronowitz helps trace the development of a particular idea that has come to rest at the bottom of our brains. The idea and its ideological function are quite similar to the thread that guided the analysis of my previous chapters, and especially in Chapter 7. He argues that hegemony operates in large part through the control of meaning, through the "manipulation" of the very categories and modes of thinking we commonsensically employ. Thus, there is an "internal tendency of capitalism to increasingly give relationships between *people* the character of relationships between *things*. Commodity production intrudes into all corners of the social world."[1] And the unequal social world that educators live in is represented by the reification, the commodification, of the very language they use. Cultural control, hence, as both Gramsci and Williams noted, acts as an important reproductive force. Through the definition, incorporation, and selection of what is considered legitimate or "real" knowledge, through positing a false consensus on what are appropriate facts, skills, hopes, and fears (and the way we all should evaluate them), the economic and cultural apparatus are dialectically linked. Here knowledge *is* power, but primarily in the hands of those who have it already, who already control cultural capital as well as economic capital.

We have come a long way in understanding the connections between what ideas are considered "real knowledge" in a society and the inequality of economic and cultural power in advanced industrial societies since Marx. *The German Ideology*, where he articulated his dictum that "the ruling class will give its ideas the form of universality and represent them as the only rational universally valid ones," still serves as one major starting point, however, in any attempt to explicate the relationships that exist among knowledge, ideology, and power. That is, however complex one's analysis is (and certainly needs to be), a fundamental guiding principle of such investigations is to establish the connections between the dominant ideas of a society and the interests of particular classes and groups.

Unfortunately, this has been interpreted by many people as something of a conspiracy theory—e.g., there is a relatively small number of men and women of power consciously conspiring to suppress the lower classes. Yet, Marx himself undoubtedly meant something more complicated than this assertion. His point, one that has provided the constitutive framework for this volume's investigation of ideology and curriculum, was that "naturally" generated out of the productive relations among individuals and social groups will be "the principles, the ideas, the categories" that conform to and support these (unequal) productive relations.[2]

My earlier sentence is somewhat misleading, however. While I said "We have come a long way . . . ," it is still problematic as to who is to be included in that group. For, as I noted in Chapters 1 and 2, the "we" here speaks to individuals and groups of concerned people who have affiliated with what might best be called the tradition of neo-Marxist scholarship. And this "we" does not usually include sociologists of education or curriculum researchers, perhaps due to the (understandable) ameliorative intent which guides both fields.[3]

As we have seen, the usual traditions in both the sociology of education and in the field of curriculum treat school knowledge, those "principles, ideas, and categories" that are preserved and reside in our educational institutions, as relatively neutral. The focus has been on measures of the acquisition of information, propensities, skills, and dispositions and the effect of such acquisition on later life. The greater the acquisition of such knowlege, the usual "paradigms" go, the greater the success of the school. The alternative tradition I have employed here, one that has deep roots in the sociology of knowledge and in critical sociology, has understood the forms of curricular knowledge somewhat differently. It has seen them as potential mechanisms of socio-economic selection and control, and thus has interpreted them, at least partially, through the lens of Marx's dictum.

This alternative tradition is not seen by its participants (the "we") as being merely one school of thought among many, though. Rather, and here I am in strong agreement, the focus has been on the necessary *prior* questions that must be asked before (and perhaps instead of) one engages in the usual types of research on school knowledge. Thus a prior set of questions to those usually asked about school success and failure (e.g., Did the students achieve such and such a level of knowledge?) has been of a different logical and political type (Whose knowledge is it? Why is it being taught to this particular group, in this particular way? What are its real or latent functions in the complex connections between cultural power and the control of the modes of production and distribution of goods and services in an advanced industrial economy like our own?). Only when we can respond to these types of questions does it make sense to inquire about our relative success in promoting the acquisition of particular forms of cultural capital.

Now it should be obvious that these kinds of prior investigations have to do with ideological questions. For political and conceptual reasons, they both criticize existing modes of research into curriculum and suggest a serious research program as an alternative. As Young and Bernstein have stressed repeatedly, while there has been some awareness of the ideological character of aspects of education, there has been little or no awareness until quite recently that the very form and content of classroom messages, of day to day school life, embody ideological "transmissions." In order to correct this, the selection and transmission of knowledge and the ideas which guide them, then, need to become a primary focus of critically oriented sociological and curricular investigation into schools.[4]

Seen in this light, the study of curriculum, of what is considered appropriate school knowledge and the principles used to select and value it, is part of a larger problem. Throughout this volume my point has been that such inquiry provides one area through which we can examine the cultural and economic reproduction of class relations in unequal societies. Because of this, it is important to note that such investigations into the creation and recreation of hegemony get their primary meaning not "merely" because of their contribution to our understanding, though this is important to be sure. Their meaning also comes from situating them into a larger politically progressive movement. In fact, there is a political point to be made here about how such a progressive political and economic movement (and its accompanying understanding) advances. Such a movement must embody a *collective commitment* toward understanding. This commitment to shared progress is something of a neo-Marxist vision, of course, when it is put in political terms and is best described by the late Lucien Goldmann.[5]

> To my mind, the principal specific characteristic of Marxist thought is the concept of the *collective subject:* the affirmation that, historically, effective action is never taken by isolated individuals but by social groups, and that it is only in relation to these that one can understand events, modes of behavior, and institutions.

For rhetorical purposes, Goldmann has overstated his argument a bit, but the implications of his point are quite important in thinking about our own work. It is only through our commitment to collectively examine each other's work, to use and go beyond what may be no longer utile or what may be weaker than it might, and then stand on each other's shoulders, that serious progress can be made in our collective understanding of and action on institutions like schools.

Thus, we should not expect that one person will answer, or even pose, all of the important questions concerning what might best be seen as the relation between power and knowledge. Certainly, I have not done so in this volume. Rather, concrete groups of people affiliated with a larger social and intellectual tradition become exceptionally important. Others, perhaps criticizing and working off of what I have written here, will lead to further political and conceptual clarity.

Obviously, there are still important steps to be taken in the program of analysis into the sociology and economics of school knowledge that I have articulated here. Therefore, I would like to suggest some paths such analyses might fruitfully take. While there is a danger of reducing all school knowledge to ideological knowledge, and this would be an analytically silly assertion (is one plus one ideological?), there is still much to be done on the question of which specific groups control curriculum selection in schools.[6] Whose cultural capital, both overt and covert, is placed "within" the school curriculum? Whose vision of economic, racial, and sexual reality, whose principles of economic reality, whose principles of social justice, are embedded in the content of schooling? These questions deal with power and economic resources and control (and with the ideology and economics of the corporate publishing industry, as well). They are probably best gotten at by a neo-Marxist analysis of *actual* cultural content. In so doing, they need to be uncovered in their concrete representations in schools.

In order to accomplish this, we need a thoroughgoing critical sociology of cultural forms that is linked to how these cultural artifacts are distributed in society. Therefore, the study of the relationship between ideology and curriculum needs to see itself as having strong connections to socio-economic appraisals of other social mechanisms that preserve and distribute popular and elite culture. The work of Lukacs, Williams, and Goldmann, for instance, becomes quite important if we are to begin to understand how both the content and form of school knowledge, like the content and form of major novels and dramas, are related to structures of the social environment of individualistically oriented advanced industrial economies like our own.[7] The knowledge that gets into school—those "legitimate principles, ideas, and categories"— grows out of a particular history and a particular economic and political reality. It needs to be understood by situating it back into that socio-economic context.

But how is this to be accomplished? To grapple more completely with the relationship between ideology and culture, between power and knowledge, such inquiries require linkages between our considerations of the forms which dominate schools and a more structural analysis of the kinds of imaginative possibilities that are seen as legitimate by the larger society. So, for example, we would have to inquire not only into overt and hidden school knowledge and the ideological, ethical, and valuative underpinnings of the ways we ordinarily think about our activity in schools as I have done here, but also into the other aspects of a society's cultural apparatus. Television and mass media, museums and billboards, films and books, all make lasting contributions to the social distribution, organization, and, above all, control of meaning.[8] These artifacts, when added to the concerns about curricula I have focused upon in this book, can then be linked in such a way that we can untangle how the cultural organization of human qualities is related to the historically evolving conditions of unequal economic systems like ours.[9]

These kinds of investigations do not stand alone, of course. A structural theory of school knowledge, and the problem of the cultural and economic reproduction of class relations that stands behind it, is part of a larger task of demonstrating both analytically and empirically that "naturally" generated out of the existing economic, social, and cultural arrangements of our society are inequalities. These inequalities are not fixable maladjustments, if you will, but instead are regularized. They are dialectically interwoven and connected to questions of economic and cultural power and control.[10] Thus, any serious concern for the relationship between ideology and curriculum is made even more potent to the extent that it aims, as well, at explicating the political economy of formal education. In fact, it may be next to impossible to do one without the other.[11]

Throughout this book, my position has embodied a political commitment. Implicit in my exploration of some aspects of the ways schools and intellectuals function in the cultural and economic reproduction of class relations is a claim that it is very difficult for educational and social theory to be neutral. Thus, as I argued in Chapter 1, curricular and more general educational research needs to have its roots in a theory of economic and social justice, one which has as its prime focus increasing the advantage and power of the least advantaged. To argue for this is also to argue that both the topics of our theories and research and the ultimate explanations of the relations among the phenomena being studied are often tacitly judgments about the kind of society in which we live.[12] Perhaps as we become clearer in our judgments about the kind of society in which we live, then our understanding of the role schools play in the reproduction of that society will become clearer as well. I have tried here to show where the collective search for such understanding might profitably go, both conceptually and politically. For, after all, the personal judgment about our role in the society in which we live is not an abstract issue. It is one we must all face. To do less is to fill the role of the abstract individual, one who does not take it upon him or herself to inquire into the actual relationships one has to the concrete groups of people who produce the conditions that enable us to do our work. To fail to think relationally about this would indeed document Williams's assertion that our very idea of community is withered at its root.

Perhaps Williams is correct. The conceptual rules we employ to define our situations, that we use to design our schools and select the traditions that are to be preserved and distributed by them, show a signal neglect of such critical appraisals. To overcome this neglect would require a critical and coherent theory of the social order in which we live. But this is exactly the point. For not only have we failed to situate the knowledge we teach, the schools we help maintain, and ourselves back into the basic structural relations of which they are a part, we have misrecognized the differential benefits of these basic structures themselves.

This is not unimportant. Just as our commonsense practices, values, and theories in education are aspects of hegemony, our awareness (or lack of it) of the workings of the structures of our political and economic system operates in a similar fashion. It also causes us to not think structurally or relationally. It sets limits on the range of interpretations we give to define our economic, cultural, and political system. Instead, we substitute an uncritical notion—one distributed by schools, the media, and other mechanisms of an effective dominant culture—of pluralistic democracy which does not provide an adequate definition of how interest and power actually operate in an advanced corporate economy.

Navarro's arguments about the nature of "pluralism" in an unequal society are instructive here, especially his points about how a vision of pluralistic democracy covers the very real conflicts that exist and the differential uses of power to get what particular groups want at the expense of other groups.[13]

> Let me stress here that the predominance of members of the corporate and upper middle classes in our political corridors of power is not the cause but rather a symptom of the pattern of class dominance in our society. Also, let me further underline that I do not assume that the corporate class, or any other class for that matter, is uniform or that all its members share the same interests. Indeed, social classes are divided according to power blocs that compete for political influence, and it is this competition that usually passes in our media and academia as the "great U.S. pluralism." But in that competition for political influence, power blocs from the upper-middle class and from the corporate class consistently wield far, far more influence over the organs of the state than power blocs belonging to the lower-middle and working classes. As Schattschneider has indicated, "The flaw in the pluralistic heaven is that the heavenly chorus sings with a very special accent . . . The system is askew, loaded, and unbalanced in favor of a fraction of a minority." Indeed, underlying and transcending these specific power bloc interests, there are far more important class interests that are paramount in explaining the political behavior of our system. Thus, more frequently than not, federal legislation produces a consistent pattern of effects that benefit the 20 per cent at the top more than the 80 per cent at the bottom of our society.

Thus, economic capital goes to economic capital. And even though our ideological persuasions make us believe otherwise, political form and the economic interests of the powerful are joined in the actual benefits naturally generated out of this conjuncture.

I have tried to illuminate how this close connection between power and control that exists between government and the dominant classes which Navarro describes also exists between the school and these groups. It is by blending together economic and cultural analysis, and by focusing on the historical and current mechanisms which allow educators and schools to continue their roles in reproducing the abstract individual, the selective tradition, ideological consensus, and hegemony, that these kinds of connections can be made clear.

Beyond Reproduction

Throughout this book, I have used the language of distribution and reproduction. This language has had the conceptual benefit of helping to disclose the power of existing institutions to enhance themselves, to set limits both on a social order and on our ways of thinking about it so that the advantages of those with cultural and economic capital are maximized. Yet, even with this kind of conceptual benefit, the very metaphors I have had recourse to here can cover something up themselves. The notion of reproduction can lead to an assumption that there is (and perhaps can be) no significant resistance to such power.[14] This is not the case. The continuing struggle for democratic and economic rights by workers, the poor, women, Blacks, Native Americans, Latinos, and others serves as a potent reminder of the possibility and actuality of concrete action. A good deal of this struggle remains relatively uncoordinated and without a coherent theory of social justice behind it. Some of it has been "incorporated" into paths which pose no threat whatsoever to established interests.[15] Much of it remains unreported in the media and unrecorded in the "legitimate knowledge" we find in schools. However, the very fact that there are once again serious democratic socialist oriented movements and study groups on the shop floor, that there are labor history study groups among teachers and administrators in numerous schools, that there is concrete scholarship, debate, and renewed interest at universities, among oppressed groups, and elsewhere about Marxist theory and collective action, all point to the problem of using the notion of reproduction uncritically.

Certainly, we must be honest about the ways power, knowledge, and interest are interrelated and made manifest, about how hegemony is economically and culturally maintained. But, we also must remember that *the very sense of personal and collective futility that may come from such honesty is itself an aspect of an effective dominant culture.* As an ideological form, it can lead us away from concrete action on the conditions which deny us "the values we most prize."

There is another side of this question of a sense of futility, however. It involves the concomitant belief that any action on a day to day ameliorative level in schools, the work place, and elsewhere merely shores up an unequal system. This position is just as problematic.

The notion that all ameliorative action is something of an unconscious bribe paid by liberal reformers to women, Blacks, workers, and others, one that keeps them from pressing for more dramatic changes, is an odd position, I think. It rests on a rather too simplistic probability assumption. It assumes there is something of a one-to-one correspondence between attempting to make life somehow better today or in the near future and preventing a revolution that will naturally arise if we just wait for conditions to get bad enough. The logic here is quite odd to say the least. The status of the word "naturally" is obviously rather strange since it implies a return to a mechanistic conception of history. It assumes that there are immutable laws of economic and political development, ones that are not shaped and reshaped by the real human practice of conscious groups of human actors.

Further, such a notion is strangely ahistorical. As Aileen Kelly has made clear in her comments on the relationship between socialist politics and ameliorative reform, such struggles to better the day to day conditions of our economic and cultural institutions are critical. They can develop into what she has called "political battles."[16] That is, only by action on day to day issues can a critical framework be made sensible. Not to engage in such well-thought-out action is to lose the opportunity for political education and for testing one's theories in actual praxis.[17]

Whither Curriculum?

These points have important implications for rethinking some of our own ideological position as curriculists, researchers, and educators aside from the suggestions for further analyses I discussed earlier in this concluding chapter. In order to take them seriously, our movement should be progressively away from the current "quasi-scientific" and management framework, one that has its roots in the achievement and socialization traditions that now guide most of the field's endeavors, and should consistently move toward a political and ethical structure. While there is certainly a need for technical expertise in the field—after all, curriculists are called upon to assist in the designing and creating of concrete environments based on our differing educational visions—all too often a technical and efficiency perspective supplies the problems, and other considerations such as those analyzed in this volume are afterthoughts, if they are indeed considered at all. A more appropriate relationship would require that educational "science" and technical competence be secured firmly within a framework that continually seeks to be self-critical and places both one person's responsibility to treat another person ethically and justly and the search for a set of economic and cultural institutions that make such collective responsibility possible at the center of its deliberations.

Habermas extends these arguments and their implications for the reconstruction of curriculum research and practice. He argues that the controlling and bureaucratized institutions of societies like our own require increasing scientific and technical knowledge. The research communities, for example, generate new rationalities and techniques that make further control and domination of individuals and groups by economic and ideological forces possible. However, while these communities produce data that support existing institutionalized rubrics and mechanisms for reproduction and control, they are also in an increasingly pivotal strategic position. Because of the structural contradictions within universities and because the basic social norms that ideally guide the various "scientific" and "intellectual" communities rest strongly upon a foundation of open and honest communication,[18] there is a potential within these groups, as well as in the working class, woman's movement, and others, for the recognition of the unnecessary control and domination that exists in many of the institutions of society. In addition, the turning around of even a small portion of the community of educational scholars and practitioners to recognize the quasi-neutral perspectives that dominate their actions, rationality, language, and investigations would have the positive effect of illuminating the way educational and other forms of social research and amelioration miss the ethical, economic and political meaning of their work.[19] In other words, the development of a critical perspective within the educational community can "contribute to the creation of alternative programs of research and development" that challenge the commonsense assumptions that underpin the field.

Just as important, in this way:[20]

> Knowledge can be generated that relates to the needs of the peoples who are trying to build social community, resist cultural manipulation, facilitate decentralization movements, and in general contribute to the actualization of human needs that are otherwise ignored. By reorienting the scientific community, or at least a significant section of it, [critical perspectives] can become a material force for change by counteracting the current drift of science toward the formation and implementation of state policy.

These arguments imply that advocacy models of research and practice are critically needed if substantial progress is to be made.

Reality has to be faced here though. To many people, the very idea of regaining any real control over social institutions and personal development is abstract and "nonsensical." In general, hegemony does exist and many people do see society's economic, social, and educational institutions as basically self-directing, with little need for their participation and with little necessity for them to communicate and argue over the ends and means of these same institutions. Even though the disintegration of aspects of family life, schools, work, health, etc., is often evident (though the centralization of control of these aspects of our collective life is becoming more covered by liberal and pluralistic rhetoric), the basic categories of corporate logic have become so commonsensical that many people no longer even see a need for emancipation, other than an anomic sense that pervades certain segments of the population. This makes the development of a *critical* curriculum community, for example, all the more essential since it is here that a *part* of the systematic criticism of the basic categories and practices that grow out of and help produce both problematic institutions and agents who fill them can originate. That is, one of the fundamental conditions of emancipation is the ability to "see" the actual functionings of institutions in all their positive *and* negative complexity, to illuminate the contradictions of extant regularities, and, finally, to assist others (and let them assist us) in "remembering" the possibilities of spontaneity, choice, and more equal models of control.[21]

This means that curriculists must take an advocacy position on a number of critical fronts, both in and outside of education. Among the most important "internal" stances would be that of support for student rights (and the democratic rights of teachers, oppressed groups, and others). Since curriculum as a field has as one of its primary concerns the task of creating access to knowledge and tradition, especially those areas that have been victims of selective tradition, the question of a student's right to have free access to politically and culturally honest information and to public expression based on this cannot be divorced from our own pursuit of just educative environments.[22]

Not only should an advocacy and critical model guide us in the economic, legal, and cultural rights questions of students, teachers, and oppressed groups, but other issues abound in the increasing use of therapeutic models in education, models that serve as excuses to change the individual child rather than the social and intellectual structure of the school to make it more responsive and responsible.

Consider, for instance, the current rapid growth of a "treatment" language on the part of educators. Behavior modification or a behavioral objectives approach again can offer good examples of this. Educators talk of giving certain specifiable "treatments" to bring about certain specifiable "results" or outcomes. Discounting the fact that the supposed cause and effect relationships between treatment and outcome are rather psychologically and logically difficult to establish, there are ethical and especially legal implications concerning the perspectives out of which clinical and therapeutic categories, labels, and procedures arise that must be brought to the fore and that can provide tactical means for challenging many of the common practices within educational institutions.

A number of legal scholars have taken the position that before therapeutic programs of any sort may be engaged in, there are a number of criteria that must be satisfied. First, we must be satisfied that the motive behind them is truly therapeutic and *that it is unlikely to be perverted into merely a mechanism of social control.* As we have seen, however, all too much of curriculum work in the past, however, has functioned in exactly this way. This is especially true of the control ideology in the evaluation and testing movement,[23] though much the same thing could be said about many educational practices we continue to employ, the types of institutions we design, and the forms of interaction that dominate them. This questioning must be seen not only in relation to the past and present but also in terms of future uses. No broad programs of diagnosis and treatment, of remediation, amelioration, and "help," should be given institutional endorsement on the grounds that practitioners require a good deal more flexibility in the methods they may use to be more effective, without at the same time showing clearly that it does not exceed what is necessary to reach its goals (if in fact the goals and means are ethically, politically, and educationally *just*).

Second, the program must demonstrate, *prior to its implementation,* that it is capable of accomplishing its goals. Without this, "the program may become an intervention into people's lives and liberties for no acceptable purpose. The individual will have been sacrificed, and society will have gained nothing." Third, and perhaps most important for my own analysis here, *any undesirable side effects, any latent outcomes of such interference into the life of an individual that can possibly be foreseen must be known beforehand and properly weighed.*[24] As I have shown here, some of the contradictions and latent ethical and political outcomes of our own work are indeed profound.

Educators have much to learn from the fact that new and increasingly subtle techniques of social and behavioral control seem to generate an impetus that causes them to be generalized beyond their immediate situation. Therefore, any proposed use of them must be examined quite carefully and at the least must embody procedural safeguards for students and parents that prevent the abuse of the programs and which guarantee that they are compatible with a (supposedly) "pluralistic" and diverse society.[25]

These legal cautions and safeguards are but one step, however, and in fact represent a limited approach to the problem of control and the ethical uses of our commonsense practices and perspectives, though as I noted they may be important in stimulating concrete action and in political education. A second step is to critically examine and raise serious questions about the very basis of these programs and processes and their role in the creation of hegemony. As one final everyday example, consider the growth of, say, a therapy model in such things as the values clarification materials and techniques found in social studies. Are they examples of the continuing transformation of overt class interests into the scientific and liberal language of neutral helping, examples of the power of schooling in extending its rationalizing ethos to even the most private and personal dispositions of students so that they can be better controlled? Are they indicative of the need on the part of a society dominated by interests in control, capital accumulation, instrumental rationality, and certainty to "produce" individuals who feel at home in institutions that have little personal meaning? Are they the equivalent, as I would suspect, of the increasing use of human relations procedures in the work place to enhance the control of blue and white collar labor?[26] While these questions are not easily answered, they must be examined if curriculists and other educators are to be aware of the latent ideological functions of their work.

It should be clear, therefore, that part of the task of establishing a firmer basis for the curriculum field and education in general is for its practitioners to distance themselves from those who control economic and political power and the now rather limited routes to them in this society. By this I do not mean that curriculists should not engage in political and economic argumentation and analysis. *Quite the contrary is the case.* Rather the members of the field need to stand back from its stance of totally accepting the ideology and institutions that prevail in corporate societies like our own. They need to *affiliate* with cultural, political, and economic groups who are self-consciously working to alter the institutional arrangements that set limits on the lives and hopes of so many people in this society. Obviously, this involves a rather difficult form of questioning. However, unless we look to other forms of action and reflection, such as those generated out of the critical traditions to which 1 have referred, ones which may enable us to raise more important issues and engage in effective collective action, we are being less than honest with ourselves. Consequently, what I am arguing for here is a redefinition of our situations, a redefinition that recognizes not the ideologically laden ideal of the unattached intellectual but instead one that takes seriously the passionate involvement Gramsci called for in his notion of the *organic* intellectual who actively participates in the struggle against hegemony.[27]

One final set of issues needs to be faced quite openly at the end, I believe. Can we as educators honestly cope with the probability that certainty will not be forthcoming, that many of our answers and our actions will be situational and filled with ambiguity? With this in mind, how do we commit ourselves to action? Part of the response to that is the realization that our very commitment to rationality in the widest sense of the term *requires* us to begin the dialectic of critical understanding that will be part of political praxis. Yet another part of the response is illuminated by my arguments in this book. Even our "neutral" activity may not be so. Our work already serves ideological interests. One has no choice but to be committed.

CHAPTER 9

Pedagogy, Patriotism, and Democracy

Ideology and Education after September 11

Introduction

Throughout this book my arguments have centered on the complex ways in which ideology works in education. As I have documented, issues of power are at the very core of our understanding (and *mis*-understanding) of the realities of curriculum, pedagogy, and evaluation and about who gets helped and hurt by our commonsense assumptions about education. Common sense is complicated. As I have documented at much greater length elsewhere,[1] it has contradictory impulses and contains element of both "good sense" and "bad sense." This means that the ways in which ideological tensions are worked out and the ways in which hegemonic relations are constituted, reconstituted, and challenged will themselves be quite complex and will change given new historical realities.

We are living in one of those times when new historical realities are being created before our very eyes. Relations of dominance and subordination are being reconstituted in truly major ways. The horrific events surrounding 9/11, the creation of a new version of a national security state, the withering of long-fought-for protections of crucial civil liberties that some of the political leaders of such a state say it requires, the invasion of Iraq without UN sanction and against the will of the majority of nations, the continued stifling of dissent and criticism of what have clearly been errors of immense proportion, the building of what seems all too much like an arrogant American empire, and the list could go on—all of these things have come together in powerful ways. It is not an overstatement to point out the very real parallels between what is happening today and the McCarthyism that was discredited years ago. All of these things are having major effects on how we think about the relationship between culture and power, about who is inside and outside of "our" community, about what we should teach and learn in schools and the cultural apparatus in general to prepare ourselves for understanding the lives and realities so many people are now facing nationally and internationally. Indeed, some of the ideological positions now circulating so widely could have been said just as easily by the historical figures discussed in this volume—Thorndike, Bobbit,

Charters, Snedden. As we are witnessing, revolutions can be conservative. They can go backwards.

After decades of struggles against the forces I identify in *Ideology and Curriculum*, many gains were made by critically oriented teachers, community activists, and members of oppressed and dispossessed groups. Such progress was hard won. Granted it was often halting, and sometimes the gains represented compromises with dominant groups that were taken back during the period of economic and ideological attack on the public sphere by neo-liberal and neo-conservative forces that we have been living under for too long a time. But spaces for counter-hegemonic work were opened up and the gains in education and other parts of society were real.[2] Yet dominant groups have used the current crisis to attempt to turn back the clock. A number of the conservative forces I analyze in this book have returned powerfully. They have returned not only because of the economic, political, cultural, and social capital that they possess, although that has played a large part in their resurgence. Nor is the only reason their very clever Gramscian understanding that to win in the state you must win in civil society. Nor is this return only due to their strategy of redefining the meanings of key ideological concepts that organize our common sense such as democracy and citizenship.[3] Each and every one of these elements is crucial of course, but sometimes dominance returns not because of clever plans, but because of historical events that are "accidental," that are not predictable. Dominant groups are able to bring large groups of people under their leadership because they have already prepared the ideological ground for our understanding of these events and have helped create what Raymond Williams called "structures of feeling," which make it harder to withstand the neo-liberal and neo-conservative elements that have slowly but effectively become integral parts of our common sense.[4] Thus, even when it is not planned, hegemonic meanings and the differential power relations that they legitimate may get reconstituted in damaging ways. This chapter takes the catastrophic horror of 9/11 as an example of how this may happen.

After 9/11

The volume of material that has been published on the September 11 tragedy has been extensive. While some of it has been filled with an uncritical acceptance of official views on the subject, a good deal of it has been considerably more nuanced and self-critical about the role that the United States may have played in helping to generate the conditions that led to the kinds of despair that might make some people believe that such action could be a legitimate response to U.S. hegemony. I do not think that there is any way to justify the acts of 9/11, but I do think that they cannot be understood in isolation from the international and national contexts out of which they arose. I will leave an exploration of the international context to others.[5]

In this chapter I want to do something else—to bring ideology up to date, so to speak, so that elements of both what I call in Chapter 1 *strain* and *conflict* theories are brought to bear on what has happened. I wish to focus on the most local of levels: the complicated ways in which 9/11 was experienced phenomenologically by teachers such as myself, and the little-known effects it had on pedagogy and on the urge to have schools participate in a complicated set of patriotic discourses and practices that swept over the United States in the wake of the disaster. Given this focus, parts of my analysis will need to be personal. I do this not because I think that I have any better purchase on reality than the reader, but because all of us may be better able to understand the lived effects of 9/11 and its participation in complex ongoing ideological transformations by exploring what it meant to identifiable social actors like myself. Thus I start at the personal level, but my aim is to participate in a collective project in which people from many different social locations and positions tell the stories of what 9/11 meant, and continues to mean, for their lives and educational practices.

I then discuss the impact of 9/11 on the politics of the local, on the school board in Madison, Wisconsin, where I live. Here we shall see that the politics of "patriotism" made it much more difficult for schools at all levels to engage in social criticism or even meaningful dialogue about U.S. policies and economic power. As we shall also see, 9/11 had powerful and worrisome effects that are often hidden in our rush to use schools for patriotic purposes in much the same ways as the more repressive parts of the Americanization project acted during previous decades of U.S. history.

Horror and Hollywood

"Damn. Who could be calling now?" My annoyance was palpable. This was one of the increasingly rare mornings that I had been able to carve out uninterrupted time to devote myself to serious writing. I ran from my computer to the phone, hoping not to lose the line of thought I was struggling with. The call was from one of my most politically active students.

"Michael, do you have your TV on? Put it on *now, quickly*! The World Trade Center is *collapsing*. It's unbelievable. We're in for a new McCarthyism! What do you think we should *do*!"

I put the TV on. You'll forgive me, but the first words out of my mouth were "Holy shit!" I sat. I watched. But this was decidedly not passive watching. Mesmerized is exactly the wrong word here. As the buildings collapsed, my mind was filled with an entire universe of competing and contradictory emotions and meanings. This wasn't the O.J. slow-motion caravan. Nor was it like my experience of being a young teacher when Kennedy was assassinated. At that time, I was giving a spelling test when the shooting was announced over the school's loudspeaker. I kept giving the test, too shocked to do anything else.

Yes, like the Kennedy experience there was the intense shock of the surreally slow-motion plane, of the collapsing towers, and worst of all of people jumping out of buildings. But I had changed and so had the cultural assemblage around which one made interpretive sense of what was happening.

At nearly exactly the same time as I felt immense horror at the World Trade Center disaster, something else kept entering into the lenses with which I saw the images on the screen. The key word here is exactly that—"screen." It seemed almost unreal. The explosions weren't large enough or dramatic enough to seem real. It was as if I expected Bruce Willis to come running out of the collapsing buildings after a fireball of gargantuan proportions lit up the sky. The fireball was too small. The scene of the plane as it headed for the second tower—a scene broadcast over and over and over again as if there was something of a perverse politics of pleasure at work—was too undramatic, to unemotional, (as if it needed a musical crescendo to tell us of the impending tragedy). The only word I can use to describe that part of this welter of meanings and emotions was that even though I had prided myself on being critically conscious of the ways that our dominant commodified cultural forms worked, I too had been "Hollywoodized". The horror of death meets *The Towering Inferno*. But the falling bodies always brought me back to reality. It was *that* sight that brought the carnage back home.

Like many people I am certain, I sat and watched—for hours. Interviews, screaming people running away, running toward, but always running—or seeking cover. Another plane—this one missing. What was its target? Then came the news that the Pentagon was hit. This created an even more complex set of interpretations and readings. Why did I have even more complicated emotions now? I had marched on the Pentagon against the Vietnam War. I had been tear-gassed there. It was the seat of American military might and power. For one fleeting moment I felt that somehow it almost *deserved* to be a target. And yet real people were killed there—real people who worked there not only out of choice but because, in a U.S. economy that was what is best called military Keynesianism (use government funding to prop up the economy—but by channeling huge amounts of that money into military-related enterprises), the Pentagon and similar sites were where many of the jobs *were*.

By that night and throughout the days and nights that followed, the ruling pundits took charge of the public expression of what were the legitimate interpretations of the disaster. The visual construction of authority on the screen and the spoken texts themselves will provide critical media analysts with enough data to once again demonstrate how power is performed in public, how the combination of somber setting, the voices of righteousness, and the tropes of patriotism and vengeance all work together to create a mighty call, not for justice but for vengeance.[6] (This is one of the reasons that I and many others joined forces to create the Justice not Vengeance movement in towns and cities throughout the nation.)

In understanding this, I try to remember that the media not only help us construct the nature of the problems we face, but they are powerful mobilizing tools. And everywhere one turns after 9/11 there are voices on the media saying the same thing. Dissident voices are not totally silent, but the shock has affected them as well, and their messages are muted. We are at war. Terrorists are here. Freedom has taken a horrible blow, but God is on our side. We cannot afford the luxury of worrying about civil liberties. Lenient policies toward immigrants, the defunding and depowering of the FBI and the CIA, our diminished military strength, all of these and so much more were nearly the only official response. There must be one unitary reply. Track *them* down in all places at all costs. Find their supporters wherever they may be, especially if they are here. Any questions about *why* so many people in so many nations might have been mistrustful of—indeed sometimes hated—the United States is seen as nearly unpatriotic; they could not be tolerated at this time. Oh, these questions might be worth asking, but after *we* had destroyed the threat to our very way of life that international terrorism represented. Of course, even asking the question "Why do they hate us?" is itself part of the problem. At the same time, I also realize that by constructing the binary of *we/they*, the very nature of the question establishes center/periphery relations that are fully implicated in the production of a reactionary common sense. Good/bad terms have always dominated the American political landscape, especially in terms of international relations.

How can we interpret this? Speaking very generally, large parts of the American public have little patience with the complexities of international relations and even less knowledge of United States' complicity in supporting and arming dictatorial regimes; nor does it have a developed and nuanced understanding of U.S. domination of the world economy, of the negative effects of globalization, of the environmental effects of its wasteful energy policies and practices, and so much more, despite the nearly heroic efforts of critics of U.S. international policy such as Noam Chomsky.[7] This speaks to the reality of the selective tradition in official knowledge and in the world beyond our borders that the news portrays. Even when there have been gains in the school curriculum—environmental awareness provides a useful example—these have been either adopted in their safest forms[8] or they fail to internationalize their discussions. Recycling bottles and cans is good; connections between profligate consumption of a disproportionate share of the world's resources and our daily behavior are nearly invisible in schools or the mainstream media. In this regard, it is helpful to know that the majority of nonbusiness vehicles purchased in the United States are now pickup trucks, minivans, and sport utility vehicles (to say nothing of the Hummer!)—a guarantee that energy conservation will be a discourse unmoored in the daily practices of the U.S. consumer and an even further guarantee that the relationship between U.S. economic and military strategies and the defense of markets and, say, oil resources will be generally interpreted as a fight to protect the "American Way of Life" at all costs.

I mention all this because it is important to place what happened in the wake of September 11 in a context of the "American" psyche and of dominant American self-understandings of the role the United States plays in the world.[9] In the domestic events surrounding September 11, *we* had now become the world's oppressed. The (always relatively weak) recognition of the realities of the Palestinians or the poor in what we arrogantly call the third world were now evacuated. Almost immediately there were a multitude of instances throughout the nation of people who "looked Arabic" being threatened and harassed on the street, in schools, and in their places of business. Less well known, but in my mind of great importance because they show the complexities of peoples' ethical commitments in the face-to-face relations of daily life, were the repeated instances of solidarity including university and community demonstrations of support for Islamic students, friends, and community members. Yet these moments of solidarity, though significant, could not totally make up for such things as Islamic, Punjabi, Sikh, and other students in high schools and at universities being threatened with retaliation, and in the case of some Punjabi secondary school students, being threatened with rape as an act of revenge for September 11. This documents the connections between some elements of national identity and forms of masculinity, a relationship that cries out for serious analysis.[10]

At the universities, some teachers ignored the horror, perhaps for much the same reason that I as a young teacher in 1963 had dealt with the Kennedy assassination by simply resorting to normality as a defense against paralysis. In other classes, days were spent in discussions of the events. Sadness, disbelief, and shock were registered, but just as often, anger and a resurgent patriotism came to the fore. Any critical analysis of the events and of their roots in the hopelessness, denial of dignity, and despair of oppressed peoples—as I and number of my colleagues put forward in our classes and seminars—had to be done extremely cautiously, not only because of the emotionally and politically charged environment even at a progressive university like my own, but also because many of us were not totally immune from some of the same feelings of anger and horror. Even for progressive educators, the events of September 11 worked off of the contradictory elements of good and bad sense we too carried within us and threatened to pull us in directions that, in other times, would have seemed to be simplistic and even jingoistic. But at least for me and the vast majority of my colleagues and graduate students, the elements of good sense won out.

Given these elements of good sense, it was clear that pedagogical work needed to be done. But this wasn't a simple issue, because a constant question, and tension, was always on my mind. How could one condemn the murderous events, give one's students an historical and political framework that puts these events in their larger critical context, and provide a serious forum where disagreement and debate could fruitfully go on so that a politics of marginalization didn't occur in the classes—and at the same time not be seen as somehow justifying the attacks which under no circumstances could be justifiable. While I had very strong feelings about the need to use this as a time both to enable students to reflect on the horrible human tragedy we had just witnessed and to show the effects of U.S. global economic, political, and cultural policies, I also had strong teacherly dispositions that this was also *not* the time to engage in a pedagogy of imposition. One could not come across as saying to students or the public, "Your understandings are simply wrong; your feelings of threat and anger are selfish; any voicing of these emotions and understandings won't be acceptable." This would be among the most counterproductive pedagogies imaginable. Not only would it confirm the already just-near-the-surface perceptions among many people that somehow the left is unpatriotic, but such a pedagogy also could push people into rightist positions, in much the same way as I had argued in my own work about why people "became right."[11] This required a very strategic sense of how to speak and act both in my teaching and in my appearances on national media.

Take my teaching as a major example. I wanted my students to fully appreciate the fact that the U.S.–led embargo of Iraq had caused the death of thousands upon thousands of children each year that it had been in place. I wanted them to understand how U.S. policies in the Middle East and in Afghanistan itself had helped create truly murderous consequences. However, unless their feelings and understandings were voiced and taken seriously, the result could be exactly the opposite of what any decent teacher wants. Instead of a more complicated understanding of the lives of people who are among the most oppressed in the world—often as a result of Western and northern economic and political policies[12]—students could be led to reject any critical contextual understanding largely because the pedagogical politics seemed arrogant. In my experiences both as an activist and a scholar, this has happened more often than some theorists of "critical pedagogy" would like to admit.[13] None of us are perfect teachers, and I am certain that I made more than a few wrong moves in my attempts to structure the discussions in my classes so that they were open and critical at the same time. But I was impressed with the willingness of the vast majority of students to reexamine their anger, to put themselves in the place of the oppressed, to take their more critical and nuanced understandings and put them into action.

Indeed, one of the things that was striking was the fact that a coalition of students in my classes was formed to engage in concrete actions in their own schools and communities, as well as in the university, to interrupt the growing anti-Islamic and jingoistic dynamics that were present even in progressive areas such as Madison and the University of Wisconsin. (This activism was extended later on to create widespread protests against the federal government's and university's imposition of a fee on all foreign students that would be used to cover the costs of their own surveillance "to protect our security." At this writing the fee has been temporarily withdrawn, at least at Wisconsin. Thus, activist coalitions that work against the increasing loss of civil liberties of foreign students and of permanent residents and citizens in the United States have lasted and have continued to engage in mobilizations in important ways. Defending our nation is important, but if we lose the reason this nation should in fact *be* defended, and hence become a very different nation in the process, then the enemies of what is best called "thick" rather than "thin" democracy have won—and we will have lost our ethical and political souls in the meantime.)

This politics of interruption became even more important because these complicated pedagogical issues and the contradictory emotions and politics that were produced in the aftermath of 9/11 were felt well beyond the walls of the university classroom. At times they also had the effect of radically transforming the politics of governance of schooling at a local level in communities throughout the United States. One example from Madison can serve as a powerful reminder of the hidden effects of the circulation of discourses of patriotism and "threat" as they move from the media into our daily lives.

Patriotism, the Flag, and the Control of Schools

On an autumn evening that hinted at the coming of cooler weather, more than 1,200 persons packed the auditorium where the Madison Board of Education had called a special meeting. Flags were everywhere, in hands, on lapels, pasted on jackets. The old and trite phrase that "you could cut the tension with a knife" seemed oddly appropriate here. The tension was somehow *physical*; it could literally be felt, almost like an electrical current that coursed through your body. And for some people present at the hearing, the figures behind the front table deserved exactly that. They needed to be electrically shocked, indeed were almost deserving of something like the electric chair.

Months before the 9/11 disaster the seeds of this conflict had been planted in what were seemingly innocuous ways. Smuggled into the state budget bill was a bit of mischief by conservative legislators seeking to gain some arguing points for the next election. There was a section in the budget authorization bill that required that students in all publicly funded schools publicly recite The Pledge of Allegiance or that schools play or sing the *The Star Spangled Banner,* a national anthem that is a strikingly militaristic song with the added benefit of being nearly impossible for most people—and certainly most children—to sing. Even though the legislation allowed for nonparticipation, given the long and inglorious history of legislation of this kind in the United States, there was a clear implication that such lack of participation was frowned upon. This was something of a time bomb just waiting to explode—and it did. In the midst of the growing patriotic fervor following 9/11, the Madison, Wisconsin, school board voted to follow the law in the most minimalist way possible. For some board members the law seemed to be the wrong way to teach patriotism.

Rote memorization was not the best approach if one actually wanted to provide the conditions for the growth of thoughtful citizenship. For others the law was clearly a political ploy by conservative legislators to try to gain more support among right-wing voters in an upcoming election that was felt to be a close call. For other board members, there were a number of principles at stake. The state should not intervene into the content of local school board decisions of this type. Further, not only had the new law not been subject to close public scrutiny and serious debate, but it threatened the cherished (at least in theory) constitutional right of freedom of dissent. For all of these reasons, a majority of people on the school board voted not to have the mandatory reciting of the pledge or the singing of the anthem in the Madison Public Schools.[14]

Within hours the furor over their decision reached a boiling point. The media made it their major story. Prominent headlines in a local conservative newspaper stated such things as "School Board Bans Pledge of Allegiance," even though the board had actually complied with the formal letter of the law, and even though the board had indeed held public hearings prior to its actions where many people had objected both to the law and to the saying of the pledge and the singing of the anthem. Conservative politicians and spokespersons, colonizing the space of fear and horror over the destruction of the World Trade Center, quickly mobilized. This could not be tolerated. It was not only unpatriotic, but it was disrespectful both to the women and men who died in the disaster and to our military overseas. To those being mobilized, it also was a signal that the board was out of touch with "real" Americans, one more instance of elite control of schools that ignored the wishes of the "silent majority" of "freedom loving" and patriotic Americans.

At the meeting of the school board, approximately fifty percent of the speakers from the audience supported the board's original decision to require neither the pledge nor the singing of the anthem, a fact that was deeply buried in the news accounts that consistently highlighted the conservative mobilization against the board. This is in part because the voices of those who supported the board's vote were often drowned out by the members of the audience who opposed it. A cacophony of hisses, boos, chants, and phrases reminiscent of earlier periods of "red-baiting" greeted each speaker who spoke in favor of the board's actions. Meanwhile, those who spoke out against the board were greeted with applause and loud cheers. (It almost sounded like an Olympics event in which the chant of "USA, USA" could be heard.)

Throughout it all, the board members tried to remain civil and not respond to what were at times quite personal attacks on their patriotism. In many ways the hours upon hours of the meeting and the intense conflicts that ensued could be interpreted as an example of democracy in action. In part, such an interpretation is undoubtedly correct. Yet the harshness of the language, the theater of patriotic symbols, the echoes of war fever, all added up to a politics of intimidation as well. Having said this, there was also a sense of genuine expression of pain and hurt, a recognition that ordinary Americans had been killed and that schools had to recognize the deaths as having occurred among people like ourselves.

The populist notes being struck here are crucial because hegemonic alliances can *only* succeed when they connect with the elements of good sense of the people.[15] Popular worries over one's children and the schools they attend, in a time of radical corporate downsizing and capital flight, worries about social stability and cultural traditions that are constantly being subverted by the commodifying processes and logics of capital, and so much more—all this allows conservative groups to suture these concerns into their own anti-public agenda. Thus, rampant and fearful conservatism and uncritical patriotism are not the only dynamics at work in this situation, even though the overt issue was about the pledge and the anthem. None of this could have happened without the growing fear of one's children's future and over the nature of an unstable paid labor market, and especially without the decades-long ideological project in which the right had engaged to make so many people believe that "big government" was the source of the social, cultural, and economic problems we face.[16]

Yet there were more conjunctural reasons for this response as well. It is always wise to remember that while the state of Wisconsin was the home of much of the most progressive legislation and of significant parts of the democratic socialist tradition in the United States, it also was the home of Senator Joseph McCarthy—yes, the figure for whom McCarthyism is named. Thus, behind the populist and social democratic impulses that have had such a long history here, there lies another kind of populism. This one is what, following Stuart Hall,[17] I have called *authoritarian populism,* a retrogressive assemblage of values that embodies visions of "the people" that have been just as apt to be nationalistic, anti-immigrant, anti-cosmopolitan, anti-communist, pro-military, and very conservative in terms of religious values.[18] In times of crisis these tendencies can come to the fore—and they did with a vengeance.

Of course we cannot understand any of this unless we understand the long history of the struggles over the very meaning of freedom and citizenship in the United States.[19] For all of the protagonists in the school board controversy, what was at stake was *freedom.* For some it was the danger of international terrorism destroying our free way of life. Nothing must interfere with the defense of American freedom, and schools were on the front lines in this defense. For others such freedom was in essence meaningless if it meant that citizens couldn't act on their freedoms, especially in times of crisis. Silencing dissent, imposing forms of compulsory patriotism—these acts were the very antithesis of freedom. A hidden curriculum of compulsory patriotism would, in essence, do exactly this.

This documents an important point. Concepts such as freedom are sliding signifiers. They have no fixed meaning, but are part of a contested terrain in which different visions of democracy exist on a social field of power in which there are unequal resources to influence the publicly accepted definitions of key words. In the words of one of the wisest historians of such concepts:

> The very universality of the language of freedom camouflages a host of divergent connotations and applications. It is pointless to attempt to identify a single "real" meaning against which others are to be judged. Rather than freedom as a fixed category or predetermined concept, . . . it [is] an "essentially contested concept," one that by its very nature is the subject of disagreement. Use of such a concept automatically presupposes an ongoing dialogue with other, competing meanings.[20]

The realization of how concepts such as democracy and freedom act as sliding signifiers and can be mobilized by varying groups with varying agendas returns us to a point I made earlier regarding the ideological project in which the economic and cultural right have engaged. We need to understand that widely successful effects of what Roger Dale and I have called "conservative modernization" have been exactly that—widely successful.[21] We are witnessing—living through is a better phrase—a social/pedagogic project to change our common sense, to radically transform our assumptions about the role of "liberal elites"; of government and the economy; about what are appropriate values; the role of religion in public affairs, gender, and sexuality; race; and a host of other crucial areas. Democracy has been transformed from a political concept to an economic one. Collective senses of freedom that were once much more widespread (although we need to be careful of not romanticizing this) have been largely replaced by individualistic notions of democracy as simply consumer choice. While this has had major effects on the power of labor unions and on other kinds of important collective social movements, it also has created other hidden needs and desires besides those of the rational economic actor who makes calculated individual decisions in a market.[22] I think that these needs and desires have also played a profound role in the mobilization of the seemingly rightist sentiment I have been describing.

Underneath the creation of the unattached individualism of the market is an almost unconscious desire for community. However, community formation can take many forms, both progressive and retrogressive. At the time of 9/11, both came to the fore. The school board's decision threatened the imagined community of the nation, at the same time as the nation actually seemed to be under physical threat.[23] It also provided a stimulus for the formation of a real community, an organization to win back the space of schooling for patriotism. The defense of freedom is sutured into the project of defending the nation, which is sutured into a local project of forming a (rightist) counter-hegemonic community to contest the antipatriotic and ideologically motivated decisions by urban liberal elites. Thus, the need to "be with others," itself a hidden effect of the asocial relations of advanced capitalism, has elements of good and bad sense within it. Under specific historical circumstances these elements of good sense can be mobilized in support of a vision of democracy that is inherently undemocratic in its actual effects on those people in a community who wish to uphold a vision of freedom that not only legitimates dissidence but provides space for its expression.[24]

In saying this, do not read me as being totally opposed to ideas of nation or of the building of imagined communities. In my mind, however, social criticism is the ultimate act of patriotism. As I say in *Official Knowledge*, rigorous criticism of a nation's policies demonstrates a commitment to the nation itself. It says that one demands action on the principles that are supposedly part of the founding narratives of a nation and that are employed in the legitimation of its construction of particular kinds of polities. It signifies that I/we live here and that this is indeed our country and our flag as well. No national narrative that excludes the rich history of dissent as a constitutive part of the nation can ever be considered legitimate. Thus, in claiming that the board had acted in an unpatriotic manner, the flag-waving crowd and the partly still inchoate movement that stood behind it was, in my mind, itself engaged in a truly unpatriotic act, one which showed that the national narrative of freedom and justice was subject to constant renegotiation and struggle over its very meaning.[25] The 9/11 tragedy provided the conditions for such struggles at a local level, not only in the classrooms at universities such as my own but in the ordinary ways we govern our schools.

Compulsory Patriotism and the Hidden Effects of Race

In Madison, even with the forces arrayed against it, the threat to call a special election to oust the board members who voted against the mandatory pledge and singing stalled. In fact, the recall campaign failed by a wide margin. The conservative organizers were not able to get anywhere near the number of votes needed to force a new election. This is a crucial element in any appraisal of the lasting effects of 9/11. In the face of resurgent uncritical patriotism and anger, in the face of calls for an enhanced national security state and for schools to be part of the first line of defense, at the local level in many communities wiser heads, ones with a more substantive vision of democracy, prevailed. Yet this is not the end of this particular story. The pressure from the right did have an effect. The board left it up to each individual school to decide if and how they would enforce the mandated patriotism. This decision defused the controversy in a way that has a long history in the United States. Local decisions will prevail, but there is no guarantee that the decisions at each local school will uphold a vision of thick democracy that welcomes dissent as itself a form of patriotic commitment.

Still, the issues surrounding thick democracy at a local level do not end with the question of whether dissent is welcome or not. To document why we must go further, I need to point to other crucial dynamics that were at work and that were the unforeseen results of this controversy. When the recall campaign failed, conservatives rededicated themselves to winning the next school board election. Two of the seats of people who had been among the majority of members who had originally made the controversial decision were to be contested. Here too, the conservatives failed and both seats were taken by progressives. This again seems as if our story had a relatively happy ending. Yet simply leaving the story there would miss one of the most important hidden effects of the September 11/pledge connection. Instead, what I shall now describe shows something very different—that often the effects of seeming victories against rightist mobilization must themselves be understood as complicated and as occurring along multiple dynamics of power.

Because of the tensions, controversies, and personal attacks that developed out of the board's deliberations, one of the members who had voted for the board's minimalist response resigned right before the closing date for registering as a candidate for the next election. That member, an African American who had been on the board for a number of years, was worn out by the controversy. In essence, while it is trite to say so, it became the straw that broke the camel's back. It had taken so much energy and time to fight the battles over funding cuts, over the development of programs that were aimed specifically at Madison's growing population of children of color, over all those things that make being one of the few minority members of a school board so fulfilling and frustrating, that the emotional labor and time commitments involved in the compulsory patriotism conflict and in its aftermath created an almost unbearable situation for him. Even though a progressive write-in candidate did win the seat that had been vacated, a cogent voice, one representing communities of color in the community, had been lost.

This points to a crucial set of unintended results. The legislation smuggled into the budget bill had echoes of dynamics that were very different from those overtly involved in the conflict over the pledge, but these echoes still were profound in their effects. In the context of 9/11, this seemingly inconsequential piece of legislation not only created the seeds of very real conflicts and conservative mobilizations, but through a long chain of events, it also led to the loss of a hard-won gain. An articulate African American elected board member who had fought for social justice in the district could take it no more. In the conjunctural and unpredictable events both of and after the horror of 9/11, a bit of mischief in which Republican legislators sought to protect their right flank, rebounds back on the realities of differential power at the local level. Obviously race was not necessarily as much on the minds of the legislators who placed that piece of legislation into the budget bill as it had been on the minds of some of the more overtly racist educators and legislators in the earlier periods of U.S. history discussed earlier in this book.[26] However, the effects to which it led ultimately were, profoundly, raced at the level of local governance.

I want to stress the importance of these effects. In any real situation there are multiple relations of power and an entire and sometimes contradictory assemblage of hegemonic and counter-hegemonic relations. Because of this, any serious understanding of the actual results of September 11 on education needs to widen its gaze beyond what we usually look for. As I have shown, in the aftermath of 9/11 the politicization of local school governance occurred in ways that were quite powerful. Yet without an understanding of other kinds of politics, in this case race, we would miss one of the most important results of the struggle over the meaning of freedom in this site. September 11 has had even broader effects than we recognize.

Conclusion

In the account I have given in the second half of this chapter, it is unclear who really won or lost here. But one thing is clear: no analysis of the effects of 9/11 on schools can go on without an understanding of the ways in which the global is dynamically linked to the local. Such an analysis must more fully understand the larger ideological work and history of the neo-liberal and neo-conservative project and its effects on the discourses that circulate and become common sense in our society. No analysis can afford to ignore the contradictory needs and contradictions that this project has created. And given the power of race in this society, any serious understanding must constantly examine the ways in which racial dynamics get played out on fields of power that don't seem to be overtly about race on first glance.

Oh, and one last thing—a complete analysis would require that we look at the effects of the commodified products of popular cultural forms of entertainment that each of us use to see the momentous events taking place all around us. Critical cultural analysts have taught us many things. Yes, we participate in guilty pleasures. (How else to explain my framing of the disastrous events of 9/11 in terms of Hollywood images?) And, yes, we can read any cultural form and content in dominant, negotiated, and oppositional ways. But it might be wise to remember that—at least in the case of the ways in which Michael W. Apple experienced the horrors of the planes and buildings and bodies on 9/11—all three went on at the same time.

Thus, I want argue that educators—whether teaching a university class or participating in local school board decision making—must first recognize our own contradictory responses to the events of September 11 and to its ongoing aftermath. We must also understand that these responses, although partly understandable in the context of tragic events, may create dynamics that have long-lasting consequences. And many of these consequences may themselves undercut the very democracy we believe that we are upholding and defending. This more complicated political understanding may well be a first step in finding appropriate and socially critical pedagogic strategies to work within our classes and communities to interrupt the larger hegemonic projects—including the redefinition of democracy as "patriotic fervor"—that we will continue to face in the future. What the present and future may hold in store—both negatively and positively—are discussed in greater detail in the interview that forms the core of the last chapter in this new edition of *Ideology and Curriculum*.

CHAPTER **10**

On Analyzing
New Hegemonic Relations
An Interview

Introduction

The text of this chapter is an interview with me conducted by Michael F. Shaughnessy, Kathy Peca, and Janna Siegel. Originally published in 2001, I have edited and updated the interview. As I mentioned in the Preface to this edition of *Ideology and Curriculum*, I believe that there are a number of very real benefits to the interview format. First, it creates the conditions in which an author has to be more clear than is usual in what are often complicated arguments and densely written prose. Such complex arguments may be necessary, and at times our language must reflect the complexities that we are trying to unpack. However, it is good for both reader—and author as well—to find ways of making one's arguments in a more approachable style.

Second, interviews are humanizing. By the very fact that they are more conversational, both reader and author participate in the form in very different ways than the more passive act of reading an academic text. Of course, no reading is actually passive. Readers read actively—they can read in dominant, negotiated, and oppositional ways, accepting all that an author has to say; partly mediating, reinterpreting, and/or taking on board parts of an author's arguments; or reading against the text, rejecting many of the claims and having an internal argument with the author. But, this said, conversations can often be productive forms of communication, ones that enhance connections among people.

The interview deals with a number of crucial issues we are facing today— the neo-liberal and neo-conservative restructuring of education, the struggle over textbooks and official knowledge, multicultural and antiracist education, national curricula, national testing, vouchers and marketization, the move toward national certification of teachers, and ultimately, the limits and possibilities of building of a more inclusive socially critical and progressive community to counter the Right and create an education worthy of its name.

The interview serves as a summary of much of the work in which I have engaged over the past ten years. Because of this, it is actually an introduction to the more nuanced forms of analysis that I and many others have developed since *Ideology and Curriculum* first appeared. *Ideology and Curriculum* was a beginning. As long as the struggle for a socially just and critically democratic education continues, there will be no end in sight. But that's the point isn't it? Education is an *inherently* political and ethical—and fully human—act. There is no way of eliding our responsibilities here. These issues will not go away and new generations will need to continue our understanding of and action on relations of dominance and inequality.

Interview

What do you see as the main issues in terms of educational policy?
There are a number of issues that I think are crucial. In my mind, the most important is what I have called in my most recent books (such as *Cultural Politics and Education, Official Knowledge, Educating the "Right" Way,* and *The State and the Politics of Knowledge*) the conservative restoration or "conservative modernization." That is, the movement more and more to redefine what education is for and how we are to proceed in education both as a practice and as a set of policies. There is a new alliance that is exerting leadership in educational policy and educational reform. In many nations there has been a shift from a limited social democratic accord or alliance to a coalition centered around three or four groups that are pushing education and social policy in general in conservative directions. This new alliance or "new hegemonic bloc" is a relatively broad umbrella; it is also tense and filled with contradictory tendencies. But taken together it has been very effective. Let me just mention something about each of the groups who are under the umbrella.

The first group is what we can call *neo-liberals.* These are economic modernizers who want educational policy to be centered around the economy, around performance objectives based on a closer connection between schooling and paid work. I want to stress the word "paid" here, because these people have a very patriarchal vision of the labor force. They tend not to think about who does the unpaid labor in this society—largely women. The economic modernizers are in leadership, by and large, in this new bloc. They see schools as connected to a marketplace, especially the global capitalist market, and the labor needs and processes of such a market. They also often see schools themselves as in need of being transformed and made more competitive by placing them into marketplaces through voucher plans, tax credits, and other similar marketizing strategies. The evidence against these positions is now nearly overwhelming. More inequalities, not fewer, are produced.

Because neo-liberals are in leadership in this alliance, using the umbrella metaphor, we might say that they are holding the handle of the umbrella. Their leadership has been successful in many ways. It is interesting, for example, that some members of dispossessed groups are being brought under the umbrella of rightist marketization, something I've written about recently with Tom

Pedroni. While I am strongly sympathetic to oppressed groups' struggles, I do not believe that in the long run marketization, vouchers, and similar policies will lead to lasting social and educational transformation and reduce the racializing results that characterize schooling.

As I mentioned, neo-liberals are not alone. A second group are what might be called neo-conservatives. In most cases it is important to make a distinction between the neo-liberal economic modernizers and neo-conservatives, although in some nations they do overlap. Neo-conservatives often agree with the neo-liberal emphasis on the economy, but their main agenda is cultural restoration. Examples in the United States are people such E. D. Hirsch, former secretary of education William Bennett, and the late Alan Bloom. Diane Ravitch also has many of the same assumptions as people within this group. These are people who want a return to a totally romanticized version of schooling in which we have a standard curriculum based on that eloquent fiction, the Western tradition. They wish a return to teacher-dominated, high-status knowledge, largely based on the traditions that have historically been seen as the most legitimate knowledge at elite universities. I mentioned that this is a romantic tradition since, by and large, there was never a time (at least certainly in the schools in the United States) where everyone learned the same curriculum, where all people spoke the same language, and where everyone agreed either on the Western tradition as the dominant model or on what should be included and excluded in that tradition. Thus, its position is based on a thoroughly romanticized version of the past, and either a romanticized vision of past students and teachers or a vision of them that assumes that without external control they will destroy "real" culture.

Because of this, neo-conservatives are deeply committed to establishing tighter mechanisms of control over knowledge, morals, and values through national or state curricula and national or state-mandated (and very reductive) testing. This is based on a very strong mistrust of teachers and local school administrators. They believe that only through establishing strong central control will the content and values of "legitimate knowledge" take its rightful place in the curriculum. Along with this is also a commitment to a supposedly more rigorous curriculum, one based on what they believe are higher standards. Thus, schooling itself must be more competitive, with students being re-stratified based on what are seen as neutral knowledge and neutral achievement tests. In essence, this has proven to be a return to Social Darwinist principles in education. It has also created a situation in which the "tail of the test wags the dog of the teacher."

There is a third group that is increasingly powerful in the United States (although they have clear counterparts in other nations). Following Stuart Hall, we can name them authoritarian populists. These are often (at least in the United States) Christian fundamentalists and evangelicals who want a return to what they believe is *the* biblical tradition as the basis of knowledge, sacred texts, and sacred authority. This part of the alliance is often very mistrustful of multiculturalism in the curriculum, although they have tried to take on the mantle of, say, Dr. Martin Luther King's authority by claiming that they are the new oppressed. This is deeply disingenuous since their situation and that of people of color who have been subjected to murderous discriminatory policies and practices have no parallels. By and large, they too want a return to a pedagogy that is based on traditional relations of authority in which the teacher and adults are always in control. But they get their warrant from inerrant readings of the Bible.

Authoritarian populist religious conservatives are extremely worried about the relationship between schools and the body and about sexuality. They are worried about the relationship between schooling and what they perceive as the traditional family. For them, the traditional family is God-given, as are relations of gender and age. God has put men in dominant positions of authority and has decreed that religious authority must supercede public policy. In the United States this has led to what have been called "stealth campaigns" in which socially and religiously conservative people hide their religious beliefs and run for election to local school boards or state school boards on a platform of fiscal responsibility. Once in power they attempt to purge the curriculum of any elements of socially liberal positions and of any elements that are not biblically based. Their mobilizations have been effective—so effective in fact that many state curricula and textbooks have become even more conservative than before and many teachers have become self-censors to avoid conflict over the curriculum.

Authoritarian populist religious conservatives are also in the forefront of the fastest growing educational "reform" in the United States—home schooling. Thus, we need to focus on their effects not only inside schools but the effects of their removal of children from the supposed evils of secular formal education.

The fourth group that has been influential in setting the agenda in educational policy does not necessarily agree with all of the positions advanced by the previous three elements of the new hegemonic bloc. It does not see itself as having an ideological agenda. This group is made up of members of the professional and managerial new middle class. If I may be permitted to speak perhaps too broadly, these people are, in essence, experts for hire.

They are often employed by the state because of their technical expertise in evaluation and testing, efficiency, management, cost-benefit analysis, and similar technical and procedural skills. These skills and knowledge are their cultural capital and have enabled them to carve out spheres of authority within the state. Their agenda is one of managerialism, and it is often their needs that are represented in the state's imposition of policies of "steering at a distance" through national and state testing and tighter control, through the use of industrial models, having more reductive curricula and pedagogy in schools, and so forth. Their cultural capital is what I called "technical administrative knowledge" in *Education and Power*. It enables the most powerful groups within the conservative modernization, neo-liberals and neo-conservatives, to tighten up the ship and to make us more accountable. In many ways these are the children and grandchildren of the efficiency experts and systems managers I analyze in *Ideology and Curriculum*.

Each of these groups has an agenda, but leadership over the main issues is exercised by the neo-liberals or economic modernizers. They, of course, have to compromise with the other groups so that the alliance includes issues of importance to neo-conservatives, authoritarian populists, and the upwardly mobile professional and managerial new middle class. But, in general, the agenda is set by these who want closer connections between schools and the (globalizing) economy. It is exactly this complex but still exceptionally conservative agenda that is present in Mr. Bush's call to "leave no child behind" (it's really simply "leave no child untested") and in the administration's policy on dismissing any research that doesn't imitate a medical or quasi-scientific model.

This taxonomy of the alliance surrounding conservative modernization is a partial view, however. There's another side about which I'll be somewhat briefer. This involves those issues surrounding a vision and a practice of democracy and social justice that is thicker than the thin vision of democracy as consumption practices advanced by neo-liberals.

These issues involve the power of (collective) local decision making, of a curriculum that comes from below rather than from above and that responds more and more to the needs, histories, and cultures of oppressed people, of people of color, and of poor people, and a more socially responsive pedagogy. In the United States, while this is less well known than, say, voucher plans and plans for "high-stakes" testing, these issues are actually becoming increasingly powerful. Thus, one of my recent books done with Jim Beane, *Democratic Schools*, portrays in detail a number of schools that are organized around this more democratic agenda. It tells their stories, as a way of interrupting the Right and showing in practice that it is possible to engage in socially and educationally critical activities that solve real problems in real schools in real communities. One of the reasons that conservative policies dominate is because teachers and others are not given realistic alternatives that actually work. *Democratic Schools* is a conscious attempt by a group of socially and educationally critical educators to answer the question "What do I do on Monday morning?" in socially just ways. Answers to "What do I do on Monday?" are powerfully answered in practice by what is happening in Porto Alegre, Brazil, as well, something that Luis Armando Gandin and I describe in detail in *The State and the Politics of Knowledge*.

When one adds in the very important work—educational and political— being done by the increasingly visible publications of *Rethinking Schools* in which social criticism is combined with serious, disciplined, and caring counter-hegemonic curricula and teaching, this does give us reason to believe that the agenda of conservative modernization can be and is being countered in important ways.

Thus, there are at least two sets of agendas, one based on the internal compromises within the forces of conservative modernization largely guided by neo-liberal assumptions, and one organized around the compromises within multiple progressive communities of educators, activists, and others. These continue to lock horns, so to speak. To be honest, right now I am not totally optimistic that the more democratic agenda will get the public notice it deserves and will become as visible as the more conservative agenda. However, the fact that *Democratic Schools* has sold hundreds of thousands copies (as have the publications of *Rethinking Schools*) and has been translated into many languages does give some reason for optimism.

Could you comment on the trend toward multicultural education?
This is complicated because I do not want to say disparaging things about people who are working so hard, especially since many of them are my friends and allies. First, we have to again understand that the way hegemonic alliances are formed and maintained by powerful groups, and the ways agendas are set and maintained, is through compromise. Further, if we want to understand why things change in American schools, by and large, it is not because of intended or internal reforms. Rather, it has been and is pressure from large-scale social movements that generate the conditions in which schools are transformed. One of the major transformative movements in the last century in the United States is the African American movement toward liberation. It pressed schools to change their pedagogy, their curriculum, and their organization. Parts of that movement often had quite a radical agenda.

Now, in order for dominant groups to maintain leadership, they must incorporate some limited segments of that agenda into their own position. And what dominant groups did do, quite remarkably, and very successfully in some ways, was to take both (how can I put this?) the most moderate and safest forms—and often the most conservative forms—of multiculturalism and put them into schools and curriculum. Therefore, we now have in textbooks, for instance, what has been called *mentioning*, where you have page after page that mention the contributions of African Americans, that mention the contributions of Latinos and Latinas, of Asians, or of women. These are most often put as special sections in the textbooks and, hence, have the status of add-ons about the culture and history of "the Other." Thus, their status as other than "real Americans" is guaranteed. In the process, students never see the world through the eyes of oppressed people. They don't see the world through the eyes of the identifiable people who are on the bottom, so to speak, socially.

So, on the one hand, multiculturalism was a gain because large social movements forced dominant groups to respond. We must always remember that.

Multiculturalism was not a gift. It took decades of struggle over a white-dominated power structure. And yet, at the same time, a good deal of multiculturalism as it has been instituted in schools is of the "safest" kind—one that does not interrupt the power of whiteness as "the human ordinary." This is one of the ways in which existing power relations recuperate oppositional movements back within dominance.

Some of these points are being constantly raised by groups of people (African American activists, Native Americans, those of Asian descent, gays and lesbians, members of the disability rights community, and many other groups) who feel that their cultures and histories are not being represented in the curriculum, Because of this, I think that multiculturalism is quite contradictory. I want to applaud it for its gains. Yet I am worried that with the conservative restoration, many of the more socially progressive gains are being washed away as we move more and more toward a curriculum that is "safer" and has very few elements of social activism in it. I would prefer that we have not just multicultural education, but specifically antiracist education. This is an education that realizes that this nation was built around racial exploitation and that it has a racial power structure. Thus, the stories of oppressed people of color then and now would not be simply an add-on. They would constitute an integral part of the way this nation was formed. This would require a recognition that the story of the United States (and I think many other nations) *is* also the story of racial oppression. Without that part of the story, there is no story. It would also require that we see the world through the eyes of people of color, not just mention their contributions as an add-ons. Of course, we have models of thinking productively about these issues and of doing policy and practice concerning them well, in the work of Gloria Ladson-Billings, Cameron McCarthy, David Gillborn, Michelle Foster, Rudolfo Torres, Heidi Safia Mirza, and others.

What is your opinion of other sociologists of education, for example, Basil Bernstein and Pierre Bourdieu?
I find the work of both of them to be extremely important. As you may know, I have criticized both of them in print, since I believe that the way to show how much you respect someone's work is to take it seriously enough to subject it to critical analysis. (This is why I actually welcome criticism. All of us have much to learn from each other.) But I will be the first to admit that I stand on their shoulders. Their recent deaths have deprived us of truly creative and powerful minds. Basil Bernstein happened to be a friend of mine and he's someone who taught me a great deal. While I knew Pierre Bourdieu, I knew him less well.

I want to separate them, but only after I say something about the commonalities they have. Both of them have very unromantic appraisals of the nature of power relations. Neither of them have been so totally taken in by some of the more aggressive forms of postmodernism, which have forgotten that this is capitalism and that this fact makes a major difference. Nor have they forgotten that there are structures that do exist. For both Bernstein and Bourdieu, the world is not simply a text; these structures are not simply discursive constructions. Further, both of them have a fairly unromantic appraisal of class relations. In my mind this is crucial, especially in a time when we are moving in the United States and in many other nations away from an analysis of class and away from structural analyses. I do not want to defend reductive structural analysis, but in this period of time when all too many people seem to have lost the collective memory of the gains made by the traditions of structural analysis, there are important positive moments in keeping alive this set of traditions.

Of course class is very complicated both empirically and conceptually, to say nothing of historically. It does not exist alone. People are classed and sexed/ gendered and raced and regioned all at the same time. Thus, you can't just talk about class as if it sat isolated from other crucial dynamics of power. Neither can you assume that everything is explained by an economy. That would be horribly reductive and essentializing.

On the other hand, to assume that class relations have somehow gone away, or that it makes no difference that there is an economy like the one we have is utterly romantic. (Of course, what Bernstein and Bourdieu *mean* by class is not necessarily what, say, the neo-Marxists mean by class and its dynamics.) Saying this, however, it is clear that both of them share a particular agenda that wants to ask: "What is the relationship between culture, power, and economy in education and the larger society?" I find this a profoundly important question. And again, each of them has taught me a good deal about how one might ask and answer this kind of question with recognition of its complexity.

Now, let me say a few words on their differences. Bernstein, I think, is much more related to the realities of schools, curricula, and teaching. For that reason I think he has probably been influential on the way I look at specific curricular and pedagogical relations. While his general agenda is similar to Bourdieu's, it is more deeply connected to the kinds of things those of us in education are about.

Bourdieu, I think, has a somewhat broader project, yet his work on various forms of capital—cultural capital, social capital, symbolic capital, economic capital, and so on—and the conversion strategies that cohere with them, is exceptional and has been a clear influence on a generation of critical research and certainly on me as well. I include myself in that group of researchers since his work provides a way of thinking about the role of education in the reproduction and transformation (Bourdieu is less good on this latter dynamic, at times) of various forms of capital and how education and these conversion strategies are situated within social fields of power. Even with my criticisms of parts of Bourdieu, I find this approach very productive. This is particularly evident in my analysis of the power of the managerial and professional new middle class in *Educating the "Right" Way*. Indeed, I do not think that you can understand why education is being reconstructed in such damaging ways right now unless you employ Bourdieu's (and Bernstein's) work.

Let me briefly mention some of my criticisms of them. Again, they're both quite brilliant. However, as I've said in print, I think that Bernstein is rather too structuralist at times. In his work you don't see real people act, nor do you see real social movements in formation and action, nor finally do you see the processes and results of social transformation. I think that these are crucial for our understanding of education. We need to focus on transformations and social movements—not only on structural forms and positions in society but on the transformative effects of the social movements. Thus, I would go considerably further than he does, as I did in my own analysis of rightist social movements and their history and effects in *Official Knowledge, Cultural Politics and Education*, and *Educating the "Right" Way*. However, the analysis of social movements and their effects in the successful struggles against colonial forms of domination that Ting-Hong Wong and I do in *The State and the Politics of Knowledge* is deeply indebted to Bernstein; so clearly his work can still be of considerable import even when I want to go further than he did.

Like Bernstein, Bourdieu is complex and at times rather unclear. However, again, we need to be patient as we read him. One of the points I have made over the years is that the reader is not the only one who should be doing all of the work. I think that it is very important that we struggle (and at times it is a struggle) to be as clear as our subject matter allows. Let me give a personal example. In both the original 1993 edition of *Official Knowledge* and the new second edition published in 2000, I did not send the volume to the publisher until I was satisfied that I had written it in as clear a manner as was possible. In the case of the 1993 version, this involved holding it back from publication for an extra year. This was not simply a concern with style. It was about the politics of representation. Given the fact that the Right is so powerful today, it is important that progressive texts not require that you read seven other books in order to understand them. Theory is absolutely crucial, but I am worried about overtheorization. At times, Bourdieu suffers from this, although as I mentioned there are times when one's subject requires a high degree of abstraction. It is exactly here where the struggle to be as clear as possible is even more important. However, again I don't want to be misunderstood. Theory *counts* and it counts in truly significant ways. After all, how could I have written books such as *Ideology and Curriculum* if I believed that new and sometimes difficult theory wasn't absolutely essential to see and understand the world in radically different ways? This realization doesn't eliminate the need to struggle with one's text to make it clearer, however, and I hope that I have gotten better at this over the years.

I have other worries about parts of Bourdieu's corpus as well: about his assumption that French culture is the culture of the world; about his multiplication of forms of capital that at times seem endless; about how far we can take market analogies as analytic tools; about his tendency on occasion to overgeneralize; and about whether one can do such work without being more deeply involved in concrete political/cultural movements. (This last criticism seems less powerful to me given the translation into English of his more political writings recently.) But on the whole, I really do want to applaud the work of both Bourdieu and Bernstein.

Why has critical theory been more readily accepted in other nations than in the United States?
In order to respond to this, I have to ask a prior question: "What do we mean by critical theory?" *Critical theory* has a very long history as a very specific kind of analytic and political approach largely in Germany and France, especially in Germany during and after Weimar and then either purged or forced to flee under the Nazi regime. Of course, names such as Benjamin, Adorno, Horkheimer, Marcuse, and others are associated with this tradition.

This form of critical theory was an attempt to think through the relationship between culture, forms of domination, and society. It began as a cultural/political analysis of capitalist mass culture and then stretched beyond capitalism and its social forms—thus its analysis, for instance, of technical knowledge and cognitive interests as forms of domination such as that done by Habermas.

This has a very specific history. I assume by the question that when we say "critical theory" we actually mean what I prefer to call "critical educational studies," which is a much broader category. It includes Marxist and neo-Marxist work and also includes work that is more related to the Frankfurt school I spoke about just a minute ago. But it also includes work in critical cultural studies, in poststructural feminist analysis, in queer theory, in critical race theory, and other critical approaches. Because of this, I'm going to define it as that broader set of approaches. The answer to the question of why it has been found less in the United States than perhaps elsewhere is very complicated and is related to the historically important question of "Why are there not large-scale socialist movements in the United States?" Much as well depends on the specifically atheoretical, positivist, and pragmatic leanings historically in the academy here. Some of it is the result of the fact that there were indigenous traditions within the United States that raised similar questions, but have not been recognized as part of critical theory. And part of it has to do with the ways in which the left has been marginalized and at times fired from universities during periods of crisis.

Has critical theory been so conceptually tied to socialism as to preclude general acceptance?
Let me merge these last two questions together. First of all, as I just said, I think that it is the case that it has been less readily accepted in the United States than elsewhere, in part because the socialist tradition in the United States has been truncated. We are the only nation of its type in the world that has never even

had a large and serious labor party. Further, one of the things we forget is that the boats that were filled with immigrants coming over were often nearly just as filled with immigrants going back. Some people who did not make it here—at times even very political people—often went back.

Added to this is the fact that with the vast openness of the West—after the murder and forced enclosure of Native Americans—people who were not making it in industrial America in the mills or in urban areas among immigrants and workers (which were often hotbeds of activism of the type we normally associate with socialism and Marxism) could leave. So we had a safety valve in the United States that was often not available in Europe and other nations. Further, the tradition here has been to *critically* use liberalism with its focus on individual rights, what I call *person rights*, in opposition to property rights. This has meant that liberalism has had a more important history here than socialism.

We need to remember that the genesis of a social and political discourse does not always preordain how it will be used socially and politically. Thus, I want to point out that liberalism has been used for quite radical purposes in the United States. It's not simply that it's been a tool of domination. (This is of course a change from the position I took in some of my earlier work.) Even with its vision of individualism, rather than seeing oneself as a member of a collective, liberalism was radicalized by men and women and used for their own purposes. In order to get person rights for you and your family, you had to join unions and you had to struggle. For women, being treated as fully functioning citizens was crucial both in the paid workplace and in the home, as well as in the state. Therefore, liberalism was reappropriated by women as a tool in their struggles over bodily control and over economic and political rights. Liberalism did and does have its contradictions, but it became a more flexible political tool than we might expect. Thus, for a variety of reasons—the geographical openness, the existence of less sympathy to more collective kinds of organizations (all too often being based on a racist nativism in which socialism was seen as an alien ideology, although socialism could also be quite racist as well as a number of historians have documented), people going back as well as staying here, and very, very importantly the repressive nature of what industrialists and the government engaged in here—all of these things and more had effects.

Take education for instance. In many communities, if you were a socialist teacher, as an example, you were fired. If you were a teacher of elementary or secondary schools and you wrote a letter to the newspaper avowing socialist ideals, you could lose your job. There were very few universities in the United States, as another example, or school systems that did not have a history of similar tragedies or of other ways of purging people on the left.

Perhaps comparing this very complicated history in the United States to other nations with their own historical complexities would be helpful. Take

Australia and England. Each has a much more overt history of nationally powerful labor union struggles. What this has meant was brought home to me during a period when I worked with teachers unions and with socially critical educators in Australia. I am a former president of a teacher's union in New Jersey and that union prided itself on its history of taking serious actions. Yet when I went to Australia for the first time, the unions there did things that seemed unthinkable in the United States. The kindergarten teachers union there went on strike and shut down the schools because the sum of $300 was cut from the teachers' budget, which had been used to buy reading materials for their classrooms. Such action is part of long tradition there. It would almost never happen in the United States, in part because for decades strikes by public employees like teachers were (and in some areas still are) illegal. The leaders of teachers unions in the United States that went on strike were jailed. Hence, there is a very different history, one that acts as both cause and effect of the fact that, say, England and Australia or other nations have a stronger tradition of Marxist and neo-Marxist analysis—although that too is changing given the attacks on unions and progressives in general in these nations as well.

Let me add a few other things. Not only does the United States have a longer history of radical populism, one with less of a theoretical background, that comes from the history of farm/labor movement; but Marx was not available in the United States. There were no United States' editions of his work. In essence, you could not buy him or read him, except with great difficulty. Now, parts of some Marxist traditions were sometimes reductive or even wrong, but without the easy availability of a good deal of the material it is difficult to develop a rich and nuanced critical position based on these traditions.

Much more needs to be said here, but let me conclude with a reminder that class has always been raced and gendered. The divisions of race and gender have always been used by dominant groups in the United States—and elsewhere—to prevent "decentered unities" from developing that might challenge hegemonic powers. This has also worked to interrupt alliances within progressive communities as well. Thus, as I noted earlier, people can be progressive about one dynamic of power and retrogressive about others. Our job is not to privilege one form of oppression over any others, but to build what used to be called a "popular front" against the multiple oppressive realities that so many of our fellow people experience daily and to build a politics of *both* redistribution and recognition (to use Nancy Fraser's insightful concepts) in ways in which each contributes to, not contradicts, each other.

Is American culture resistant to seeking the underlying political meanings of education and curriculum?
Each of these questions is quite complicated. I'm aware that I do not have a whole book to answer them so sometimes I must simply give an outline of an answer.

There is a history in the United States that makes "American" culture resistant to seeking political meanings. (I've put the word "American" in quotation marks because it's important that people in the United States realize that all of the people in North, Central, and South America have just as much claim to being "American" as we do. The arrogance of claiming to be the real Americans speaks to imperial tendencies. I'll continue to use the word, but whenever you see it please mentally put it in quotes.) Let me explain this strand of resistance. I hinted earlier that there is a history in the United States that has positive and negative moments surrounding what might be called anti-theory and anti-intellectualism. Now in some ways, that is a very progressive moment. Historically, the tradition of aristocratic culture is underdeveloped in the United States. Thus, one of the positive moments of American culture is its populist form. In general, there is a real dislike of elitism. This means that theoretically complex apparatuses like the kinds of ways of looking at the politics of education and the curriculum that requires a great deal of discipline and study actually are seen as simply "mere theory." These traditions are tarred with the theory brush. This is connected to an anti-theory tradition, which again as I've mentioned, is partly contradictory. It has some quite positive moments because of the American experience with pragmatism. It rests on a demand that says "I want these things to be able to be used in my daily life." In many ways, I respond very positively to that.

However, there's a negative moment to that as well. It does require even harder work to examine things politically here because the kinds of political and theoretical resources that are available "naturally" in the universities or in the press and the media in, for example, Europe and Latin America, have much less of a lengthy history here, because, again, they were either actively purged or were harder to find. Think of social reality as something of a Sony Walkman in which there are one hundred stations. Ninety-nine are playing the messages that support or do not question dominant interpretations of the world. It takes hard and conscious effort to find the one station that challenges these commonsense understandings.

There's one last thing I want to say about this question. I actually don't think that it is the case that American culture is necessarily resistant to understanding political meanings. It may be that what we count as politics is somewhat different or even perhaps wider. An example would be something like this. Many people in the United States historically *have* argued, often quite powerfully, against the ways schools operate and the curriculum and pedagogy that dominate them. These critiques have been couched largely in the language of individualism. That is just as political and does have its own tradition here in schools. But the dominance of individualism as a discourse and as a set of structural conditions in the United States has made it hard for these criticisms to be turned into politically collective questions. However, you can't understand, for instance, the history of women or the history of people of color, or the history of working-class and ethnic struggle in the United States without saying that for the vast majority of people of color and for many women and working-class people and gays and lesbians and indigenous people in the United States, the meanings of education and the curriculum have constantly been criticized. It is often the dominant culture that does not recognize the political nature of the curriculum in American education.

What current political and sociological issues are now affecting education?
I've partly answered that in my first response, but let me go further here. As I noted, right now there are major transformations going on. As an example, we are changing education into a commodity to be purchased. The very meaning of democracy now is consumption practices. What was once a political concept and practice, one based on collective dialogue and negotiation, is now a wholly *economic* concept. Under the influence of neo-liberalism now, the very meaning of citizenship is being radically transformed. The citizen is now simply the consumer in all too many countries. The world is seen as a vast supermarket. Schools, and even our students as in the case of Channel One in the United States where children are sold as a captive audience for commercial advertisers who market their products in schools, become commodities that are bought and sold in the same way everything else is bought and sold.

That is a major transformation in the way we think of ourselves. Thinking about citizenship as a political concept meant that to be a citizen was to participate in building and restructuring your institutions. To be a consumer is to be a possessive individual who is known by her or his products. You are defined by what you buy, not by what you do. Thus, the general sociological and economic movement that redefines democracy and citizenship into being a set of consumptive practices, and in which the world is seen as a vast supermarket, is having a major effect on education. This is one of the major effects of things such as voucher plans and it is a disaster in terms of the restructuring of our common sense. If I'm correct that it's social movements that transform education, then thinking of oneself as simply an individual consumer in a market— where social justice in essence will take care of itself through our purchasing activities—is the ultimate demobilizing ideology. It's the best thing that neo-liberals could wish for.

There is another movement, or rather movements, that I think are having a major effect as well. These movements are what some postmodern and post-structural theories are trying to represent. These movements are aimed more and more toward what we might call de-centered unities, that is political movements that are no longer centered only around class, labor unions, and our traditional assumptions about who the real historical actors are. Yet, these do not assume that a simple additive model is sufficient. Thus, they do not assume that adding race and then simply adding sex or gender or disability is enough.

We are no longer centered around only race lines; we are no longer centered around only class lines; we are not only centered around lines of sex/gender.

This partly responds to the partial fragmentation of social movements. There are black lesbian social movements; there are gay Hispanic and Latino social movements; there are movements based upon environmental destruction that combine race and class in complex ways. Therefore, there are large-scale collective movements, ones that most of us would associate with needed progressive transformations in society and education, but which our accepted theories may not recognize as major actors. This sense of fragmentation of *the* emancipatory project is unsettling for many critical educators. What were once certain as the defining issues (class, the economy, the state) have been added to. Issues of sexuality and the body, disability, postcolonialism, and many more have been not simply added but have been taken up, sometimes as substitutes for struggles that many people have given their entire lives to. This situation has created a real crisis because the rightist movements are relatively coherent and the politics of the left are now extremely fragmented.

In a number of recent books I've argued that I am not in a church so I am not worried about heresy. But I do have some reservations about some aspects of both postmodern politics and postmodern theories, especially when they lead us as I said earlier to ignore class and political economy and treat the world as a text. These forms of romantic possibilitarianism are worrisome to me. My own position is that I would hope for what I call a de-centered unity—groups and movements that work together on a number of broad fronts. This has some similarity to past popular front politics that enabled people to join together rather than fighting against each other. But I would broaden the range of politics and issues that are seen as important. The politics of the body around HIV/AIDS, for example, combines international economic struggles, the dominance of profit in the pharmaceutical and medical industries, the exploitation of third world peoples, neo-liberal policies, masculinities and cultural struggles for women's rights, gay and lesbian rights, the control of the media and of the politics of representation, education in sexuality and its suppression by conservative movements, to name but some of the issues and movements that must be jointly involved if progress is to be made. HIV/AIDS is not a minor issue. It is having a truly devastating effect on entire continents and is one of the areas in which class, race, gender, sexuality, anti-imperialism, colonial and postcolonial realities, and religion intersect. Economic, political, cultural, and educational struggles are all joined together here. It is no more and no less important than class and labor struggles or other battles over school policies and practices. It is not a replacement for other crucial issues, but one example of how certain issues require the building of coalitions across difference in order to effectively create counter-hegemonic alternatives. This is why the work of writers such as Nancy Fraser, Judith Butler, bell hooks, and others becomes so important. They are trying to chart an intellectually/politically/culturally defensible path that provides ways of understanding and acting on what are dynamics that now too often divide people who need to come together to deal with a range of oppressions nationally and internationally.

Let us be honest. This will be very hard to do, as will be the maintenance of equally important class, race, and sex/gender movements inside and outside of education. One of the major reasons for this is the increasing power of the new hegemonic movements that I talked about at the beginning of this interview. Ideological transformations that redefine citizenship, that redefine democracy, have as one of their effects the de-classing, de-racing, and de-gendering of people. That is, to define everyone as a consumer and democracy as individual consumer choice is a radically individuating project with a radically individuating set of identities attached to it. As I mentioned a minute ago, a politics of the left, or multiple politics of the left, then becomes even more difficult.

In what other ways does the resurgence or the strength of the current political right affect education?
I would like to talk here more proximally, more practically, closer to the realities of classrooms. Let's take textbooks as an example. More and more as the Right gains power, especially the religious Right as well as the neo-conservative and neo-liberal Right, what we all too often find is the following at the level of the curriculum.

In the United States, even though there is no official rule that states this should be the case, the curriculum *is* the textbook in a large number of classes. Even though we don't have a national curriculum in the United States, and we don't have a national ministry of education that says that all teachers must use textbooks, it is quite clear that whether we like it or not, most teachers use textbooks. While they can choose among many texts, nearly all the textbooks look basically the same. This has to do with the political economy of textbook publishing. Textbooks are sold on a market and written to the specifications of what the most populous states want. Because of this market, any content that is politically or culturally critical or can cause a negative reaction by powerful groups is avoided. Thus, at the level of the textbook we are witnessing a growing movement away from any kind of provocative material. Anything that can jeopardize sales is to be avoided. This has created a situation of what has been called "dumbing down" (meaning trying to make the textbooks quite simple and bland). Another effect of the increasing power of the Right is the movement toward quite conservative positions, or away from many social democratic or certainly any radical position that might have been found in the core of the curriculum in earlier periods. Since the American curriculum was always a result of compromises over what and whose knowledge should be declared legitimate, it always had some progressive elements in it. Partially progressive discussions of race, sex/gender, disability, environment, and class dynamics and histories had found their way into the curriculum after decades of effort. While these elements are not now removed, they are made much "safer" and are integrated under much more conservative themes and perspectives.

These are important points because in order for dominant groups to maintain their leadership, they had to compromise. They had to have some content about unions, about women, about the lamentable past (and even present) of racial dynamics in their history. Currently we are seeing a movement away from that, but we are also seeing a movement toward certain other kinds of things. For example, for the neo-conservative Right, the notion of tight control over schools becomes crucial as a way to make certain that the appropriate values and knowledge are taught to everyone. Of course, their definition of "appropriate" is very different than, say, an antiracist perspective or one that assumes that knowledge is constructed through action, not pre-given and simply taught in such a way that the role of the student is only to master whatever content is given. Neo-conservatives are pressing for "a curriculum of facts." They want a national or state curriculum and national or state testing, and these in turn should be centered around the "accepted" facts that make up "real" knowledge and on the measurement of outcomes in which students and teachers are to be held strictly accountable for such mastery.

But facts are not alone as an emphasis. Accompanying this is a neo-conservative emphasis on re-instilling values in the curriculum of a conservative kind, and also having these values emphasized in the curriculum, in our teaching practices, and on the tests. All of this is indicative of the fact that, while some of the latest reform rhetoric stresses decentralization, just as often in reality, control is just as likely to be going more and more toward the center.

Neo-conservatives are not alone here, as I said. At the same time, the most powerful element within the new alliance surrounding conservative modernization—neo-liberals—want a closer connection between schools, and the (paid) economy. (This again demonstrates that underpinning neo-liberal positions are patriarchal assumptions—and racial ones as well—a fact that is documented at much greater length in *Educating the "Right" Way* and *The State and the Politics of Knowledge*.) One of the effects of this has been the growth of school-to-work programs.

Such things are contradictory. They have elements of good sense and bad sense within them. They involve positive possibilities in some ways, since many curricula are aimed toward university-bound students and the majority of poor students and/or even working-class students will never go beyond secondary school (Whether or not you feel that it is essential for all students to go beyond secondary is not the issue here). This provides an opening for a discussion of a focus on a polytechnic education as something that is probably wise for *everyone*, not just the working class. There is a long history of such discussions, including the work of John Dewey and others. Thus, oddly enough, neo-liberal positions can provide space for a different kind of debate about the ends of education.

But the way this discussion has been defined is exactly the opposite. Neo-liberals are critical of existing definitions of important knowledge, especially that knowledge that has no connections to what are seen as economic goals and needs. They want creative and enterprising (but still obedient) workers. Flexibility and obedience go hand in hand here. Due to this, a creative and critical polytechnic education that combines "head, heart, and hand" is not sponsored by neo-liberals. The possible space for that discussion is closed down by an emphasis on an education whose role is primarily (and sometimes only) economic.

The movements associated with this aspect of the Right are having a profound effect at the level of textbooks, at the level of testing, and at the level of curriculum. To give another example, one of the mandatory courses that all teachers had to take in my own home state, Wisconsin, in order to become licensed or certified as a teacher was "Education for Employment." The legislation that mandated this also mandated that every curriculum unit in every subject from kindergarten to secondary school must have identifiable elements concerning education for employment. Wisconsin has historically been one of the most progressive states in the entire nation. The fact that it had such legislation speaks to the growing power of the hegemonic discourse of neo-liberalism. One can see, again, that movement toward the Right is having a profound effect.

Finally, there is the authoritarian populist Right. They are making their position known quite strongly, and are increasingly influential in conflicts over texts, over teaching and evaluation, and over the place of religion in the schools. (They want a return to fundamentalist and conservative evangelical religious emphases in the curriculum and/or a de-emphasis on secular perspectives in schooling.)

State-sponsored prayer in schools is illegal in the United States. (In some states you have moments of silence or the prohibition of state-sponsored school prayers is simply ignored.) The re-emphasis of conservative religious impulses by authoritarian populists is making teachers quite fearful of being attacked. In many school districts, teachers are increasingly cautious about what they teach and how they teach it, since they are deeply worried that the curriculum has become subject to severe criticism by religious conservatives, many of whom want to radically alter the curriculum to bring it into line with their own theological and moral positions. So, with the rapid growth of such rightist populism, there is a growing feeling right now of mistrust of teachers, mistrust of the curriculum, and mistrust of the very idea of public schools among such conservative advocates. Not only do teachers throughout the United States feel that they are under attack from these various groups, but there has also been a rapid increase in the number of conservative parents who are now engaged in home schooling. It is estimated that between 1.5 and 2 million children are now being schooled at home to protect them from the supposed ideological, spiritual, and moral dangers of public schooling. This number is many more than children in, say, charter schools, schools that get much more publicity but may be considerably less important than the growth of home schooling.

To this we need to add the repressive forms of compulsory patriotism that have now surfaced and the attacks on dissent in education, the media, and other institutions, and the hidden effects that this movement has had, similar to what I describe in Chapter 9, "Pedagogy, Patriotism, and Democracy." As I've stated time and again, criticism is the sincerest form of patriotism. It means that "This is our country as well" and we expect, demand, that it live up to the ideals for which it supposedly stands.

Obviously, I've only been able to give a bare outline of what is a very complicated, contradictory, and tense situation here. But I've discussed this is at much greater depth in *Cultural Politics and Education* and especially in *Educating the "Right" Way.*

What restrictions do you now see as being imposed upon the research community in education? What will be the results?

I think that here too there exists quite a contradictory situation right now. That is, what is considered as science and as important and legitimate research has been impressively transformed, not only in this nation but elsewhere. For instance, in 1970 when I gave my first address at the American Educational Research Association, I was one of the only persons out of seven or eight thousand researchers who were doing not only ethnographic research at the time, but ethnographic research that was socially and culturally critical. Now there are many such researchers. Hence, when I look around this nation and many others, it would be impossible not to see the transformation that has occurred in what counts as science.

Now there is ethnographic work (both descriptive and critical) and critical historical work; and there is much greater emphasis on conceptual work, narrative work, on life histories, analyses based on cultural studies, and so much more—all of which are now generally seen as legitimate. When you add to this the existence and rapid growth of multiple kinds of feminist research, postcolonial research, critical disability studies, critical race theory, critical discourse analysis, and many other exciting areas and approaches, I think there have been major gains.

However, as in my previous discussion, things do not only go in one direction. These emerging perspectives have also led to a certain kind of fragmentation. There has been an accompanying growth of "private" languages and esoteric ways of expressing our theories that only specialists in a small area can understand. Thus, while the growth of multiple research perspectives has been for the good, one of the dangers has been that it has gotten harder for generally progressive researchers to communicate with each other easily. This must be overcome if we are not only to advance toward a more critically democratic set of perspectives and research agendas, but also to combine research approaches that enable activists and scholars to combine their efforts to clarify what needs to be defended and what needs to be changed in current educational policies and practices.

At the same time as this is going on, there are pressures due to restricted funding to limit what counts as legitimate inquiry, what counts as science, in the academy to only that which helps in an industrial project—or to the priorities and concerns of traditional positivist forms of inquiry. One example is if we look at the emerging patterns of funding in educational research, those who are more deeply involved in testing, evaluation, and assessment or are interested in issues of achievement, not in whose knowledge is actually being taught, are much more likely to get funded than those people who are more socially critical. This is not always the case since some real gains have been made, but the general tendencies are clear. This situation is clearly worsened by the institutionalization within the Bush administration's educational research agenda of the most reductive forms of research as the only legitimate ones.

Hence, there are visible transformations and pressures that are imposed both because of the fiscal crisis in research funds and because of the ideological agenda of the current administration. Thus, while what passes as research has been broadened, whether you ever get a chance to do it and whether it gets published are dependent in part on whether you have funds to be able to carry out the work. Once again there's a political economy of research funding, one that is organized around particular senses of what is important to know and what the legitimate procedures are to know it.

I need to make one other point so that I am not misunderstood. I am not arguing that quantitative research is unimportant. Nor am I arguing against the use of the best of statistical social and psychological tools and perspectives. Indeed, critical qualitative scholarship often smuggles in statistical claims through the back door, so to speak. (Think of critical qualitative research on children in poverty where data on poverty rates, income, and so on provide the foundation for who one studies, or in which poor women, say, have their voices heard in one's research on the effects of the growing impoverishment of women.) To be honest, I am coming to think that critical researchers and activists have actually participated in their own de-skilling by labeling any quantitative work as "polluted." This as been a disaster in some ways, since it often leaves critical work at a disadvantage when public debates occur.

Think of the book *The Bell Curve* by Herrnstein and Murray (funded in large part by the very same conservative foundations that are currently funding the push toward voucher plans), which sought to show that genetically blacks were on average inferior to whites in intelligence and that women were inferior to men mathematically. (Steven Selden's work in *Inheriting Shame* and elsewhere on the history of such funding is very important in this regard.) Not only was the volume fundamentally racist and sexist, it was statistically horribly flawed. No reputable population geneticist would ever make such claims on such poor data. In the public debates, Herrnstein and Murray were able to make their case into a seemingly more powerful one because few critical scholars were actually able to show how bad it was empirically as well.

Has the long U.S. history of opposition to communism caused a skepticism or outright rejection of critical theory due to its basis in Marxist assumptions?
In many ways, yes. But it's important to remember that the United States has its own traditions of radicalism. I've said some things about this earlier when I spoke about why the left was underdeveloped and weaker here. However, it's equally important to understand how crucial race was (and is) in the United States. Class was often racialized and many radical movements grew up around issues of the intersection of class and race.

What is your opinion of the movement toward national certification for teachers?
Let me make a prefatory remark. I think that this issue has to be seen as coming at a particular time. I am not, in principle, opposed to national movements that are aimed at truly democratic reforms. The United States has a history of decentralization. Yet when we decentralize things—for instance, decentralizing decisions from the national level to the state level—capital and business interests sometimes have much more power actually at the state level than the federal level in Washington. As an example, at a state level a large corporation can say to a state government "Unless you give us major tax breaks, we will take our factories and move to another state or Mexico." This continues to happen repeatedly.

In this way, both global and local capital are, in essence, able to hold up, almost to rob, the tax system and use it for their own benefit. It's more hidden than going into a bank with guns, saying "Give me all your money." But in the long run, in terms of the destruction of local communities, in terms of shifting the tax burden and the balance of power in their favor, they can do that more at a local or especially state level than they could at a national level where national unions can intervene. Because of this, some issues are better dealt with at a national level (although this too is changing given the fact that lobbyists for capital and conservative foundations are actually helping to write legislation on economic policy, the environment, and so much more in this administration).

Now on to the issues surrounding national certification of teachers. At the same time as we are moving toward national certification of teachers—and this is supposedly part of a movement away from paper-and-pencil testing of teachers toward more performance-based evaluation of teachers—there are other movements to which it is linked that may make it less progressive. If we are going to do this nationally, we should want a way to know not just whether teachers know their subject matter, but also whether they can actually do creative and socially and educationally critical things with students in schools. But let us be honest—in order for that to work we would have to spend probably a billion dollars that we do not have now. For instance, in the public schools of many of our cities, such as New York or Los Angeles, there are classes being held in toilets and in hallways. In many urban and rural school systems, three elementary classes must share one set of mathematics textbooks.

In the long run then, given the fact that we do not have sufficient money to provide the bare necessities for many of our children in urban and rural areas, either we will then have a national certification model that will be hardly enforceable and based on paper-and-pencil tests as usual, or we will establish two classes of teachers—a small one seen as elite and talented and a considerably larger one (the vast majority of teachers) seen as untalented and less worthy of respect, higher pay, and support. This could be a real disaster, given teachers' working conditions right now in all too many school districts in impoverished areas.

It could reproduce previous negative experiences and effects. It can have the same effect as the National Teachers Examination has had. This test almost had a label attached to it that said, "If you are black, or Native American, or Latino/a or simply poor, you will score more poorly on this test and it will not respond to your culture or your abilities, and it will increase the probability and possibility of having a more affluent, largely white Anglo-Saxon middle-class teaching force even though the demographics of the United States are moving in exactly the opposite direction." This can also be especially dangerous at a time when at the national level, the neo-liberal and neo-conservative Right is growing in power and in its ability to control the goals, means, and content of education.

I am not in any way opposed to increasing the skills and experiences of teachers. But I am asking us if national certification, at a time of resurgent national power of groups who have redefined the meaning and the means and ends of democracy, is wise. There are more participatory alternatives to this, similar to what my colleague Kenneth Zeichner is doing on the development of critical and democratic models of teacher education and teacher development; models that are discussed in his book with Dan Liston, *Teacher Education and the Social Conditions of Schooling* [New York: Routledge, 1991].

You have discussed several issues concerning textbooks used in schools today. How can we improve the way the material included in textbooks is either selected or taught? Would we be better off without textbooks altogether?

Let me answer the first one because it is easier to begin there. I am not usually a believer in textbooks. I think that often they are stultifying. On the other hand, and again I argue this in my book *Official Knowledge*, you have to understand that one of the reasons that textbooks became dominant in the United States is because we had a young teaching force made up mostly of (often very smart) young women in the elementary schools. There were multi-aged, often very crowded, classrooms where the teachers were responsible for every subject area. Given these conditions, teachers insisted on getting some help. They called for standardized materials so that they would have time to actually do some teaching. The textbook was a progressive response, not just a regressive response. Oddly enough, then, it has a partly democratic history in terms of the labor of teachers. Teachers were saying "You can't expect us to teach everything when we don't even have a library in these schools." Due to this, at the turn of the nineteenth to the twentieth century, textbooks and the advice of experts became even more powerful.

Thus, even though textbook publishers were quick to exploit these conditions for their own benefit, the dominance of the standardized textbook came not just from the publishers. It was also a response to a demand from teachers saying "I'm being exploited in this situation; I don't have time to do all this." (Of course, the development of the standardized textbook was also due to other dynamics: from worries about Americanizing the immigrants, to administrators assuming that women weren't talented enough to develop their own material, and to patriarchal assumptions about the need to control women's labor as I show in *Teachers and Texts*, to worries that racially "dangerous" material could be taught that would undercut the prevailing racial order of the United States.)

On the whole, I think a textbook-based curriculum is a curriculum that tends to be boring and uncritical. It tends to not be democratic. To quote Stephen Ball, it is "a curriculum of the dead." In *Democratic Schools* [Alexandria, VA: ASCD, 1995], one of the things that James Beane and I try to do is to show a number of classrooms where teachers have moved to a negotiated curriculum where the materials are built by teachers and students in direct response to local community problems. This seems to me to be a much more dynamic process than reliance on standardized materials that are too often outdated and conservative. *Rethinking Schools* and other publishers have provided powerful examples of ways that teachers can move beyond standardized curricular material to honestly confront important issues.

This does not mean that we can't intervene to make textbooks much better. There are things that we can do. But this intervention must be done with full realization of how the economics and politics of textbooks operate. In the United States, texts are determined at a local or at a state level, depending on the state in which one lives. However, the southern tier of states (about 20 states) have state textbook adoption policies. They have established rigorous criteria that must be met for a book to be approved in those states. Three of the states—Texas, California, and Florida—control much of what will be published in the entire nation.

Since these are among the most populous states and, in essence, they buy their textbooks statewide, publishers will only publish what sells in Texas, California, and Florida. (Together, these three states make up around 35% of the textbook market. They are also the home of powerful conservative movements. Remember, Ronald Reagan was the governor of California before becoming president. Bush was the governor of Texas and his brother is currently the governor of Florida.) Due to this, if you wanted to make a difference in the contents of textbooks and in their organization, you would have to organize in those three states. This means progressive movements must learn what the Right has learned: to organize and target your movement well; to focus on those areas that have the largest potential for transformative effect; and to realize that it will take years of cultural efforts and political organizing. The Right did the hard work. So must we.

What is your feeling about a national curriculum?
Again, let me preface this by saying I am not, in principle, opposed to the idea of things being democratically decided and then being institutionalized at a national level. However, in my mind, the only reason for a national curriculum, the *only* reason, is to stimulate debate over what knowledge is important at every level from local schools to cities to states to regions. The only reason for even talking about it is to stimulate a national debate!

In the United States, the movement toward a national curriculum, by and large, is a conservative movement, although it has more liberal and more progressive elements in it. An example would be that some African American scholars want a national curriculum because for the first time it would guarantee that in very conservative, often racist school districts, you would have to teach the histories of people of color.

On the other hand, however, I think that moving toward a national curriculum at this time in the United States would be quite dangerous. One of the effects of having a national curriculum at this time in the United States is to legitimate and institutionalize a system of national testing. Both the neo-conservatives and the neo-liberal aspects of conservative modernization are strongly in favor of such a test. Once a national test is instituted, based on a national curriculum, in general the knowledge of elite economic and cultural groups will dominate. We know from past experiences in a number of nations that they have more of a voice and more power to get their knowledge into the test.

Thus I predict that a national curriculum will inexorably lead to a national test. I would also predict that the national test would be used, in Washington and at the state level, to justify cost cutting and expediency. Rather than showing which students need extra funding and support, it would confirm common sense by tacitly underpinning a position that holds that poor and working-class children are less intelligent.

Once this is established as the common sense again at a national level, there will be no more money given to those schools which in many places are in such economic crisis that many school districts in the United States will have to close their doors earlier in the school year and not have children attend them the required 180 days a year. There would be no money to do anything else.

There is another danger in a time of neo-liberal reforms and that is that a national curriculum and a national test will exacerbate even more the process of turning schools into commodities. The neo-liberal emphasis, remember, is on making the school either part of the economy or making it into a commodity itself.

As has happened in England, where their national curriculum is sutured into the national test (the results of which are published as "league tables" in the press and elsewhere in which schools are compared), this provides a direct mechanism that enables the Right, in essence, to put price tags on schools and say "This is a good school, this is a bad school." In essence, it enables them to say "There's no more money to support real efforts at democratic school reform, so what we need to do then is marketize."

This is a direct link to voucher plans, which give parents a small amount of money for them to choose marketized schools. Soon we will have a system in which, if you have higher incomes, you can supplement the public money from these vouchers and you can go to any school you want. It is a formula for disaster.

These are complicated dynamics. A national curriculum and a national test will oddly lead both to increasing privatization on the one hand and increasing centralization of control over official knowledge on the other. It will place price tags on schools so that the market can function. The private sector for the affluent will expand and there will be a fiction of choice for the poor and working class. This is exactly what Whitty, Power, and Halpin found in their book, *Devolution and Choice in Education* [Bristol, PA: Open University Press, 1998] and what Lauder and Hughes found as well in their own recent examination of the connections among neo-liberal markets, neo-conservative policies on curricula and testing, and inequality, *Trading in Places* [Philadelphia: Open University Press, 1999]. The truly damaging effects inside classrooms of this combination are demonstrated graphically as well in Gillborn and Youdell's excellent book, *Rationing Education* [Philadelphia: Open University Press, 1999].

The implications of this are profound. Federal and state money will go to private schools; more affluent parents will move their children out of underfunded public schools that will be falling apart and place them in private schools. They will refuse to pay taxes to make the remaining schools better. What we will have is highly controlled, highly policed, and decaying schools in the inner cities. That will be destructive for all concerned. In my mind, then, a national curriculum at a time of neo-liberal and neo-conservative hegemony is a formula for what I will call very bluntly simply "educational apartheid."

Do you feel that NCATE (National Council for Accreditation of Teacher Education, a bureaucratic organization that evaluates the quality of teacher education programs) *and the other accrediting bodies have too much power?*

Definitely. As a matter of fact, the University of Wisconsin withdrew from NCATE more than a decade ago. One of the reasons being that accrediting agencies such as this have a universal model that they think they can impose on every education program at every institution. Since at that time and now, we were considered in the national ratings to be one of the very highest rated schools of education in the United States, the kinds of programmatic and bureaucratic reports and changes that they were requesting seemed to be taking an enormous amount of time and money and were not thought to be very helpful. In our own deliberations, we were certain that we could do better on our own given our very real commitment to build a high-quality undergraduate and graduate program in education.

Hence, we did withdraw. But later on we were under considerable pressure to re-join because of the problem of portability of credentials. Could the graduates of our teacher education program have their credentials nationally recognized? This national recognition is important of course, but it often substitutes for a more serious and less bureaucratic response to the problem of building a socially and educationally critical teacher education program. And I am not at all certain that NCATE and similar organizations actually assist us in doing that. Thus, while I think that there are elements of NCATE that are partly progressive, I think that in general NCATE and similar bureaucratic accrediting agencies deserve the criticism they often get.

What are the implications of Herrnstein and Murray's book, The Bell Curve *for education?*
At first I was amazed that it was published! Clearly, as I mentioned earlier, all of its logic and all of its data have been discredited before. As I said, no reputable geneticist would make the claim they are making. There is no genetic argument you can make about large populations based on their analysis. We have been through the Arthur Jensen period before and we know that these kinds of claims are methodologically, ethically, and theoretically wrong. Statistically, as well, it's simply bad science.

What it proves is that the American Enterprise Institute, the Heritage Foundation, the Bradley Foundation, and other neo-liberal and neo-conservative think tanks are incredibly influential and very highly funded. They helped place Murray (Herrnstein had died before the book was published) on what seemed to be every talk show on television and radio and in every newspaper and magazine throughout the United States. They had millions of dollars behind the scenes sponsoring this. Its overt effects on educational policy, in the short term, have been relatively minimal. The longer term ideological consequences may be more hidden, but may have more lasting implications.

Even if it were true that on the average, say, African Americans by and large have a lower IQ (a simply disgustingly racist claim), we know that the tails of the curve overlap to such an extent that there's no educational policy you could make that would be different. Therefore, even if the book's claims were true, it would make no difference. On the other hand, what the book has done, in this time of growing reactionary politics, racist nativism, economic uncertainties, and possessive individualism, is to exacerbate these tendencies. People blame minority groups and immigrants for the problems of the economy. Economic fears are organized around rightist themes. Affirmative action for "unworthy groups" (both biologically and morally) and similar policies are seen as the root causes of social and educational problems. This enables dominant groups more and more to shift the blame away from their own culpability in making crucial economic and political decisions.

In essence, what this does is establish one more brick in a wall that is being built between dominant groups and the rest of us. By exacerbating a situation where people blame all of their problems in the economy, with crime, with a loss of security and tradition on even less powerful groups than themselves, this can destroy communities and any real sense of the common good. I find that very destructive. Its long-term effects on education, then, may be in justifying even more cuts in funding for social services, health care, programs to expand educational opportunities, and so on. It will do this by confirming and legitimating in certain people intuitions about the Other that they had before, intuitions that often are quite racist. These hidden effects may be harder to see, but they are significant. Thus, even though things like *The Bell Curve* itself may not have a major effect on education in terms of obvious changes in policy and practice, this doesn't mean that its effects aren't there. And these effects are international as well as national since if these arguments based on "saying the unsayable" are seen as legitimate in the United States, they are also then seen as increasingly legitimate in other nations.

Should there be a unified system of education? In this regard, let us give you some background. We have gifted education, and special education, reading education, and vocational education. Should we have a unified system of education or should we have all these "splinter educations"?

In part, we already have a unified system of education right now, but in a very odd way. That is, schools function to sort and select. That's not all they were built to do, but it certainly was one of the reasons they were built and organized the way they were. Just read Horace Mann's original work—or any of the original early school builders—and you will understand that schools were there in part to be "vast engines of democracy." But these engines would be based on a vision of democracy in which some people would be leaders and some people would be followers. The unified notion of schools as sorting and selecting is very much alive and well.

We also have another strong element of uniformity, one based on the textbook. As I mentioned before, we have a national curriculum in the United States, but it's unofficial. It is almost as if we had a ministry of education mandating that particular things be taught, but by "ability."

More directly related to the interest behind your question, what should we have? My own position on this was stated earlier. In an ideal world I think that a good education is a polytechnic education for everyone—that is an education of heart, head, and hand for *all* people. We would not have tracking and screening. We would not have a differential curriculum that says that specific types of students will go to vocational training and others will go somewhere else. I find that very dangerous. In a time of declining resources, no matter what the rhetoric behind it, this differential vision simply leads to the rebuilding through the school of traditional hierarchical models of the social division of labor. Thus, I want a uniform model in terms of the way we think about an education for everybody. I want us not to negatively differentiate. I also am usually strongly in favor of inclusive education, that is of not having separate special education classes for students who are labeled as having emotional disabilities or physical disabilities. I think that's important not just for the children who are labeled as having disabilities, but it is just as important for the children who are not labeled that way. What kind of society are we producing when we separate out and do not have collective responsibilities so that our children don't know how to interact with everyone else?

On the other hand, while in an ideal situation I would prefer to have inclusive schools, on the other hand, in the realities of too many classrooms what we have now are rising class sizes, decreasing budgets, more social problems in the schools, and the intensification of teachers' labor. To quote from one of my friends who teaches in the schools of my own city, "Michael, I don't have time even to go to the bathroom during the day." Given this kind of situation, what is happening in many ways to teachers is that the rhetoric is saying "inclusion," but the reality says "Dump these children into a regular classroom, and give no help, no assistance, no resources to teachers who are already in conditions that make life extremely difficult." Hence, in the real situation in a considerable number of schools and classrooms, what we have is often equivalent to what we did when we closed mental hospitals in the United States. We dumped people back into the communities and let them sink or swim, with little long-term support. And by and large, they sank.

What impact do you think the current U.S. Republican Congress and the popular conservative radio commentator Rush Limbaugh [an ultra-conservative who is the most widely listened-to radio personality in the United States] *will play in enacting a conservative agenda on education? What do you see as the components of their impact?*
In many ways, I've have answered some of this earlier. I think that all the trends toward privatization, marketization, tighter control of knowledge and values, blaming the schools for everything, and so much more will just be continued and will fester. We will have even better schools for rich children and even poorer schools for poor children. The gap between rich and poor schools will

widen measurably, as it already is doing. I also think that there will increasingly be the creation of a rightist "common sense" that is once again exactly what we are seeing right now. In *Official Knowledge* and *Educating the "Right" Way,* I argue that one of the major things the Right has realized is that to win in the state, you must win in civil society. That is, you must change a society's fundamental ideas about what schools (and all social policies) are for.

I think that Rush Limbaugh and similar conservative radio and TV personalities are spokespersons for much of the very large movement I've been talking about here. What people like him are now saying continues to be immensely damaging. Much of what they are saying is patently racist and sexist. But it does speak to the anger that has been organized around the themes that the Right has taken up. It speaks to a populist impulse, but that impulse has been colonized by the Right in powerful ways so that people who are angry about the ways they are treated and worried (justifiably) about their future and that of their children are brought under the leadership of the conservative alliance. There has been a very clever use of the discourse of individual responsibility here—a discourse that says that *we* are responsible and moral and *they* (people of color, the poor, immigrants, gays and lesbians, state employees, etc.) are not. What radio personalities such as Limbaugh do is legitimate the notion that people are poor because it's their fault, that people don't do well in school not because there are no jobs and no economic future, or because of horrible inequalities in resources, but because again they are stupid and have no character or morals. He and many others like him also then characterize anyone who has principled disagreement with conservatives as ideologues or as unpatriotic or as "special interests." Various fractions of capital aren't special interest groups? The oil company executives at the center of our government aren't a special interest group? The corporations that are weakening our environmental laws aren't a special interest group? The Christian Right isn't a special interest group? Conservative foundations don't speak for special interest groups? Well funded, largely white and conservative anti–affirmative action organizations aren't special interest groups? It's always interesting to me to see how this works. Language has real power here.

This has meant and will mean the same in the future. I fear that we will have city, state, and national administrations who, in order to win the votes of those who are generating what might best be called "white anger," will be even more uncaring about the plight of those who are really on the bottom. The results of these policies will be covered up, using as rhetoric words that used to be socially democratic (democracy, freedom, etc.). In fact, one of the most powerful (and at times brutal) things the Right has done—and Rush Limbaugh has been effective in popularizing this strategy—is to take populist sentiments that are so popular and powerful in the United States (the language of the people) and give them a rightist turn. A situation has been created in which the increasingly dominant perspective is it's us against them, with the "we" being the supposedly hardworking Americans who somehow made it out of poverty by their own efforts, and the "they's" are African American, Latino/a, and other people of color. This is creating a climate in which racial and economic segregation is now called "choice." And it is justified using the rhetoric of democracy as consumption practices. It's a brilliant strategy and the effects of it are all too visible all around us. It does point, however, to the crucial importance of progressives learning how to employ the media in creative ways to counter the messages of people such as Limbaugh and others like him. Talk shows, the Internet, and films and even popular books as Michael Moore has shown—all of these are crucial and the progressive communities are just beginning to learn how to use them effectively.

Given what is happening in general, however, I am very, very worried about the future of American education. The transformations we are experiencing are very real. Yet, conditions have been bad before and the forces of thick democracy have won major gains then as well. I don't want to be rhetorical here. What is happening for example in Porto Alegre in Brazil with the growth of participatory budgeting and Citizen Schools gives us reason for hope. This is where the South has much to teach the North. Thus, I am an optimist without illusions. Raymond Williams was wise when he said that hope is one of our most valuable resources. Now we have to act on that hope.

Notes

Preface to the 25th Anniversary Third Edition

1. In the order in which they were written, the books that followed *Ideology and Curriculum* include *Education and Power* (New York: Routledge, 1982; revised Ark Edition, 1985; 2nd ed. 1995), *Teachers and Texts* (New York: Routledge, 1986), *Official Knowledge* (New York: Routledge, 1993; 2nd ed. 2000), *Cultural Politics and Education* (New York: Teachers College Press, 1996), *Educating the "Right" Way: Markets, Standards, God, and Inequality* (New York: RoutledgeFalmer, 2001), and Michael W. Apple, et al., *The State and the Politics of Knowledge* (New York: RoutledgeFalmer, 2003). The latter volume was a collective project and extends and deepens the arguments made in *Educating the "Right" Way*. There is a volume of a number of my other essays that may be useful to examine as well. See *Power, Meaning, and Identity* (New York: Peter Lang, 1999).
2. Pierre Bourdieu, *The State Nobility* (Stanford: Stanford University Press, 1996).
3. Apple, *Educating the "Right" Way*.
4. Pauline Lipman, *High Stakes Education* (New York: RoutledgeFalmer, 2004) and Linda Mc-Neil, *The Contradictions of School Reform* (New York: Routledge, 2000).
5. Mary Lee Smith, et al., *Political Spectacle and American Education* (New York: Routledge-Falmer, 2004).
6. See Apple, *Educating the "Right" Way*, McNeil, *The Contradictions of School Reform*, and David Gillborn and Deborah Youdell, *Rationing Education* (Philadelphia: Open University Press, 2000).
7. Michael B. Katz, *The Price of Citizenship* (New York: Metropolitan Books, 2001, p. 2).
8. Ibid, p. 37.
9. Charles Mills, *The Racial Contract* (Ithaca: Cornell University Press, 1997).
10. Katz, *The Price of Citizenship*, pp. 43–44.
11. For a much more detailed examination of this, see Apple, et al. *The State and the Politics of Knowledge*.
12. Ibid.
13. Michael W. Apple and James A. Beane, eds. *Democratic Schools* (Alexandria, VA: Association for Supervision and Curriculum Development, 1995).

Preface to the Second Edition

1. See, for example, Michael W. Apple, *Teachers and Texts* (New York: Routledge, 1986).
2. Marcus Raskin, *The Common Good* (New York: Routledge, 1986).
3. See Kenneth Teitelbaum, "Contestation and Curriculum: The Efforts of American Socialists, 1900–1920," in Landon E. Beyer and Michael W. Apple, eds., *The Curriculum: Problems, Politics and Possibilities* (Albany: State University of New York Press, 1988), pp. 32–55.
4. This is discussed at greater length in Landon E. Beyer and Michael W. Apple, "Values and Politics in Curriculum," in Beyer and Apple, eds., *The Curriculum*, pp. 3–16.
5. Apple, *Teachers and Texts*.
6. Raskin. *The Common Good*, p. 8.
7. Ibid.
8. Michael W. Apple, *Education and Power* (Boston: Routledge, ARK Edition, 1985).
9. Apple, *Teachers and Texts*.
10. Michael W. Apple, ed., *Cultural and Economic Reproduction in Education* (Boston: Routledge, 1982), Michael W. Apple and Lois Weis, eds., *Ideology and Practice in Schooling* (Philadelphia: Temple University Press, 1983), and Beyer and Apple, eds., *The Curriculum*.
11. Pierre Bourdieu, quoted in Loie J. D. Wacquant, "Toward a Reflexive Sociology: A Workshop With Pierre Bourdieu," *Sociological Theory* 7 (Spring 1989), p. 24. For a detailed analysis of some of the limitations of even this reformulation, see Philip Wexler, *Social Analysis of Education* (New York: Routledge, 1987).

12. See, for example, Apple, *Education and Power*, Apple, *Teachers and Texts*, and Cameron McCarthy and Michael W. Apple, "Class, Race and Gender in American Educational Research," in Lois Weis, ed., *Class, Race and Gender in American Education* (Albany: State University of New York Press, 1988), pp. 9–39.

13. I have analyzed this in considerably greater depth in Michael W. Apple, "Redefining Equality," *Teachers College Record* 90 (Winter 1988), pp. 167–184.

14. See Herbert Gintis, "Communication and Politics," *Socialist Review* 10 (March/June 1980), pp. 189–232. Samuel Bowles and Herbert Gintis, *Democracy and Capitalism* (New York: Basic Books, 1986), and Ernesto Laclau and Chantal Mouffe, *Hegemony and Socialist Strategy* (London: Verso, 1985).

15. William Bennett, *Our Children and Our Country* (New York: Simon & Schuster, 1988).

16. Raymond Williams, *Resources of Hope* (New York: Verso, 1989), p. 35–36.

17. Ibid, p. 37–38.

18. Ibid, p. 38.

19. Ibid, p. 216.

20. Ibid, p. 14.

21. See Ira Shor, *Culture Wars* (New York: Routledge, 1986).

22. Stanley Aronowitz and Henry Giroux, "Schooling, Culture, and Literacy in the Age of Broken Dreams," *Harvard Educational Review* 58 (May 1988), pp. 172–194.

23. Pierre Bourdieu quoted in Wacquant, "Toward a Reflexive Sociology," p. 46.

24. Ibid.

25. Williams, *Resources of Hope*, p. xxi.

26. Raymond Williams, *The Long Revolution* (London: Chatto and Windus, 1961).

Chapter 1

1. Michael W. Apple, "Personal Statement," *Curriculum Theorizing: The Reconceptualists* (Berkeley: McCutchan, 1975), pp. 89–93.

2. Donald Lazere, "Mass Culture, Political Consciousness, and English Studies," *College English*, XXXVIII (April 1977), 755.

3. Ibid.

4. See, for example, Basil Bernstein, *Class, Codes and Control, Volume 3: Towards a Theory of Educational Transmissions* (London: Routledge & Kegan Paul, 1975), p. 158.

5. Samuel Bowles and Herbert Gintis, *Schooling in Capitalist America* (New York: Basic Books, 1976).

6. The research on this is described rather clearly in Caroline Hodges Persell, *Education and Inequality* (New York: Free Press, 1977).

7. Roger Dale, *et al.*, eds, *Schooling and Capitalism: A Sociological Reader* (London: Routledge & Kegan Paul, 1976), p. 3.

8. See the analysis of Althusser's notion of "overdetermination" in Miriam Glucksmann, *Structuralist Analysis in Contemporary Social Thought* (London: Routledge & Kegan Paul, 1975).

9. Raymond Williams, "Base and Superstructure in Marxist Cultural Theory," *Schooling and Capitalism*, Roger Dale, *et al.*, eds, op. cit., p. 202.

10. Ibid., pp. 204–5.

11. Ibid., p. 205.

12. See, for example, Michael F. D. Young, ed., *Knowledge and Control* (London: Collier-Macmillan, 1971).

13. Michael W. Apple, "Power and School Knowledge," *The Review of Education III* (January/Feburary, 1977), 26–49, and Chapters 2 and 3 below.

14. Seymour Sarason, *The Culture of the School and the Problem of Change* (Boston: Allyn & Bacon, 1971).

15. Trent Schroyer's account of this process is helpful here. See his *The Critique of Domination* (New York: George Braziller, 1973).

16. Part of what follows here appears in expanded form in Michael W. Apple, "Humanism and the Politics of Educational Argumentation," *Humanistic Education: Visions and Realities*, Richard Weller, ed. (Berkeley: McCutchan, 1977), pp. 315–30.

17. Raymond Williams, *The Long Revolution* (London: Chatto & Windus, 1961, pp. 298–300.

18. Apple, "Power and School Knowledge," op. cit.

19. Ian Hextall and Madan Sarup, "School Knowledge, Evaluation and Alienation," *Society, State and Schooling,* Michael Young and Geoff Whitty, eds (Guildford, England: Falmer Press, 1977), pp. 151–71.

20. Carl Boggs, *Gramsci's Marxism* (London: Pluto Press, 1976), p. 9 and Persell, op. cit., pp. 7–11.

21. See Paul Baran and Paul Sweezy, *Monopoly Capital* (New York: Monthly Review Press, 1968). See also the exemplary analysis in Vicente Navarro, *Medicine Under Capitalism* (New York: Neale Watson Academic Publications, 1976).

22. John Rawls, *A Theory of Justice* (Cambridge, Mass.: Harvard University Press, 1971).

23. For an interesting discussion of the debate in education over the social principle of equality of opportunity, see Walter Feinberg, *Reason and Rhetoric: The Intellectual Foundations of Twentieth Century Liberal Educational Policy* (New York: John Wiley, 1975). See also, the articles on worker control of the workplace that have appeared in *Working Papers for a New Society* over the past few years.

24. Navarro, op. cit.

25. Louis Wirth, "Preface" to Karl Mannheim, *Ideology and Utopia* (New York: Harcourt, Brace & World, 1936), pp. xxii–xxiii.

26. Philip Wexler, *The Sociology of Education: Beyond Equality* (Indianapolis: Bobbs-Merrill, 1976).

27. Michael W. Apple, "Curriculum as Ideological Selection," *Comparative Education Review,* XX (June, 1976), 209–15, and Michael W. Apple and Philip Wexler, "Cultural Capital and Educational Transmissions," *Educational Theory,* XXVII (Winter, 1978).

28. Michael F. D. Young, ed., *Knowledge and Control* (London: Collier-Macmillan, 1971), Richard Brown, ed., *Knowledge, Education and Cultural Change* (London: Tavistock, 1973), Basil Bernstein, *Class, Codes and Control Volume 3: Towards a Theory of Educational Transmissions* (2nd edn: London: Routledge & Kegan Paul, 1977), Michael Flude and John Ahier, eds, *Educability, Schools and Ideology* (London: Halstead, 1974), and Rachel Sharp and Anthony Green, *Education and Social Control: A Study in Progressive Primary Education* (London: Routledge & Kegan Paul, 1975). A review of much of this work can be found in John Eggleston, *The Sociology of the School Curriculum* (London: Routledge & Kegan Paul, 1977).

29. Young, op. cit., p. 24.

30. Feinberg, op. cit., p. vii.

31. Roger Dale, *et al.,* op. cit., p. 1.

32. Ibid., pp. 1–2.

33. Ibid., p. 2.

34. In the examination that follows, I am drawing upon the excellent treatment of ideology by Helen M. McClure and George Fischer, "Ideology and Opinion Making: General Problems of Analysis" (New York: Columbia University Bureau of Applied Social Research, July, 1969, mimeographed).

35. See, for example, Clifford Geertz, "Ideology as a Cultural System," *Ideology and Discontent,* David Apter, ed. (New York: Free Press, 1964), pp. 47–76.

36. McClure and Fischer, op. cit., pp. 7–10.

37. For further discussion of the problem of ideology, one of the more analytically interesting treatments can be found in Nigel Harris, *Beliefs in Society: The Problem of Ideology* (London: C. A. Watts, 1968).

Chapter 2

1. Thomas R. Bates, "Gramsci and The Theory of Hegemony," *Journal of the History of Ideas,* XXXVI (April–June 1975), 36.

2. Karl Mannheim, *Ideology and Utopia* (New York: Harcourt, Brace & World, 1936).

3. This is of course best laid out by Peter Berger and Thomas Luckmann, *The Social Construction of Reality* (New York: Doubleday, 1966). The most articulate challenge to the use of such "phenomenological" formulations in education is found in Rachel Sharp and Anthony Green, *Education and Social Control: A Study in Progressive Primary Education* (London: Routledge & Kegan Paul, 1975).

4. Geoff Whitty, "Sociology and the Problem of Radical Educational Change," *Educability, Schools and Ideology,* Michael Flude and John Ahier, eds (London: Halstead Press, 1974), p. 125.

5. Raymond Williams, *The Long Revolution* (London: Chatto & Windus, 1961), pp. 119–20.

6. Herbert M. Kliebard, "Persistent Curriculum Issues in Historical Perspective," *Curriculum Theorizing: The Reconceptualists,* William Pinar, ed. (Berkeley: McCutchan, 1975), pp. 39–50.

7. Taped interview given at the University of Wisconsin, Madison. The necessity for large-scale educational reform movements to have this cautious penumbra of vagueness is analyzed further in B. Paul Komisar and James McClellan, "The Logic of Slogans," *Language and Concepts in Education,* B. Othanel Smith and Robert Ennis, eds (Chicago: Rand Mc-Nally, 1961), pp. 195–214.

8. See, for example, Raymond Williams, *The Country and the City* (New York: Oxford University Press, 1973), Pierre Bourdieu and Jean Claude Passeron, *Reproduction in Education, Society and Culture* (London: Sage, 1977) and Basil Bernstein, *Class, Codes and Control, Volume 3: Towards a Theory of Educational Transmissions* (2nd edn; London: Routledge & Kegan Paul, 1977).

9. Joseph Schwab, *The Practical: A Language for Curriculum* (Washington: National Education Association, 1970), and Dwayne Huebner, "Implications of Psychological Thought for the Curriculum," *Influences in Curriculum Change,* Glenys Unruh and Robert Leeper, eds (Washington: Association for the Supervision and Curriculum Development, 1968, pp. 28–37).

10. These issues are discussed further in Chapter 3 below and in Geoff Whitty and Michael Young, eds, *Explorations in the Politics of School Knowledge* (Nafferton, England: Nafferton Books, 1976).

11. I am drawing on the insightful exposition of these two research traditions in Philip Wexler, "Ideology and Utopia in American Sociology of Education," *Education in a Changing Society,* Antonia Kloskowska and Guido Martinotti, eds (London: Sage, 1977), pp. 27–58.

12. Robert Dreeben, *On What is Learned in Schools* (Reading, Mass.: Addison Wesley, 1968).

13. Michael F. D. Young, "On the Politics of Educational Knowledge," *Education in Great Britain and Ireland,* R. Bell, ed. (London: Oxford, 1973), p. 201.

14. Wexler, op. cit.

15. For further examination of the roots of this tradition see Michael W. Apple, "Power and School Knowledge," *The Review of Education,* III (January/February 1977), 26–49, and Michael W. Apple and Philip Wexler, "Cultural Capital and Educational Transmissions," *Educational Theory,* XXVIII (Winter 1978).

16. Michael F. D. Young, "Knowledge and Control," *Knowledge and Control,* Michael F. D. Young, ed. (London: Collier-Macmillan, 1971), p. 8.

17. Bourdieu and Passeron, op. cit., p. 5.

18. I have analyzed the conceptual and political commitments further in Apple, "Power and School Knowledge," op. cit.

19. Madeleine MacDonald, *The Curriculum and Cultural Reproduction* (Milton Keynes: Open University Press, 1977), p. 60.

20. Samuel Bowles and Herbert Gintis, *Schooling in Capitalist America* (New York: Basic Books, 1976).

21. MacDonald, op. cit., p. 309. This piece also provides a number of interesting criticisms of Bowles and Gintis's reliance on a correspondence theory.

22. John W. Meyer, "The Effects of Education as an Institution," *American Journal of Sociology,* LXXXIII (July 1977), 64.

23. MacDonald, op. cit.

24. Roger Dale, *et al.,* eds. *Schooling and Capitalism: A Sociological Reader* (London: Routledge & Kegan Paul, 1976), p. 4.

25. Ibid.

26. R. W. Connell, *Ruling Class, Ruling Culture* (New York: Cambridge University Press, 1977), p. 219. How this actually operates, especially through the complex process of labeling that goes on in schools, will be explored further in Chapter 7.

27. MacDonald, op. cit.

28. The two way nature of this relationship—how culture and economics interpenetrate and act on each other in a dynamic fashion—is best examined in Raymond Williams, "Base and Superstructure in Marxist Cultural Theory," *New Left Review,* LXXXII (November/December 1973).

29. Ibid. See also the final chapter, "Aspects of the Relations between Education and Production," in Bernstein, op. cit.

30. Michael F. D. Young, "Taking Sides Against the Probable," *Rationality, Education and The Social Organization of Knowledge* (London, Routledge & Kegan Paul, 1977), pp. 86–96 and Michael W. Apple, "Curriculum as Ideological Selection," *Comparative Education Review,* XX (June, 1976), 209–15.

31. See, for example, Albrecht Wellmer, *Critical Theory of Society* (New York: Herder and Herder, 1971), especially Chapter 1. See also the discussion of the position taken by the French Marxist philosopher of science Louis Althusser in Miriam Glucksmann, *Structuralist Analysis in Contemporary Social Thought* (London: Routledge & Kegan Paul, 1974). Though it may be difficult to deal with "proving" critically oriented social assertions using the positivist tradition, this does not mean that empirical documentation of aspects of the problem is inconsequential. This is nicely argued in Connell, op. cit.

32. Ian Hextall and Madan Sarup, "School Knowledge, Evaluation and Alienation," *Society, State and Schooling,* Michael Young and Geoff Whitty, eds (London: Falmer Press, 1977), pp. 151–71.

33. See the articles by Mehan and McKay in Hans Peter Dreitzel, ed., *Childhood and Socialization* (New York: Macmillan, 1973), and Linda M. McNeil, "Economic Dimensions of Social Studies Curricula: Curriculum as Institutionalized Knowledge" (unpublished doctoral thesis, University of Wisconsin, Madison, 1977).

34. Whitty, op. cit.

35. Michael F. D. Young, "An Approach to the Study of Curricula as Socially Organized Knowledge," in Young, *Knowledge and Control,* op. cit. There are interesting parallels here between the work of Young and Huebner in their joint focus on curricular accessibility. Compare Dwayne Huebner, "Curriculum as the Accessibility of Knowledge" (unpublished paper presented at Curriculum Theory Study Group, Minneapolis, 2 March 1970, mimeographed).

36. Bernice Fischer, "Conceptual Masks: An Essay Review of Fred Inglis, *Ideology and The Imagination,*" *Review of Education,* I (November 1975), 526. See also Hextall and Sarup, op. cit.

37. The principle that schools serve to maximize the production of technical knowledge was first noted by Walter Feinberg in his provocative chapter "A Critical Analysis of the Social and Economic Limits to the Humanizing of Education," *Humanistic Education: Visions and Realities,* Richard H. Weller, ed. (Berkeley: McCutchan, 1977), pp. 249–69. My analysis here is indebted to his own.

38. Andrew Hacker, "Cutting Classes," *New York Review of Books,* XXIII (May, 1976), 15. Hacker notes that at full employment our economy can usefully use only about 43 per cent of the work age population. It is not profitable to employ more than that. "Some of the unnecessary 57 per cent become housewives, college students, or retire on moderate pensions. Others, however, must settle for a lifetime of poverty because the economic system offers them no alternatives."

39. Geoff Whitty and Michael F. D. Young, "The Politics of School Knowledge," *Times Educational Supplement,* September 1973, 20.

40. This is an empirical claim, of course, and is falsifiable. There are a number of educators and scientists who would take issue with such a simplification of science and mathematics. See, for example, Thomas Kuhn, *The Structure of Scientific Revolutions* (University of Chicago Press, 1970). What aspects of scientific "paradigms" *are* stable is being argued right now. See Imre Lakatos and Alan Musgrave, eds, *Criticism and the Growth of Knowledge* (Cambridge University Press, 1970) and Stephen Toulmin, *Human Understanding* (Princeton University Press, 1972).

41. Harry Braverman, *Labor and Monopoly Capital* (New York: Monthly Review Press, 1975).

42. The close relationship between academic curricula, the distribution of scarce resources, and the labeling and tracking of high school students is documented in James E. Rosenbaum, *Making Inequality* (New York: John Wiley & Sons, 1976).

43. Young, "An Approach to the Study of Curriculum as Socially Organized Knowledge," op. cit., p. 34.

44. Habermas's analysis of how purposive/rational or instrumental forms of language and action have come to dominate our consciousness is illuminating here. Cf., Jürgen Habermas, *Knowledge and Human Interests* (Boston: Beacon Press, 1971) and Michael W. Apple, "The Process and Ideology of Valuing in Educational Settings," *Educational Evaluation: Analysis and Responsibility,* Michael W. Apple, *et al.,* eds (Berkeley: McCutchan, 1974), pp. 3–34. We would want to trace the growth in status of purposive/rational forms of action within the

concomitant growth of particular economic systems. Raymond Williams's corpus of work provides essential models for this kind of inquiry. See his *The Long Revolution,* op. cit. and *The Country and the City,* op. cit.

45. Reviews of some of the relevant research on the question of hegemony can be found in David W. Livingston, "On Hegemony in Corporate Capitalist States," *Sociological Inquiry,* XLVI (nos 3 and 4, 1976), 235–50 and R. W. Connell, op. cit., especially Chapters 7–10.

46. See also, Herbert Gintis and Samuel Bowles, "Educational Reform in the U.S.: An Historical and Statistical Survey" (New York: The World Bank, March 1977, mimeographed).

47. Raymond Williams, *The Long Revolution,* op. cit., pp. 298–9.

48. Henry M. Levin, "A Radical Critique of Educational Policy" (Stanford, California: Occasional Paper of the Stanford University Evaluation Consortium, March, 1977, mimeographed), pp. 26–7.

49. Basil Bernstein has made some intriguing inroads into this area in his "Aspects of the Relations Between Education and Production" in Bernstein, op. cit. See also, Nicos Poulantzas, *Classes in Contemporary Capitalism* (London: New Left Books, 1975) and Burton Bledstein, *The Culture of Professionalism* (New York: Norton, 1976).

50. See the interesting essay by John W. Meyer, op. cit. Randall Collins's attempt to articulate a theory of cultural markets, in "Some Comparative Principles of Educational Stratification," *Harvard Educational Review,* XLVII (February, 1977), 1–27, is also of some assistance here. It is a bit conceptually confused, though. See my reply to him in *Harvard Educational Review,* XLVII (November 1977), 601–2.

51. William Pinar, ed., *Curriculum Theorizing: The Reconceptualists* (Berkeley: McCutchan, 1975).

52. Walter Feinberg, *Reason and Rhetoric: The Intellectual Foundations of Twentieth Century Liberal Educational Policy* (New York: John Wiley, 1975).

Chapter 3

1. Charles Silberman, *Crisis in the Classroom* (New York: Random House, 1970).

2. Herbert Gintis and Samuel Bowles, "The Contradictions of Liberal Educational Reform," *Work, Technology, and Education,* Walter Feinberg and Henry Rosemont, Jr, eds (Urbana: University of Illinois Press, 1975), p. 109.

3. That this is not merely an "intellectual" interest, but embodies social and ideological commitments will be examined in greater depth in Chapter 6.

4. Michael F. D. Young, "Knowledge and Control," *Knowledge and Control,* Michael F. D. Young, ed. (London: Collier-Macmillan, 1971), p. 8.

5. John Kennett, "The Sociology of Pierre Bourdieu," *Educational Review,* XXV (June, 1973), 238.

6. On the necessity of seeing institutions relationally, see Bertell Ollman, *Alienation: Marx's Conception of Man in Capitalist Society* (New York: Cambridge University Press, 1971).

7. Daniel Kallos, "Educational Phenomena and Educational Research" (Report from the Institute of Education, Number 54, University of Lund, Lund, Sweden, mimeographed), p. 7.

8. Dennis Warwick, "Ideologies, Integration and Conflicts of Meaning," *Educability, Schools and Ideology,* Michael Flude and John Ahier, eds, (London: Halstead Press, 1974), p. 94. See also, Michael W. Apple, "Curriculum as Ideological Selection," *Comparative Education Review,* XX (June 1976) 209–15.

9. Bill Williamson, "Continuities and Discontinuities in the Sociology of Education," in Flude and Ahier, op. cit., pp. 10–11.

10. Ibid.

11. Barry Franklin, "The Curriculum Field and the Problem of Social Control, 1918–1938: A Study in Critical Theory," (Unpublished doctoral dissertation, University of Wisconsin, Madison, 1974), pp. 2–3.

12. Ibid., pp. 4–5. See also, Steven Selden, "Conservative Ideologies and Curriculum," *Educational Theory,* XXVII (Summer 1977), 205–22. It should be noted here that scientific management itself was not necessarily a neutral technology for creating more efficient institutions. It was developed as a mechanism for the further division and control of labor. This is provocatively portrayed in Harry Braverman, *Labor and Monopoly Capital: The Degradation of Work in the Twentieth Century* (New York: Monthly Review Press, 1974).

13. Ibid.

14. Ibid., p. 317.

15. Walter Feinberg, *Reason and Rhetoric: The Intellectual Foundations of Twentieth Century Liberal Educational Policy* (New York: John Wiley, 1975).
16. Philip Jackson, *Life in Classrooms* (New York: Holt, Rinehart & Winston, 1968).
17. Elizabeth Vallance, "Hiding the Hidden Curriculum," *Curriculum Theory Network,* IV (Fall, 1973/1974), 15.
18. Ibid.
19. Ibid., 18–19.
20. Gintis and Bowles, op. cit., p. 133. These normative meanings and personality attributes are distributed unequally to different "types" of students, often by social class or occupational expectation, as well. Not all students get the same dispositional elements nor are the same meanings attached to them by the distributor of cultural capital. See Gintis and Bowles, op. cit., p. 136.
21. See, for example, Michael W. Apple, "Ivan Illich and Deschooling Society: The Politics of Slogan Systems," *Social Forces and Schooling,* Nobuo Shimahara and Adam Scrupski, eds (New York: David McKay, 1975), pp. 337–60 and Michael F. D. Young, "An Approach to the Study of Curricula as Socially Organized Knowledge," in Young, *Knowledge and Control,* op. cit., pp. 19–46.
22. Nell Keddie, "Classroom Knowledge," in Michael F. D. Young, *Knowledge and Control,* op. cit., pp. 133–60.
23. See John Eggleston, *The Sociology of the School Curriculum* (London: Routledge & Kegan Paul, 1977).
24. This, of course, is a fundamental tenet of ethnomethodological studies, as well. See Peter McHugh, *Defining the Situation* (Indianapolis: Bobbs-Merrill, 1968), Roy Turner, ed. *Ethnomethodology* (Baltimore: Penguin, 1974), and Aaron Cicourel, *Cognitive Sociology* (New York: Free Press, 1974).
25. For further explication of this point, see Basil Bernstein, "On The Classification and Framing of Educational Knowledge," in Michael F. D. Young, ed., *Knowledge and Control,* op. cit., pp. 47–69.
26. Robert MacKay, "Conceptions of Children and Models of Socialization," *Childhood and Socialization,* Hans Peter Drietzel, ed. (New York: Macmillan, 1973), pp. 27–43.
27. An excellent treatment of this "ethnographic" tradition can be found in Philip E. D. Robinson, "An Ethnography of Classrooms," *Contemporary Research in the Sociology of Education,* John Eggleston, ed. (London: Methuen, 1974), pp. 251–66. For further discussion of these methodological issues, and for further analysis of the data on which this section of the chapter is based, see Nancy R. King, "The Hidden Curriculum and the Socialization of Kindergarten Children" (unpublished Ph.D. thesis, University of Wisconsin, 1976).
28. Thomas R. Bates, "Gramsci and the Theory of Hegemony," *Journal of the History of Ideas,* XXXVI (April-June, 1975), 360.
29. Habermas's arguments about patterns of communicative competence in advanced industrial "orders" are quite interesting as interpretive schema here. See, for example, Jürgen Habermas, "Towards a Theory of Communicative Competence," *Recent Sociology,* no. 2, Hans Peter Dreitzel, ed. (New York: Macmillan, 1970), pp. 115–48, and Trent Schroyer, *The Critique of Domination* (New York: George Braziller, 1973).
30. Rachel Sharp and Anthony Green, *Education and Social Control: A Study in Progressive Primary Education* (Boston: Routledge & Kegan Paul, 1975), p. 8.
31. Ibid., p. 13.
32. Ibid., pp. 110–12. See also, the provocative analysis found in Basil Bernstein, *Class, Codes and Control, Volume 3: Towards a Theory of Educational Transmissions* (2nd edn; London: Routledge & Kegan Paul, 1977).
33. Ibid., p. 116.
34. Sharp and Green, op. cit., p. x.

Chapter 4

1. Here I am using Dawe's notion that control involves the imposition of meaning on a dominated group by a dominant group. See, Michael F. D. Young, ed., *Knowledge and Control* (London: Collier-Macmillan, 1971), p. 4.
2. Pierre Bourdieu, "Intellectual Field and Creative Project," in Young, *Knowledge and Control,* op. cit., pp. 161–88.

3. Basil Bernstein, *Class, Codes and Control, Volume 3: Towards a Theory of Educational Transmissions* (2nd edn: London: Routledge & Kegan Paul, 1977). See also, Samuel Bowles and Herbert Gintis, *Schooling in Capitalist America* (New York: Basic Books, 1976).

4. Cf., Chapter 7 in this volume and Michael W. Apple, "Power and School Knowledge," *The Review of Education*, III (January/February 1977). See also, James E. Rosenbaum, *Making Inequality: The Hidden Curriculum of High School Tracking* (New York: John Wiley, 1976) and Herbert Gintis and Samuel Bowles, "The Contradictions of Liberal Educational Reform," *Work, Technology and Education*, Walter Feinberg and Henry Rosemont, Jr., eds (Urbana: University of Illinois Press, 1975), pp. 92–141.

5. Carl F. Kaestle, *The Evolution of an Urban School System* (Cambridge, Mass.: Harvard University Press, 1973), p. 141.

6. Ibid., pp. 141–2.

7. Ibid., p. 161.

8. Marvin Lazerson, *Origins of the Urban School* (Cambridge: Harvard University Press, 1971), p. xv. See also, Elizabeth Vallance, "Hiding The Hidden Curriculum" *Curriculum Theory Network*, IV (Fall, 1973/1974), 5–21.

9. Ibid., pp. x-xi.

10. I have selected these individuals as the most important formative members of the curriculum field because I believe that their identification with the social efficiency movement and a behavioristic psychology place them in the mainstream of the field. I am not including John Dewey and others identified with child-centered education and the child's needs/interest tradition. Although their ideas are interesting and important, they had little impact on either the curriculum field as it developed or for that matter on school practice. For a discussion of this position with reference to Thorndike see Clarence J. Karier, "Elite Views on American Education," *Education and Social Structure in the Twentieth Century*, Walter Laquer and George L. Mosse, eds (New York: Harper Torchbooks, 1967), pp. 149–51.

11. Franklin Bobbitt, *The Curriculum* (New York: Arno Press, 1971), Chapter 9.

12. Ibid., p. 95.

13. Ibid., p. 42, Franklin Bobbitt, *How to Make A Curriculum* (Boston: Houghton Mifflin, 1924), pp. 29, 97, W. W. Charters, *Curriculum Construction* (New York: Arno Press, 1971), Chapters 4–5.

14. Harold Rugg, *et al.*, "The Foundations of Curriculum-Making," *The Foundations of Curriculum-Making, The Twenty-Sixth Yearbook of the National Society for the Study of Education, Part II*, Guy Montrose Whipple, ed. (Bloomington: Public School Publishing, 1926), p. 16.

15. Bobbitt, *The Curriculum*, op. cit., Chapter 12.

16. Bobbitt, *How to Make A Curriculum*, op. cit., p. 281.

17. Bobbitt, *The Curriculum*, op. cit., p. 131.

18. My analysis here does not reflect support for the late Richard Hofstadter's status anxiety thesis as an explanation for middle-class support of the social reforms of the progressive movement. Rather, I am simply reflecting the views, which I do document throughout this chapter, of the early leaders of sociology, psychology, and education. For a presentation of the thesis see Richard Hofstadter, *The Age of Reform* (New York: Vintage Books, 1956), Chapter 4. For an interesting analysis and critique of the status anxiety thesis see Robert W. Doherty, "Status Anxiety and American Reform: Some Alternatives," *American Quarterly*, XIX (Summer, 1962), 329–36.

19. These fears about industrialization and urbanization had important implications for the development of the curriculum field as well as for the social sciences generally. See Barry M. Franklin, "The Curriculum Field and the Problem of Social Control, 1918–1938: A Study in Critical Theory" (unpublished Ph.D. dissertation, University of Wisconsin, 1974). For a similar analysis of the development of the field of educational sociology, see Philip Wexler, *The Sociology of Education: Beyond Equality* (Indianapolis: Bobbs-Merrill, 1976).

20. Edward A. Ross, *Social Control* (New York: Macmillan, 1912), pp. 432–6; R. Jackson Wilson, *In Quest of Community: Social Philosophy in the United States, 1860–1920* (New York: Oxford University Press, 1968), pp. 89–99.

21. Robert A. Nisbet, *The Quest for Community* (New York: Oxford University Press, 1967), p. 54.

22. Robert H. Wiebe, *The Search for Order* (New York: Hill & Wang, 1967), Chapter 5.

23. Ibid., p. 44.

24. Edward A. Ross, *Foundations of Sociology* (5th edn; New York: Macmillan, 1919), pp. 382–5.

25. Charles A. Ellwood, *Sociology and Modern Social Problems* (New York: American Book Co., 1913), p. 220.

26. Ibid., pp. 217–21, Edward A. Ross, *Principles of Sociology* (New York: Century, 1920), pp. 36–7.

27. Ross, *Principles of Sociology*, ibid., p. 409.

28. Ross L. Finney, *Causes and Cures for the Social Unrest: An Appeal to the Middle Class* (New York: Macmillan, 1922), pp. 167–72.

29. Ibid., p. 43.

30. Ross L. Finney, *A Sociological Philosophy of Education* (New York: Macmillan, 1928), pp. 382–3.

31. Ibid., p. 428.

32. Charles C. Peters, *Foundations of Educational Sociology* (New York: Macmillan, 1924), p. 25.

33. Thorndike seemingly accepted the views of the American anthropologist, R. H. Lowie, that "the Negroes evince an inveterate proclivity for at least the forms of monarchical government." See Edward L. Thorndike, *Your City* (New York: Harcourt, Brace, 1939), pp. 77–80. For an examination of Thorndike's behaviorism and its impact on the curriculum field, see Barry M. Franklin, "Curriculum Thought and Social Meaning; Edward L. Thorndike and the Curriculum Field," *Educational Theory*, XXVI (Summer, 1976), 298–309.

34. Finney, *Causes and Cures for the Social Unrest*, op. cit., p. 180.

35. Finney, *A Sociological Philosophy of Education*, op. cit., p. 386.

36. Thorndike, *Human Nature and the Social Order*, op. cit., p. 440.

37. Bobbitt, *The Curriculum*, op. cit., p. 158; William Chandler Bagley, "Supplementary Statement," in Rugg, op. cit., p. 38.

38. Bobbitt, *How to Make A Curriculum*, op. cit., pp. 41–2, 61–2; Edward L. Thorndike, *Individuality* (Boston: Houghton Mifflin 1911), p. 51; Edward L. Thorndike, *Education: A First Book* (New York: Macmillan, 1912), pp. 137–319; David Snedden, *Sociological Determination of Objectives in Education* (Philadelphia: Lippincott, 1921), p. 251; Peters, *Foundations of Educational Sociology*, op. cit., p. vii.

    Finney took a somewhat different view of differentiation than the other formative theorists of the field. He advocated what appeared to be a common curriculum dominated by the emerging social science disciplines. But he made a critical distinction on how these subjects were to be taught to individuals of differing ability. Those of high intelligence would be taught their social heritage through a study of the social sciences. It would be a study that would teach them to understand not only their heritage but the social demands it would make on them. Those of low intelligence would only be taught the social sciences themselves but would be conditioned to respond to appropriate slogans that reflected the content of these disciplines and the social demands embedded in them. See Finney, *A Sociological Philosophy of Education*, op. cit., Chapter 15, pp. 393–6, 406, 410. For the importance of curriculum differentiation in the contemporary curriculum field see Herbert M. Kliebard, "Bureaucracy and Curriculum Theory," *Freedom, Bureaucracy, and Schooling*, Vernon F. Haubrich, ed. (Washington: Association for Supervision and Curriculum Development, 1971), pp. 89–93.

39. Finney, *A Sociological Philosophy of Education*, op. cit., pp. 388–9; Thorndike, *Human Nature and the Social Order*, op. cit., pp. 77–9, 792–4, 800–802; Edward L. Thorndike, "A Sociologist's Theory of Education," *The Bookman*, XXXV (November, 1906), pp. 290–1; Edward L. Thorndike, *Selected Writings from a Connectionist's Psychology* (New York: Appleton-Century-Crofts, 1949), pp. 338–9.

40. Finney, *A Sociological Philosophy of Education*, op. cit., pp. 386, 389; Edward L. Thorndike, "How May We Improve the Selection, Training, and Life Work of Leaders," *How Should a Democratic People Provide for the Selection and Training of Leaders in the Various Walks of Life* (New York: Teachers College Press, 1938), p. 41; Walter H. Drost, *David Snedden and Education for Social Efficiency* (Madison: University of Wisconsin Press, 1967), pp. 165, 197.

41. Finney, *A Sociological Philosophy of Education*, op. cit., p. 395.

42. Ibid., pp. 397–8.

43. Bobbitt, *The Curriculum*, op. cit., pp. 78–81, 95.

44. Edward L. Thorndike, "The Psychology of the Half-Educated Man," *Harpers*, CXL (April, 1920), 670.

45. Bobbitt, *The Curriculum*, op. cit., pp. 78–86.

46. Ibid., p. 42; David Snedden, *Civic Education* (Yonkers on Hudson: World Book Co., 1922), Chapter 14.

47. Thorndike, *Human Nature and the Social Order*, op. cit., pp. 86–7, 783–5, 963.
48. For an examination of this tendency in social thought see Trent Schroyer, "Toward a Critical Theory for Advanced Industrial Society," *Recent Sociology* No. 2, Hans Peter Dreitzel, ed. (New York: Macmillan, 1970), p. 212. For the appropriateness of this view for interpreting American education see Walter Feinberg, *Reason and Rhetoric* (New York: John Wiley, 1975), p. 40.
49. Kliebard, "Bureaucracy and Curriculum Theory," op. cit., pp. 74–80 and Raymond E. Callahan, *Education and the Cult of Efficiency* (University of Chicago Press, 1962), Chapter 4.
50. Finney, *A Sociological Philosophy of Education*, op. cit.
51. John Higham, *Strangers in the Land* (New Brunswick: Rutgers University Press, 1955), pp. 51, 187, 257, 303–10, Chapter 9.
52. Ross, in similar circumstances, lost his job at Stanford University because he angered Mrs Leland Stanford, the wife of the founder of the university and its chief authority after his death. He attacked the business community for its support of unrestricted Chinese immigration. See Walter P. Metzger, *Academic Freedom in the Age of the University* (New York: Columbia University Press, 1955), pp. 164–71 and Bernard J. Stern, ed., "The Ward-Ross Correspondence II 1897–1901," *American Sociological Review*, VII (December, 1946), 744–6.
53. Higham argues that in the decade of the 1920s, the period in which curriculum emerged as a field of study and in which the educators I am considering did their most important work, American nativist sentiments turned away from attempts at assimilation through Americanization programs and instead turned to support of immigration restriction. It was in 1924 that the Johnson-Reed Act was passed which firmly established the "national origins principle," with the restrictions it applied to Eastern and Southern European peoples, into American law. See Higham, *Strangers in the Land*, op. cit., Chapter II.
54. Dwayne Huebner, "The Tasks of the Curricular Theorist," *Curriculum Theorizing: The Reconceptualists*, William Pinar, ed. (Berkeley: McCutchan, 1975), p. 256.
55. Ibid., p. 255.
56. On the uses of hortatory language to create imagery see Murray Edelman, *The Symbolic Uses of Politics* (Urbana: University of Illinois Press, 1964).
57. For further explication of this relationship, see Michael W. Apple and Philip Wexler, "Cultural Capital and Educational Transmissions," *Educational Theory*, XXVIII (Winter, 1978).

Chapter 5

1. See especially Basil Bernstein's analysis in his new chapter, "Aspects of the Relation between Education and Production," *Class, Codes and Control, Volume 3: Towards A Theory of Educational Transmissions* (2nd edn; London: Routledge & Kegan Paul, 1977).
2. Philip Jackson, *Life in Classrooms* (New York: Holt, Rinehart & Winston, 1968), pp. 3–37.
3. Cf., Peter K. Eisinger, "Protest Behavior and the Integration of Urban Political Systems" (Madison: University of Wisconsin Institute for Research on Poverty, 1970, mimeographed).
4. Roberta Sigel, ed., *Learning About Politics* (New York: Random House, 1970), p. xiii.
5. Ibid., p. 104.
6. Ibid., p. 316. Such a statement is both realistic and rather critical. In a way, critics of the schools (and the present author to a large extent) are caught in a bind. It is rather easy to denigrate existing "educational" structures (after all, everyone seems to do it); yet, it is not quite as easy to offer alturnative structures. The individual who attempts to ameliorate some of the more debilitating conditions runs the risk of actually helping to shore up and perpetuate what may very well be an outmoded set of institutional arrangements. Yet, not to try to better conditions in what are often small and stumbling ways is to neglect those real human beings who now inhabit the schools for most of their pre-adult lives. Therefore, one tries to play both sides of the battle often. One criticizes the fundamental ideological and economic assumptions that undergird schools as they exist today and, at the same time, paradoxically attempts to make these same institutions a bit more humane, a bit more educative. It is an ambiguous position, but, after all, so is one's total situation. My discussion of the fundamental glossing over of the nature and necessity of conflict and the tacit teaching that accompanies it shows this ambiguity. However, if education in particular can make a difference (and here we should read politically and economically), then concrete

changes must be effected now *while* the more basic criticisms are themselves being articulated. One is not an excuse for the other.

7. See, for example, Edith F. Gibson, "The Three D's: Distortion, Deletion, Denial," *Social Education*, XXXIII (April, 1969), 405–9 and Sidney M. Willhelm, *Who Needs the Negro?* (Cambridge, Mass.: Schenkman, 1970).

8. Helen McClure and George Fischer, "Ideology and Opinion Making: General Problems of Analysis" (New York: Columbia University Bureau of Applied Social Research, July, 1969, mimeographed).

9. The language of "rules of activity" is less analytically troublesome than the distinction often made between thought and action, since it implies that the distinction is somewhat naive and enables action—perceptual, conceptual, and bodily—to be the fundamental category of an individual's response to his or her situation. While we often use rules of activity and assumptions interchangeably, the point should be made that assumptions usually connote a less inclusive category of phenomena and are actually indicative of the existence of these socially sedimented rules and boundaries that seem to affect even our very perceptions. Further work on such rules can be found in the ethnomethodological literature and, of course, in the later Wittgenstein. See, for example, Harold Garfinkel, *Studies in Ethnomethodology* (Englewood Cliffs, N.J.: Prentice-Hall, 1967) and Ludwig Wittgenstein, *Philosophical Investigations* (New York: Macmillan, 1953).

10. In essence, the "system" that many individuals decry is *not only* an ordered interrelationship of institutions, but a framework of fundamental assumptions that act in a dialectical relationship with these institutions.

11. Robert Dreeben, *On What is Learned in Schools* (Reading, Mass.: Addison-Wesley, 1969), pp. 144–5.

12. Michael W. Apple, "Community, Knowledge and the Structure of Disciplines," *The Educational Forum*, XXXVII (November, 1972), 75–82.

13. Michael Polanyi, *Personal Knowledge* (New York: Harper & Row, 1964).

14. Warren Hagstrom, *The Scientific Community* (New York: Basic Books, 1965) p. 256.

15. Ibid., p. 264.

16. Alvin Gouldner, *The Coming Crisis of Western Sociology* (New York: Basic Books, 1970), pp. 102–3. See also, Polanyi, op. cit. On the relations between positivistic conceptions of objectivity and economic and communicative forms, see Jürgen Habermas, *Toward a Rational Society* (Boston: Beacon Press, 1970).

17. Thomas Kuhn, *The Structure of Scientific Revolutions* (second edition: University of Chicago Press, 1970). Kuhn's seminal work is subjected to rather acute analysis, and discussed with rebuttal and counter rebuttal in Imre Lakatos and Alan Musgrave, eds, *Criticism and the Growth of Knowledge* (New York: Oxford University Press, 1970). The entire volume is devoted to the issues—epistemological and sociological—raised by Kuhn's book. See also, Stephen Toulmin, *Human Understanding* (Princeton University Press, 1972).

18. Imre Lakatos, "Falsification and the Methodology of Scientific Research Programmes," *Criticism and the Growth of Knowledge*, Imre Lakatos and Alan Musgrave, eds, (New York: Oxford University Press, 1970), p. 155. Normal science refers to that science that has agreement (consensus) on the basic paradigms of activity to be used by scientists to interpret and act on their respective fields. See Kuhn, op. cit., for an intensive analysis of normal and revolutionary science.

19. Apple, op. cit., and Michael Mulkay, "Some Aspects of Cultural Growth in the Natural Sciences," *Social Research*, XXXVI (Spring, 1969), 22–52.

20. Hagstrom, op. cit., p. 81. It is important to distinguish between conflict and competition, however. While conflict seems to stem from a number of the conditions we have examined or will examine—new paradigms, disagreements over goals, methodology, etc.—competition seems to have its basis in the "exchange system" of science. See, for example, Storer's examination of the place of professional recognition and commodity exchange in the scientific community, in Norman W. Storer, *The Social System of Science* (New York: Holt, Rinehart & Winston, 1966), pp. 78–9.

21. Hagstrom, op. cit., pp. 130 and 173.

22. Hilary Rose and Steven Rose, eds, *The Radicalization of Science* (London: Macmillan, 1976).

23. Hagstrom, op. cit., pp. 82–3.

24. See, Robert Olby, *The Path to the Double Helix* (Seattle: University of Washington Press, 1974).

25. Storer, op. cit., pp. 78–9.

26. Hagstrom, op. cit., pp. 193–4. Journals such as *Science for the People, Marxist Perspectives, Radical Science, and Dialectical Psychology* provide interesting and important examples of such politically affiliated discussion and debate.

27. Ralf Dahrendorf, *Essays in the Theory of Society* (London: Routledge & Kegan Paul, 1968), p. 112.

28. Gouldner, op. cit., p. 193.

29. Ibid., p. 48.

30. Ibid., pp. 210–18.

31. Ibid., p. 206.

32. Ibid., p. 427. See also the interesting but at times acritical discussion in Peter Berger and Thomas Luckmann, *The Social Construction of Reality* (New York: Doubleday, 1966).

33. Lawrence Senesh, "Recorded Lessons," *Our Working World: Families at Work,* Lawrence Senesh, ed. (Chicago: Science Research Associates, 1964).

34. Center for the Study of Instruction, *Principles and Practices in the Teaching of the Social Sciences: Teacher's Edition* (New York: Harcourt, Brace & World, 1970), p. T-17. It is questionable whether many Blacks or Latinos in the ghettos of the USA would give unqualified support to this "description."

35. Ibid., p. T-26.

36. Maxine Durkin, *et al., The Taba Social Studies Curriculum: Communities Around Us* (Reading, Mass.: Addison-Wesley, 1969), p. v.

37. Nathan Hare, "The Teaching of Black History and Culture in the Secondary Schools," *Social Education,* XXXIII (April, 1969), 385–8, and Preston Wilcox, "Education for Black Liberation," *New Generation,* L1 (Winter 1969), 20–1.

38. Ralf Dahrendorf, *Class and Class Conflict in Industrial Societies* (Stanford: Stanford University Press, 1959), p. 27. For concrete studies of conflict both within and among classes in corporate society, see R. W. Connell, *Ruling Class, Ruling Culture* (Cambridge: Cambridge University Press, 1977) and Nicos Poulantzas, *Classes in Contemporary Capitalism* (London: New Left Books, 1975).

39. Jack Walker, "A Critique of the Elitist Theory of Democracy," *Apolitical Politics,* Charles A. McCoy and John Playford, eds (New York: Crowell, 1967), pp. 217–18.

40. Quoted in Dahrendorf, *Class and Class Conflict,* op. cit., p. 207.

41. Lewis Coser, *The Functions of Social Conflict* (Chicago: Free Press, 1956), p. 31.

42. Ibid., p. 126. Perhaps the best illustration of material on the law-breaking dimension of conflict is a primary-grade course of study, "Respect for Rules and Law" (New York State Bureau of Elementary Curriculum Development, 1969). One set of curricular materials does take some interesting and helpful steps in allowing for a more honest appraisal of conflict. See Donald Oliver and Fred Newmann, eds, *Harvard Social Studies Project: Public Issues Series* (Columbus, Ohio: American Educational Publications, 1968).

43. Ibid., pp. 124–5.

44. Ibid., p. 90.

45. Peter Berger, *The Sacred Canopy* (New York: Doubleday, 1967), pp. 24–5, and Clifford Geertz, "The Integrative Revolution: Primordial Sentiments and Civil Politics in the New States," *Old Societies and New States,* Clifford Geertz, ed. (New York: Free Press, 1963), p. 118.
    The literature on the history of women's struggles to gain such autonomy is, thankfully, becoming much more extensive. Some of the more interesting recent contributions to the history of this conflict can be seen in Gerda Lerner, *The Female Experience: An American Documentary* (Indianapolis: Bobbs-Merrill, 1977), Nancy F. Cott, *The Bonds of Womanhood* (New Haven: Yale, 1977), Linda Gordon, *Woman's Body, Woman's Right* (New York: Grossman, 1976), and Mary P. Ryan, *Womanhood in America* (New York: New Viewpoints, 1975).

46. Coser, op. cit., p. 33. This is perhaps one of Piaget's most fruitful insights.

47. Mulkay, op. cit.

48. See, for example, Mary Roth Walsh, *Doctors Wanted. No Women Need Apply* (New Haven: Yale, 1977), Edward T. James, Janet Wilson James and Paul S. Boyer, *Notable American Women 1607–1950* (Cambridge, Mass.: Belknap Press, 1971), and H. J. Mozans, *Woman in Science* (Cambridge, Mass.: Massachusetts Institute of Technology, 1974).

49. See, for example, Ariel Dorfman and Armand Mattelart, *How to Read Donald Duck* (New York: International General, 1975) and Martin Carnoy, *Education as Cultural Imperialism* (New York: David McKay, 1974). One of the more interesting books for children which

deals with some of these issues is Pal Rydlberg, *et al. The History Book* (Culver City, California: Peace Press, 1974).

50. Among the available bibliographies are *Women in U.S. History: An Annotated Bibliography* (Cambridge, Mass.: Common Women Collective, 1976) and Jim O'Brien, *et al. A Guide to Working Class History* (2nd edn: Somerville, Mass.: New England Free Press, n.d.).

51. The proposals for social action curriculum by Fred Newmann are interesting here. See his *Education for Citizen Action* (Berkeley: McCutchan, 1975). For a discussion of some of the problems with such proposals, see Michael W. Apple, "Humanism and the Politics of Educational Argumentation," *Humanistic Education: Visions and Realities*, Richard Weller, ed. (Berkeley: McCutchan, 1977), pp. 315–30.

52. David Easton and Jack Dennis, *Children in the Political System* (New York: McGraw-Hill, 1969), p. 162.

53. Ibid., pp. 271–6.

54. Dwayne Huebner, "Politics and the Curriculum," *Curriculum Crossroads*, A. Harry Passow, ed. (New York: Teachers College Press, 1962), p. 88.

55. Shlomo Avineri, *The Social and Political Thought of Karl Marx* (New York: Cambridge University Press, 1968), p. 137.

56. Ibid., p. 148.

Chapter 6

1. W. James Popham, "Probing the Validity of Arguments Against Behavioral Goals," reprinted in Robert J. Kibler, *et al., Behavioral Objectives and Instruction* (Boston: Allyn & Bacon, 1970), pp. 115–16.

2. Joseph J. Schwab, *The Practical: A Language for Curriculum* (Washington, D.C.: National Education Association, 1970), p. 18.

3. Cf., the analysis of the relationship between knowledge and institutions in Peter L. Berger and Thomas Luckmann, *The Social Construction of Reality* (New York: Doubleday Anchor Books, 1966).

4. Abraham Kaplan, *The Conduct of Inquiry* (San Francisco: Chandler, 1964), pp. 3–11.

5. Dwayne Huebner, "Curricular Language and Classroom Meanings," *Language and Meaning*, James B. Macdonald and Robert R. Leeper, eds (Washington, D.C.: Association for Supervision and Curriculum Development, 1966), pp. 8–26.

6. Cf., Gilbert Ryle, *The Concept of Mind* (New York: Barnes & Noble, 1949), Michael Polanyi, *the Tacit Dimension* (New York: Doubleday Anchor Books, 1966), and Hannah Arendt, *The Human Condition* (New York: Doubleday Anchor, 1958).

7. See, for example, the discussion of wave *v.* particle theories of light in Thomas S. Kuhn, *The Structure of Scientific Revolutions* (University of Chicago Press, 1970). See also Imre Lakatos and Alan Musgrave, eds, *Criticism and the Growth of Knowledge* (Cambridge University Press, 1970) and Michael Polanyi, *Personal Knowledge* (New York: Harper Torchbooks, 1964).

8. J. O. Urmson, *Philosophical Analysis* (London: Oxford University Press, 1956), p. 146.

9. Trent Schroyer, "Toward a Critical Theory for Advanced Industrial Society," *Recent Sociology*, 2, Hans Peter Dreitzel, ed. (New York: Macmillan, 1970), p. 215 and Jürgen Habermas, "Knowledge and Interest," *Sociological Theory and Philosophical Analysis*, Dorothy Emmet and Alasdair Macintyre, eds (New York: Macmillan, 1970), pp. 36–54.

10. Peter L. Berger and Thomas Luckmann, op. cit., p. 129.

11. Richard Sennett, *The Uses of Disorder* (New York: Vintage Books, 1970), p. 94.

12. Ibid., p. 96.

13. Bela H. Banathy, *Instructional Systems* (Palo Alto, California: Fearon, 1968), p. 22.

14. Cf., Donald Arnstine, *Philosophy of Education: Learning and Schooling* (New York: Harper & Row, 1967) and Stuart Hampshire, *Thought and Action* (New York: Viking Press, 1959).

15. This naive separation and the destructive aspects of behavioral specification can often best be seen in discussions of scientific thought, especially that of Michael Polanyi, op. cit. Susanne Langer's analysis of "mind" in *Philosophy in a New Key* (New York: Mentor, 1951), is also quite helpful here.

16. Schroyer, op. cit., p. 212.

17. Alvin W. Gouldner, *The Coming Crisis of Western Sociology* (New York: Basic Books, 1970), p. 50.

18. Schroyer, op. cit., p. 210.
19. Banathy, op. cit., p. 10.
20. Gouldner, op. cit., p. 161.
21. Banathy, op. cit., p. 13.
22. Herbert M. Kliebard, "Bureaucracy and Curriculum Theory," *Freedom, Bureaucracy, and Schooling,* Vernon Haubrich, ed. (Washington, D.C.: Association for Supervision and Curriculum Development, 1971), pp. 74–93. This is not an unconscious linkage to the work of early theorists such as the sometimes quite problematic work of Bobbitt. See, for example, Robert Kibler, *et al., Behavioral Objectives and Instruction* (Boston: Allyn & Bacon, 1970), p. 105.
23. Banathy, op. cit., p. 1 7.
24. Ibid., p. 2.
25. Perhaps one of the more interesting examples of this is reflected in the work of Snedden. His appropriation of the worst of sociology served conservative ideological concerns. See Walter Drost, *David Snedden and Education for Social Efficiency* (Madison: University of Wisconsin Press, 1967).

    Yet another instance is our increasing use of learning theory. Not only has it told us little that is applicable to the complex day-to-day reality of educational life but we have been persistently unaware of the problems learning theory itself has within its own scholarly community. The most complete analysis of the conceptual difficulties can be found in Charles Taylor, *The Explanation of Behavior* (New York: Humanities Press, 1964), and Maurice Merleau-Ponty, *The Structure of Behavior* (Boston: Beacon Press, 1963).
26. Schwab, op. cit., pp. 33–5.
27. Bruce R. Joyce, *et al., Implementing Systems Models for Teacher Education* (Washington, D.C.: U.S. Department of Health, Education and Welfare, 1971).
28. See Raymond Callahan, *Education and the Cult of Efficiency* (University of Chicago Press, 1962).
29. This political and economic history is clearly documented in Harry Braverman, *Labor and Monopoly Capital* (New York: Monthly Review Press, 1975) and Stanley Aronowitz, *False Promises* (New York: McGraw-Hill, 1973).
30. Cf., Derek J. De Solla Price, *Little Science, Big Science* (New York: Columbia University Press, 1963) and Warren O. Hagstrom, *The Scientific Community* (New York: Basic Books, 1965).
31. For a rather poetic rendering of this problem see Maxine Greene, "The Matter of Mystification: Teacher Education in Unquiet Times," *Identity and Structure: Issues in the Sociology of Education,* Denis Gleason, ed. (Driffield: Nafferton Books, 1977), pp. 28–43.
32. Gouldner, op. cit., p. 445. A provocative view of how these "determinations" function in the control of educational action can be found in the work of the French Marxist philosopher Louis Althusser. See Alex Callinicos, *Althusser's Marxism* (London: Pluto Press, 1976). See also Michael Erben and Denis Gleason, "Education as Reproduction," *Society, State and Schooling,* Michael Young and Geoff Whitty, eds (Guildford, England: Falmer Press, 1977), pp. 73–92, and Erik Wright, *Class, Crisis and the State* (London: New Left Books, 1978).
33. Colin Greer, "Immigrants, Negroes, and the Public Schools," *The Urban Review,* III (January, 1969), 9–12.
34. The use of the language of "relevance" by school people to feed back to educational critics in the ghetto to bring about quiescence is extremely similar in this respect. Michael W. Apple, "Relevance—Slogans and Meanings," *The Educational Forum,* XXXV (May, 1971), 503–7.
35. Murray Edelman, *Politics as Symbolic Action* (Chicago: Markham, 1971).
36. Compare here to the discussion of systems theory in sociology as being a tacit theory of conservative politics as well in Gouldner, op. cit.
37. Ibid., p. 105.
38. Ibid., p. 105.
39. Erving Goffman, *The Presentation of Self in Everyday Life* (New York: Doubleday Anchor, 1959).
40. Berger and Luckmann, op. cit., pp. 72–9.
41. For a concrete study of how intense conflict and a rejection of an imposed symbolic order can lead to a people's "demonstration of the beauty and power of the human spirit," see the masterful analysis of the development of black culture and consciousness in Eugene Genovese, *Role, Jordan, Role* (New York: Random House, 1974).

42. See, for instance, the provocative but often overdrawn and politically and analytically troublesome examination in Jacques Ellul, *The Technological Society* (New York: Vintage, 1964).

43. Berger and Luckmann, op. cit., p. 105.

44. Kuhn op. cit. For a more in depth discussion of the place of conflict in science, one that suggests a Darwinian rather than revolutionary model, see Stephen Toulmin, *Human Understanding* (Princeton University Press, 1972).

45. Norman W. Storer, *The Social System of Science* (New York: Holt, Rinehart & Winston, 1966), pp. 78–9.

46. Polanyi, op. cit., p. 171.

47. Historical analyses of this problem can be found in Carl Kaestle, *The Evolution of an Urban School System* (Cambridge, Mass.: Harvard University Press, 1973) and David Tyack, *The One Best System* (Cambridge, Mass.: Harvard University Press, 1974).

48. Michael W. Apple, "Behaviorism and Conservatism," *Perspectives for Reform in Teacher Education,* Bruce R. Joyce and Marsha Weil, eds (Englewood Cliffs, N.J.: Prentice Hall, 1972).

49. Arendt's, op. cit., treatment of the forms of argumentation and political and personal action of the polis is helpful here.

50. John Rawls, *A Theory of Justice* (Cambridge, Mass.: Harvard University Press, 1971).

51. See the interesting debate *in Interchange,* II (no. 1, 1971) on alternatives to existing modes of schooling. Nearly the entire issue is devoted to the topic. On the necessity of imaginative vision in education, see William Walsh, *The Use of Imagination* (New York: Barnes & Noble, 1959) and Fred Inglis, *Ideology and the Imagination* (New York: Cambridge University Press, 1975).

52. Habermas, op. cit., p. 45.

53. Two papers by Huebner are quite important in this regard. See Dwayne Huebner, "Curriculum as the Accessibility of Knowledge" (paper presented at the Curriculum Theory Study Group, Minneapolis, 2 March, 1970) and "The Tasks of the Curricular Theorist," *Curriculum Theorizing: The Reconceptualists,* William Pinar, ed. (Berkeley: McCutchan, 1975), pp. 250–70.

Chapter 7

1. Alan F. Blum, "Sociology, Wrongdoing, and Akrasia: An Attempt to Think Greek about the Problem of Theory and Practice," *Theoretical Perspectives on Deviance,* Robert A. Scott and Jack D. Douglas, eds (New York: Basic Books, 1972), p. 343.

2. Cf., Jürgen Habermas, *Knowledge and Human Interests* (Boston: Beacon Press, 1971) and Peter Berger and Thomas Luckmann, *The Social Construction of Reality* (New York: Doubleday, 1966).

3. See, for example, Hannah Arendt, *The Human Condition* (New York: Doubleday, 1958) and Albrecht Wellmer, *Critical Theory of Society* (New York: Herder & Herder, 1971).

4. Jack D. Douglas, *American Social Order* (New York: Free Press, 1971), pp. 9–10.

5. William Ryan, *Blaming the Victim* (New York: Random House, 1971), pp. 21–2.

6. Anthony Platt, *The Child Savers: The Invention of Delinquency* (Chicago: University of Chicago Press, 1969). See also, Steven L. Schlossman, *Love and the American Delinquent* (Chicago: University of Chicago Press, 1977).

7. Edwin M. Schur, *Labeling Deviant Behavior* (New York: Harper & Row, 1971), p. 33.

8. On the dominance of a social control ethic in schools see Clarence Karier, Paul Violas, and Joel Spring, *Roots of Crisis* (Chicago: Rand McNally, 1973) and Barry Franklin, "The Curriculum Field and Social Control" (unpublished doctoral thesis, University of Wisconsin, 1974).

9. Douglas, op. cit., p. 181. See also the discussion of interpretive and normative rules in Aaron Cicourel, "Basic and Normative Rules in the Negotiation of Status and Role," *Recent Sociology,* no. 2. Hans Peter Dreitzel, ed. (New York: Macmillan, 1971), pp. 4–45.

10. Herbert M. Kliebard, "Persistent Curriculum Issues in Historical Perspective," *Curriculum Theorizing: The Reconceptualists,* William Pinar, ed. (Berkeley: McCutchan, 1975), pp. 39–50.

11. I am again using the concept of ideology here to refer in part to commonsense views of the world held by specific groups, not merely as "politically" biased views. This follows from Harris's statement that "Ideologies are not disguised descriptions of the world, but rather real descriptions of the world from a specific viewpoint, just as all descriptions of the world

are from a particular viewpoint." Nigel Harris, *Beliefs in Society: The Problem of Ideology* (London: A. Watts, 1968), p. 22.

12. See Susanne Langer's articulate treatment of the necessity of discursive *and* nondiscursive forms of rationality in her *Philosophy in a New Key* (New York: Mentor, 1951).

13. Stephen Toulmin, *Human Understanding: The Collective Use and Evolution of Concepts* (Princeton University Press, 1972), p. 84.

14. Ibid., p. 96.

15. Alice Miel, *Changing The Curriculum: A Social Process* (New York: D. Appleton-Century, 1946).

16. I have discussed this elsewhere in Michael W. Apple, "The Process and Ideology of Valuing in Educational Settings," *Educational Evaluation: Analysis and Responsibility*, Michael W. Apple, Michael J. Subkoviak, and Henry S. Lufler, Jr., eds (Berkeley: McCutchan, 1974), pp. 3–34.

17. Insightful treatments of this thesis can be found in Roger Dale, *et al.*, eds, *Schooling and Capitalism* (London: Routledge & Kegan Paul, 1976), Denis Gleeson, ed., *Identity and Structure* (Driffield: Nafferton Books, 1977) and Trent Schroyer, "Toward a Critical Theory for Advanced Industrial Society," *Recent Sociology*, no. 2, Hans Peter Dreitzel, ed. (New York: Macmillan, 1970), pp. 210–34.

18. Ian Hextall, "Marking Work," *Explorations in the Politics of School Knowledge*, Geoff Whitty and Michael Young, eds (Driffield: Nafferton Books, 1976), p. 67.

19. Apple, "The Process and Ideology of Valuing in Educational Settings," op. cit.

20. See Phil Slater, *Origin and Significance of the Frankfurt School* (London: Routledge & Kegan Paul, 1977). See also Marx's discussion of the *dialectical* relationship between infrastructure and superstructure in *Capital*, vol. I (New York: New World, 1967), pp. 459–507.

21. Cf., Jean-Paul Sartre, *Search For a Method* (New York: Vintage Books, 1963) and Andre Gorz, *Strategy For Labor* (Boston: Beacon Press, 1967).

22. See, for example, the well-written portrayal of Marx's own lack of rigid dogmatism in Michael Harrington, *Socialism* (New York: Bantam Books, 1972). For a reappraisal of Marx's supposed economic determinism, one that argues against such an interpretation, see Bertell Ollman, *Alienation: Marx's Conception of Man in Capitalist Society* (Cambridge University Press, 1971).

23. This subtle interplay between cultural and class interpretations is described quite nicely in Terry Eagleton, *Marxism and Literary Criticism* (Berkeley: University of California Press, 1976). For a discussion of the phenomenological theory of "truth," see Aron Gurwitsch, *The Field of Consciousness* (Pittsburgh: Duquesne University Press, 1964), p. 184.

24. Charles Taylor, "Marxism and Empiricism," *British Analytic Philosophy*, Bernard Williams and Alan Montifiore, eds (New York: Humanities Press, 1966), pp. 227–46.

25. Bertell Ollman, op. cit., p. 18.

26. Ibid., p. 15. This position has been given the name of a "philosophy of internal relations." Oddly, such a view *has* had an extensive history in American thought, even somewhat in educational thought. See, for example, the work of Whitehead such as *Process and Reality*.

27. Ibid., p. 90.

28. Martin Jay, *The Dialectical Imagination* (Boston: Little, Brown, 1973), p. 83. For a history of the ideological position taken by many of the pragmatists in education, see Walter Feinberg, *Reason and Rhetoric* (New York: John Wiley, 1975).

29. Ibid., p. 268.

30. Trent Schroyer, *The Critique of Domination* (New York: George Braziller, 1973), p. 30–1.

31. Shlomo Avineri, *The Social and Political Thought of Karl Marx* (Cambridge University Press, 1968), p. 117. Avineri puts it this way, "Ultimately, a commodity is an objectified expression of an intersubjective relationship."

32. Michael F. D. Young, "Knowledge and Control," *Knowledge and Control*, Michael F. D. Young, ed. (London: Macmillan, 1971), p. 2.

33. On the relationship between this transformation of human interaction into other reified forms and an ideological political, and economic framework, see Ollman, op. cit., pp. 198–9.

34. Douglas, op. cit., pp. 70–1.

35. Robert A. Scott, "A Proposed Framework for Analyzing Deviance as a Property of Social Order," Scott and Douglas, op. cit., p. 15.

36. Bonnie Freeman, "Labeling Theory and Bureaucratic Structures in Schools" (unpublished paper, University of Wisconsin, Madison, n.d.).

37. Scott, op. cit., p. 14. See also the discussion of deviance as a threat to taken for granted perspectives in Berger and Luckmann, op. cit.
38. Cf., Aaron Cicourel and John Kitsuse, *The Educational Decision-Makers* (Indianapolis: Bobbs-Merrill, 1963). That this labeling process begins upon the students' initial entry into schools, with the initial labels becoming increasingly crystallized, is documented in Ray C. Rist, "Student Social Class and Teacher Expectation: The Self-Fulfilling Prophecy in Ghetto Education," *Harvard Educational Review,* XL (August, 1970), 411–51.
39. Thomas S. Szasz, *Ideology and Insanity* (New York: Doubleday, 1970), p. 149. The fact that once students are so labeled, other educational and economic opportunities are quite firmly closed off is clearly documented in James Rosenbaum, *Making Inequality* (New York: John Wiley, 1976).
40. Erving Goffman, *Asylums* (New York: Doubleday, 1961).
41. Szasz, op. cit., p. 58.
42. Jane R. Mercer, *Labeling the Mentally Retarded* (Berkeley: University of California Press, 1973).
43. Ibid., pp. 96–123.
44. Hugh Mehan, "Assessing Children's School Performance," *Childhood and Socialization,* Hans Peter Dreitzel, ed. (New York: Macmillan, 1973), pp. 240–64. For further discussion of how dominant modes of educational evaluation and assessment ignore the concrete reality of students and function in a conservative political and epistemological manner, see Apple, "The Process and Ideology of Valuing in Educational Settings," op. cit.
45. Mercer, op. cit., p. 96.
46. Ibid., pp. 60–1.
47. Michael F. D. Young, "Curriculum and the Social Organization of Knowledge," *Knowledge, Education, and Cultural Change,* Richard Brown, ed. (London: Tavistock, 1973), p. 350.
48. Some of the best work of this type in education can be found in David Hargreaves, *et al. Deviance in Classrooms* (London: Routledge & Kegan Paul, 1975).
49. A number of the political difficulties of labeling theory are laid out in Ian Taylor and Laurie Taylor, eds, *Politics and Deviance* (London: Pelican, 1973) and Ian Taylor, Paul Walton, and Jock Young, *Critical Criminology* (London: Routledge & Kegan Paul, 1974).
50. Rachel Sharp and Anthony Green, *Education and Social Control* (London: Routledge & Kegan Paul, 1975), p. 25. My discussion here draws upon the exceptional theoretical analysis in their first two chapters.
51. Ibid., p. 6.
52. Freeman, op. cit. and Herbert M. Kliebard, "Bureaucracy and Curriculum Theory," *Freedom, Bureaucracy, and Schooling,* Vernon Haubrich, ed. (Washington: Association for Supervision and Curriculum Development, 1971), pp. 74–93.
53. Murray Edelman, "The Political Language of the Helping Professions," (unpublished paper, University of Wisconsin, Madison, n.d.) pp. 3–4.
54. Ibid., p. 4.
55. Ibid., pp. 7–8.
56. Goffman, op. cit., p. 115.
57. Jane R. Mercer, "Labeling the Mentally Retarded," *Deviance: The Interactionist Perspective,* Earl Rubington and Martin S. Weinberg, eds (New York: Macmillan, 1968). For a more complete treatment of the conservative posture of clinical and helping viewpoints, see Apple, "The Process and Ideology of Valuing in Educational Settings," op. cit.
58. One interesting point should be made here. Persons employing clinical perspectives in dealing with health or deviance are apt to label people as "sick" rather than "well" in most instances to avoid the danger of what might happen to the "patient" if they are wrong. Here, one more motivation for "finding" individuals to fit institutional categories can be uncovered. Thomas Scheff, *Being Mentally Ill: A Sociological Theory* (Chicago: Aldine, 1966), pp. 105–6.
59. A number of critical researchers have argued that the "discipline and achievement problems" of schools are, in fact, indications of nascent class conflict. See Christian Baudelot and Roger Establet, *La Escuela Capitalista* (Mexico City: Siglo Veintiuno Editores, 1975).
60. Schur, op. cit., p. 51. This is not to say that all labeling can be done away with. It is to say, however, that we must begin to raise serious critical questions on how specific labels and the massiveness of the reality these categories represent function in school settings.
61. James E. Curtis and John W. Petras, eds, *The Sociology of Knowledge* (New York: Praeger, 1970), p. 48.

62. Jack D. Douglas, "Freedom and Tyranny in a Technological Society," *Freedom and Tyranny: Social Problems in a Technological Society,* Jack D. Douglas, ed. (New York: Alfred A. Knopf, 1970), p. 17.

63. See the discussion of the role of the expert in Alfred Schutz, "The Well-informed Citizen: An Essay on the Social Distribution of Knowledge," *Collected Papers II: Studies in Social Theory* (The Hague: Martinus Nijhoff, 1964), pp. 120–34.

64. Michael W. Apple, "Power and School Knowledge," *The Review of Education,* III (January/February 1977), 26–49 and Michael W. Apple, "Making Curriculum Problematic," *The Review of Education,* II (January/February 1976), 52–68.

65. Florian Znaniecki, *The Social Role of the Man of Knowledge* (New York: Harper & Row, 1968), pp. 45–9.

66. Douglas, *American Social Order,* op. cit., p. 49. See also the discussion of how engineering expertise was used to support a management ideology to control the work force, in David Noble, *America By Design: Science, Technology, and the Rise of Corporate Capitalism* (New York: Knopf, 1977).

67. This is not to say that one ignores official data. As Marx showed in *Capital,* official data may be exceptionally important in illuminating the actual workings of, and assumptions behind, an economic system.

68. Ian Taylor, Paul Walton, and Jock Young, "Advances Towards a Critical Criminology," *Theory and Society,* I (Winter 1974), 441–76.

69. The term "strict science" refers here to fields whose fundamental interests reflect and are dialectically related to the dominant interests of advanced industrial economic systems and thus are grounded in process-product or purposive-rational logic. These interests are in technical rules, control, and certainty. Among the fields one could point to are behavioral psychology and sociology. See Jürgen Habermas, "Knowledge and Interest," *Sociological Theory and Philosophical Analysis,* Dorothy Emmet and Alasdair MacIntyre, eds (New York: Macmillan, 1970), pp. 36–54 and Michael W. Apple, "Scientific Interests and the Nature of Educational Institutions," *Curriculum Theorizing: The Reconceptualists,* William Pinar, ed. (Berkeley: McCutchan, 1975), pp. 120–30.

70. Szasz, op. cit., p. 2.

71. Robert W. Friedrich, *A Sociology of Sociology* (New York: Free Press, 1970), pp. 172–3.

72. Lewis A. Dexter, "On the Politics and Sociology of Stupidity in Our Society," *The Other Side,* Howard S. Becker, ed. (New York: Free Press, 1964), pp. 37–49.

73. Jules Henry, *Culture Against Man* (New York: Random House, 1963) and Philip Jackson, *Life in Classrooms* (New York: Holt, Rinehart & Winston, 1968). Goffman's notion of "secondary adjustments" is quite helpful in interpreting parts of the hidden curriculum. Goffman, op. cit., p. 189. Some alternatives to these pedagogical practices can be found in William Kessen, ed., *Childhood in China* (New Haven: Yale University Press, 1975), and Geoff Whitty and Michael Young, eds, *Explorations in the Politics of School Knowledge* (Driffield: Nafferton Books, 1976).

74. Schur, op. cit., p. 96.

75. Kliebard, "Bureaucracy and Curriculum Theory," op. cit.

76. Pierre Bourdieu and Jean-Claude Passeron, *Reproduction in Education, Society and Culture* (London: Sage, 1977) p. 5.

77. A recent and exceptionally interesting ethnographic study of how this production of agents operates on a day-to-day level, one that gets away from viewing schools as black boxes, can be found in Paul Willis, *Learning to Labour* (Westmead: Saxon House, 1977).

Chapter 8

1. Stanley Aronowitz, *False Promises* (New York: McGraw-Hill, 1973), p. 95. Aronowitz's stress.

2. Rob Burns, "West German Intellectuals and Ideology," *New German Critique,* VIII (Spring, 1976), 9–10.

3. This is *not* meant to imply that amelioration is necessarily neutral. As I have demonstrated in this volume, the possible latent political, economic, and ethical consequences of ameliorative practices should make us less than sanguine about many ameliorative activities.

4. Dennis Warwick, "Ideologies, Integration and Conflicts of Meaning," *Educability, Schools, and Ideology,* Michael Flude and John Ahier, eds (London: Halstead Press, 1974), p. 89.

5. Lucien Goldmann, *Power and Humanism* (London: Spokesman Books, 1974), p. 1.

6. I have advanced some research proposals into this in Michael W. Apple, "Politics and National Curriculum Policy," *Curriculum Inquiry*, VII (no. 4, 1978), 355–61.

7. See, for example, Fredric Jameson, *Marxism and Form* (Princeton University Press, 1971), Raymond Williams, *Marxism and Literature* (New York: Oxford University Press, 1977), Raymond Williams, *The Long Revolution* (London: Chatto & Windus, 1961) and Lucien Goldmann, *Towards a Sociology of the Novel* (London: Tavistock, 1975). I have examined this at greater depth in Michael W. Apple, "Ideology and Form in Curriculum Evaluation," *Qualitative Evaluation*, George Willis, ed. (Berkeley: McCutchan, 1978).

8. See, for example, Michael W. Apple and Jeffrey Lukowsky, "Television and Cultural Reproduction," *Journal of Aesthetic Education*, in press.

9. Eberhard Knödler-Bunte, "The Proletarian Sphere and Political Organization," *New German Critique*, IV (Winter, 1975), 53.

10. For an interesting glimpse at how this perspective has been applied to an area of social policy other than education, see Ian Taylor, Paul Walton, and Jock Young, "Towards a Critical Criminology," *Theory and Society*, I (Winter 1974).

11. Samuel Bowles and Herbert Gintis, *Schooling in Capitalist America* (New York: Basic Books, 1976) is the first step in a political economy of education, of course. It is flawed, however, in that it neglects to account for cultural reproduction outside of its discussion of the norms and character traits that schools both teach and reinforce.

12. Taylor, Walton, and Young, op. cit., 463.

13. Vicente Navarro, *Medicine Under Capitalism* (New York: Neale Watson Academic Publications, 1976), p. 91.

14. I am indebted to Professor Yolanda Rojas of The University of Costa Rica for a number of these points.

15. See the discussion of the history of some aspects of the American labor movement in Aronowitz, op. cit.

16. Aileen Kelly, "A Victorian Heroine: A Review of *Eleanor Marx*," *New York Review of Books*, XXIV (26 January 1978), 28.

17. This combination of action on day to day issues with long term goals is exceptionally well portrayed in William Hinton, *Fanshen* (New York: Vintage, 1966).

18. Cf., Norman Storer, *The Social System of Science* (New York: Holt, Rinehart & Winston, 1966).

19. Schroyer, *The Critique of Domination* (New York: George Braziller, 1973), pp. 165–6.

20. Ibid., p. 172.

21. Schroyer, op. cit., p. 248. See also Hinton, op. cit. and Joshua S. Horn, *Away With All Pests* (New York: Monthly Review Press, 1969).

22. Michael W. Apple, "Justice As A Curriculum Concern," *Multicultural Education*, Carl Grant, ed. (Washington: Association for Supervision and Curriculum Development, 1977), pp. 14–28.

23. Clarence Karier, "Ideology and Evaluation," *Educational Evaluation: Analysis and Responsibility*, Michael W. Apple, Michael J. Subkoviak, and Henry S. Lufler, Jr., eds (Berkeley: McCutchan, 1974), pp. 279–320.

24. Nicholas N. Kittrie, *The Right to be Different: Deviance and Enforced Therapy* (Baltimore: John Hopkins, 1971), p. 336.

25. Ibid., p. 339.

26. Harry Braverman, *Labor and Monopoly Capital* (New York: Monthly Review Press, 1975).

27. Carl Boggs, *Gramsci's Marxism* (London: Pluto Press, 1976), especially Chapter V. This is not merely a theoretical ideal. Models of such a role that we may wish to ponder upon can be found in Cuba.

Chapter 9

1. See Michael W. Apple, *Official Knowledge*, 2nd edition (New York: Routledge, 2000), Michael W. Apple, *Educating the "Right" Way: Markets, Standards, God, and Inequality* (New York: RoutledgeFalmer, 2001), and Michael W. Apple, et al., *The State and the Politics of Knowledge* (New York: Routledge, 2003).

2. See Michael W. Apple and James A. Beane, eds. *Democratic Schools* (Alexandria, VA: Association for Supervision and Curriculum Development, 1995), Apple, *Educating the "Right" Way*, and Apple, et al., *The State and the Politics of Knowledge*.

3. Ibid.
4. Raymond Williams, *Marxism and Literature* (Oxford: Oxford University Press, 1977).
5. See, for example, Noam Chomsky, *9–11* (New York: Seven Stories Press, 2002).
6. For how critical media analysis might interrogate such representations, see Apple, *Official Knowledge*.
7. Noam Chomsky, *Profit over People* (New York: Seven Stories Press, 1999).
8. See the discussion of needs and needs discourses in Nancy Fraser, *Unruly Practices* (Minneapolis: University of Minnesota Press, 1989).
9. Even though I have used this word before in my text, I have put the word "American" in quotation marks for a social purpose in this sentence, since it speaks to the reality I wish to comment on at this point in my discussion. *All* of North, Central, and South America are equally part of the Americas. However, the United States (and much of the world) takes for granted that the term refers to the United States. The very language we use is a marker of imperial pasts and presents. See Edward Said, *Orientalism* (New York: Pantheon, 1978) for one of the early but still very cogent analyses of this.
10. Marcus Weaver-Hightower, "The Gender of Terror and Heroes?" *Teachers College Record*, in press.
11. Michael W. Apple, *Cultural Politics and Education* (New York: Teachers College Press, 1996). See also Apple, et al., *The State and the Politics of Knowledge*.
12. William Greider, *One World, Ready or Not* (New York: Simon and Schuster, 1997).
13. This is one of the reasons that, even though parts of the points may have been based on only a limited reading of parts of the critical pedagogical traditions, I have some sympathy with a number of the arguments made in Carmen Luke and Jenny Gore, eds. *Feminisms and Critical Pedagogy* (New York: Routledge, 1992)—and not a lot of sympathy for the defensive overreactions to it on the part of a number of writers on "critical pedagogy." Political/educational projects, if they are to be both democratic and effective, are always collective. This requires a welcoming of serious and engaged criticism, even when one may not agree with all of it.
14. The reality was actually a bit more complicated than such a simple act of prohibition. The Madison School Board *did* actually comply with the law by having the music of the anthem played over the loudspeaker. Thus, if a school was determined to, say, have the anthem, only an instrumental version was to be played. This would eliminate the more warlike words that accompanied the music. Some members of the board felt that in a time of tragedy in which so many innocent lives had been lost, the last thing that students and schools needed were lyrics that to some glorified militarism. The solution was a compromise: play an instrumental version of the anthem. This too led to some interesting and partly counterhegemonic responses. At one school, a famous Jimi Hendrix rendition of *The Star Spangled Banner* was played over the loudspeaker system. This version—dissonant and raucous—was part of the antiwar tradition of music during the Vietnam-era protests. This raised even more anger on the part of the "patriots" who were already so incensed about the board's vote.
15. See Apple, *Cultural Politics and Education*, and Apple, *Educating the "Right" Way*.
16. Ibid. See also Michael B. Katz, *The Price of Citizenship* (New York: Metropolitan Books, 2001).
17. Stuart Hall, "Popular Democratic vs. Authoritarian Polulism," in Alan Hunt, ed. *Marxism and Democracy* (London: Lawrence and Wishart, 1980).
18. Apple, *Educating the "Right" Way*.
19. Eric Foner, *The Story of American Freedom* (New York: Norton, 1998).
20. Ibid, p. xiv.
21. See Apple, *Educating the "Right" Way* and Roger Dale, "The Thatcherite Project in Education," *Critical Social Policy* 9:4–19 (1989/90).
22. See Apple, *Official Knowledge*, Apple, *Educating the "Right" Way*, and Linda Kintz, *Between Jesus and the Market* (Durham, N.C.: Duke University Press, 1997).
23. Benedict Anderson, *Imagined Communities* (New York: Verso, 1991).
24. Of course, the conservative groups that mobilized against the board's initial decision claimed that they were exercising dissent, that their members were also engaged in democratic action. This is true as far as it goes. However, if one's dissent supports repression and inequality, and if one's dissent labels other people's actions in favor of their own constitutional rights as unpatriotic, then this is certainly not based on a vision of thick democracy. I would hold that its self-understanding is less than satisfactory.

25. In this regard it is important to know that the Pledge of Allegiance itself has *always* been contested. Its words are the following: "I pledge allegiance to the flag of the United States of America, and to the republic for which it stands, one Nation, under God, with liberty and justice for all."

   Yet, the phrase "under God" was added during the midst of the McCarthy period in the early 1950s as part of the battle against "God-less communists." Even the phrase "to the flag of the United States of America" is a late addition. The pledge was originally written by a well-known socialist and at first only contained the words "I pledge allegiance to the flag." In the 1920s a conservative women's group, the Daughters of the American Republic, successfully lobbied to have the words "of the United States of America" added as part of an anti-immigrant campaign. They were deeply fearful that immigrants might be pledging to another nation's flag and, hence, might actually be using the pledge to express seditious thoughts.

26. As I have argued in *Educating the "Right" Way*, however, that race and the politics of "whiteness" have played a significant role in the historical development of neo-liberal, neo-conservative, and authoritarian populist anger at the state and in the development of their proposals for school reform.

Index